BIG HISTORY IN FLIGHT

From the Creation of our Universe to the Crafts Built to Explore it

by **Wendy Curtis**
and **Evan Penn Serio**

Glad to
see all your
work on
getting people to
Think & discuss
aviation concept.
Wendy Curtis

Concept Illustrations by Wendy Curtis
Principally Illustrated by Evan Penn Serio

With Contributions by:

Katie Hennessey, Andrew LeVierge

Kathryn Woods, Lauren Anderson, Chris Bowen, Arianna
Bruno, Carl Caivano, Ernie Carbone, Michael Kelley, Mike
Kuehlmuss, Michelle Kroll, Jay Rathaus, Jingyu Rhine, Jason
Root, Steffani Scheer, Dan Taibbi, Mike Thorn, Bianca Wedge.

ABOUT THIS BOOK

This book presents state-of-the-art scientific and historic theories concerning flight. It explains the dynamics of fluids, gravity, and other scientific principles integral to flight, and describes the development of flying animals and the historic journey of humans as they take to the skies. It begins with the Big Bang and, using a Big Picture format, continues to the present time in chronological order. Alternative theories and previous theories that have been superseded are included when notable.

The immense scope of this book and its limited number of pages allow for the inclusion of only the most important ideas and events. The resulting overview is designed to help the reader keep the principal ideas in mind. The main idea on each page is presented in large type, and supporting facts and details are included in smaller type. Other material, including additional footnotes and references, is available from our website at **www.GeoBookStudio.org**.

Paragraphs of supporting detail are labeled by topic with icons to help the reader identify areas of interest. Here are some of those topics and their icons:

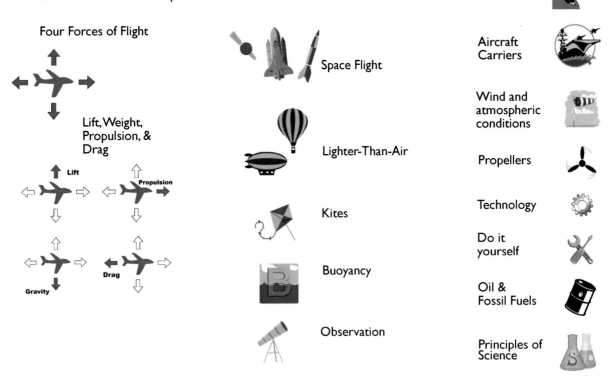

Four Forces of Flight

Lift, Weight, Propulsion, & Drag

Space Flight

Lighter-Than-Air

Kites

Buoyancy

Observation

Explorers

Aircraft Carriers

Wind and atmospheric conditions

Propellers

Technology

Do it yourself

Oil & Fossil Fuels

Principles of Science

GeoBook Studio

Thank you for your interest in this book. Your feedback and suggestions are welcomed and may be included with proper acknowledgment in subsequent editions. Please contact us with any questions, comments, or feedback:

TeamGeo@GeoBookStudio.org

To order additional copies and other products:

www.GeoBookStudio.org

Version 3.4 © Wendy Curtis • June 4 2018

An interactive version of this book is also available as an Apple iBook.

CONTENTS

Long have we marveled.

Human beings have watched the birds, felt the wind, and watched the seeds of plants riding on currents of air. We watched the sun make its daily transit across the sky and watched clouds build. We saw falling stars and the moon hanging in its orbit in space.

All through the ages, we have wondered and thought and marveled.

Bound to the Earth as we are, we find an analog of flight in water. We can feel fluid motion as water molecules slide past other water molecules.

When we immerse ourselves in water, it suspends us and we feel as if we have partially escaped gravity. We can drift in a current and we can push against the water with our hands and feet, sending some of it backward as we glide forward. Is this what birds feel with every beat of their wings in the vast gaseous ocean of the sky?

Air, which is almost transparent, is clearer than water and a thousand times less dense. It is a fluid so ethereal that it is not easily apparent that it is a fluid at all.

Air is so light and so free that it is easy to think there is nothing there at all.

Before we could fly, we dreamed of flying.

All through history, humans have told tales of unusual flying creatures and have sculpted wings onto beasts.

Perhaps humans have always dreamed of flying as they watched birds and other animals glide and soar through the sky.

Since antiquity, great thinkers have proposed that matter is made of atoms, have pondered the difference between solids, liquids, and gasses, and have tried to describe the force of gravity.

The more we know, the more marvelous the picture becomes.

We wonder now just as much as ever. Now we wonder how to better use gravity to assist our spacecraft, or if the Universe will expand forever.

Our quest continues, as one theory is replaced by a better one.

Science enriches wonder; it never replaces it.

In the beginning, according to the Big Bang Theory, the Universe was gathered into a small, dense clump known as a singularity.

The Big Bang Theory is still the most accurate and comprehensive model of the Universe that science has to offer. It has so far answered the criticisms of most skeptical scientists and continues to be largely consistent with new observations. Scientific theories evolve in order to best describe the facts that we observe. The Big Bang Theory has endured for more than half a century but will likely be modified, perhaps even replaced, sometime in the future.

Everything is contained within the singularity. Nothing can escape it. Even light rays are not able to fly away from it.

Chapter 1: Energy Expands in a Big Bang

A singularity is paradoxically small. It contains everything, making its gravity so strong that it crushes itself into a tiny clump that is smaller than a pinhead. It is too densely packed for atoms to exist within it. As a result, a singularity contains energy but no matter.

Time is linked to space. Within the singularity, where everything is crushed small, there is no space and time is set at zero.

The singularity might have always existed or it could be the result of a previous Universe that collapsed back upon itself, a concept called the Big Bounce. Some scientists speculate that there could even be or have been other singularities that exist or became other Universes; making for a Multiverse.

The evidence that our Universe was once a singularity is described in more detail in the last few chapters of this book. There are three separate lines of evidence, postulated by scientists in the 20th century, that support *the Big Bang Theory*. The first is that all of the galaxies we observe are moving away from one another, indicating that space is expanding. The second is that the different kinds of atoms we observe and detect throughout the Universe are found in proportions that are consistent with expansion from a singularity and the subsequent influence of gravity and other laws of physics. The third is the relic signature or afterglow of the Big Bang, called the Cosmic Background Radiation, which was sought for and later found by astronomers in the last half of the 20th century.

A singularity is governed by the crazy laws of the quantum world.

The Universe escapes the confines of the Singularity in a quantum flash.

This hypothetical event is referred to as The Big Bang.

13.7
Billion Years Ago

The four forces in physics become distinct.

Scientists suspect that, in the early stages of the Big Bang, only a single super-force operates. As temperature and density diminish, the four forces of physics - Gravity, the Strong and Weak Nuclear forces, and Electromagnetism - manifest themselves.

Although the four forces seem separate and distinct to us now, scientists endeavour to discover relationships between them. This is known as the Quest for a Unified Theory.

The Universe expands, unfurling space and filling it with an energetic, brilliant haze.

As space continues to expand, the thundering haze becomes less dense and it cools.

As the haze cools, tiny particles condense out.

Light rays are trapped within the haze. Each light ray flies straight until it collides with the next particle and bounces off in a new direction. The ricocheting light rays make the space brilliant but opaque.

As space expands, the waves of energy within it stretch. Energy with a longer wavelength is less intense. As the energy of the waves subsides, the first tiny sub-sub-atomic particles appear.

Electrons are among the first particles to form. Quarks form shortly thereafter, and later they begin to bond together. Three quarks bonded together form a proton.

As the Universe continues to cool, the particles move at slower speeds and individual electrons settle down with individual protons, creating neutral atoms of matter.

A single proton with an electron makes the smallest kind of atom, which is called hydrogen. At this point, hydrogen is the only kind of atom that has formed. Soon, some of the hydrogen atoms collide with one another and merge together to make helium, a slightly larger atom.

Light rays fly free and the Universe becomes transparent.

As soon as the electrons became incorporated into atoms of matter,
the light rays, which had been bouncing off of them, fly unobstructed.
Each light ray flies off in the direction it happened to be heading. This
release of light is called the **Cosmic Background Radiation**.
Scientists also call this the time of The Last Scatter.

As the light rays continue to
fly, the Universe darkens.

Only the smallest kinds of atoms
have formed and they gather
together as they drift.

The atoms of matter drift separately in the still expanding
space. Each atom is an independent system of sub-atomic
particles that are bound together and each one has a tiny
effect on the gravitational fabric of space.

At this time, the Universe contains only hydrogen and
helium atoms (and a faint trace of lithium, the next largest
element). Hydrogen is the smallest and simplest of all the
elements; it consists of just one proton and one electron.
Helium, which formed when hydrogen atoms collided
and fused together, is only slightly larger. The synthesis of
helium was a process that could only happen when the
Universe was really hot because at lower temperatures,
atoms bounce off one another without fusing.

Large collections of drifting atoms become stars and brighten up the darkened Universe.

The stars create new kinds of atoms out of the small atoms.

Stars fuse some of the many small atoms into a fewer number of larger atoms. They create carbon, oxygen, aluminum, silicon, and other atoms as large as iron.

In the cores of stars, gravity forces atoms so close together that some of them merge. This is called nuclear fusion, a process that liberates energy, causing stars to shine.

Iron, which is in the lowest energy state, is the most stable atom created by nuclear fusion. Smaller elements release energy when they are fused together, but an input of energy is required to create atoms larger than iron.

Carbon, another atom created by nuclear fusion, is a versatile building block that can readily bond with a variety of other atoms, including itself. Carbon-to-carbon chains will make the framework of living organisms and the fossil fuels that will power airplanes. Carbon fiber composites are light but strong.

Oxygen, which is also created by nuclear fusion, typically bonds so readily with other atoms that it is highly reactive.

Aluminum is created by nuclear fusion as well. It makes a strong but lightweight metal that will support the development of airplanes.

Stars can't make atoms that are larger than iron.

Only when stars explode are the largest elements finally created.

After forging iron, a star reaches the end of the nuclear fusion cycle. If the star is not gigantic, it becomes a dim cloud surrounding a core of iron. If a star is large enough, it explodes in a **supernova.** Only in supernova explosions are the rest of the elements finally created.

In a supernova explosion, many kinds of particles are released at high speeds and existing atoms are bombarded and pumped up with them. Every kind of atomic configuration comes into existence as atoms swell with extra particles. Many of these big, new atoms are unstable and lose particles through radioactive decay until

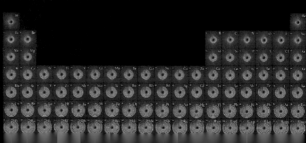

The Universe also contains a lot of **Dark Matter.**

Visible matter, which is the matter we generally refer to, is made up of atoms. As astronomy techniques improve and astronomers catalogue galaxies and collect data on speed of spin rotation, they realize that some galaxies appear to be surprisingly small, considering how fast they spin. To spin fast, a galaxy must have a hub that is massive enough to keep stars in the outer regions from drifting off. This leads astronomers to speculate about the existence of matter that is not visible, which becomes known as Dark Matter. Scientists suspect that Dark Matter is far more abundant in the Universe than regular matter and that they coexist. One analogy is that, while only the tip of an iceberg is visible to us, it indicates the presence of the whole iceberg. Another is that phosphorescence, when visible in the sea on a dark night, makes us aware of the water in which it is immersed. Evidence suggests that Dark Matter eventually becomes segregated into a halo around each galaxy. While atoms are the basic units of regular matter, we don't yet know what the units of Dark Matter are.

The galaxies become separated by great voids of empty space.

The galaxies are not evenly distributed, but are gathered into clusters and along linear bands. The spaces between galaxies expand fully, blowing up like soap bubbles to form vast voids. The galaxies remain between the voids and thus come to be arranged in clusters or arrayed in linear swaths known as filaments at the intersections of voids.

The Universe contains the full variety of atoms of matter, but not in equal proportions.

Hydrogen and helium, which formed in the early stages of the Big Bang, make up 98% of all matter. Atoms that were created by fusion in stars make up most of the remaining 2%.

When a star is active and shining, it is converting small elements together into mid-sized elements, including sodium, carbon, oxygen, and silicon.

The rarest of all elements are created only in supernova explosions and are heavier than iron.

Atoms can combine to form molecules.

The electrons of an atom orbit its nucleus in a series of shells, which are arrayed outward like the layers of an onion. The first shell has room for only two electrons. Hydrogen and helium have one and two electrons, respectively. The shell of the hydrogen atom is half filled while the shell of the helium atom is completely filled. Larger atoms have more shells and are able to hold more electrons.

When atoms approach one another, the electrons in the outermost shell of each atom interact. If the shell of an atom is completely full, the atom will not bond and react with other atoms. Hydrogen readily bonds with other atoms (even other hydrogen atoms) while helium is inert.

Carbon is a versatile building block. It has a medium level of reactivity, and can bond with a variety of other atoms, including itself, but is fairly stable by itself and doesn't quickly bond with just any other atom. Carbon-to-carbon chains will eventually make the frameworks of living organisms.

Oxygen bonds so readily with so many other kinds of atoms that it forms many kinds of oxides; rust is iron oxide, glass is silicon dioxide, and water is made of hydrogen and oxygen. Oxygen is so reactive that it can sometimes cause problems for living organisms.

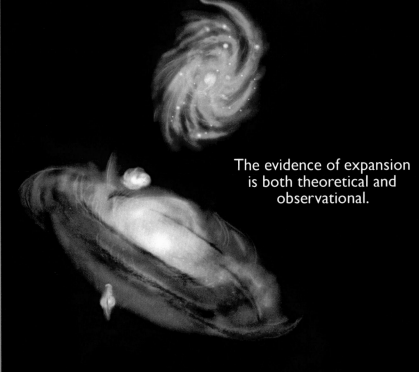

The evidence of expansion is both theoretical and observational.

Not only are the galaxies all moving away from us, but the galaxies farthest away are moving away fastest. The speed at which a galaxy is moving away from us is directly proportional to its distance from us (a galaxy twice as far away is moving twice as fast; and a galaxy three times as far away is moving three times as fast). Lemaître and Hubble noticed this relationship and realized that it is indicative of general overall expansion. It is well described by an analogy of raisins in a rising loaf of raisin bread. The raisins move away from one another as the whole loaf expands.

The point of view from any galaxy (like any raisin in the dough) is that everything is **moving** away from it. The outermost raisins move much farther away from one another because there is more dough between them to expand. It all happens over one interval of time (the time that the universe has been expanding or the dough rising) so the raisins that move farthest also move at the fastest rates. While it may at first seem that the other galaxies are moving away from us because we are at the center of a giant explosion, this is not the case and neither is a loaf of bread exploding.

The observational evidence that the galaxies are moving away from us is that the spectra of the light coming from each of them is shifted toward the red end of the spectrum. This is called **redshift** or **Doppler shift.**

The spectra of a light source (which can be a galaxy) contains a rainbow of colors and individual dark lines which indicate specific elements, like hydrogen. When the source of light is moving toward or away from the viewer, the light waves are either bunched up or spread out respectively causing the positions of the spectral lines to shift slightly. Telescopes of Doppler's day were not yet refined enough to discern the effect that Doppler sought, but he hypothesized that the effect could also be demonstrated with sound waves. In 1845, Doppler shift was demonstrated by musicians playing from a moving train while observers listened at the station. You can hear the effect for yourself in the volume of an ambulance siren, which increases as the ambulance approaches and decreases as it travels away.

The Milky Way is within a
cluster we call The Local Group.
Our local group is within the
Virgo Super Cluster.

Chapter 2: Planets Orbit Stars

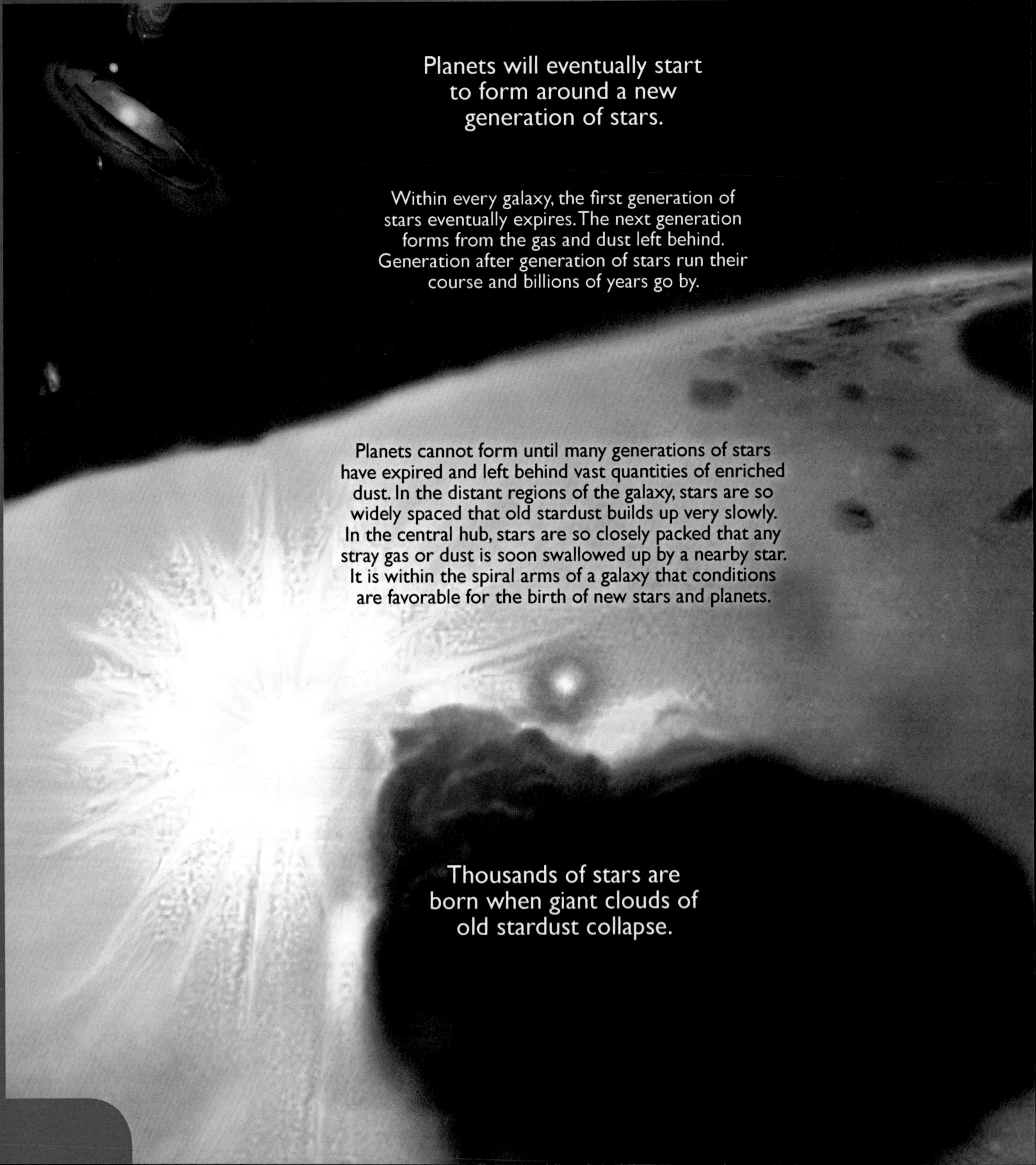

Planets will eventually start
to form around a new
generation of stars.

Within every galaxy, the first generation of
stars eventually expires. The next generation
forms from the gas and dust left behind.
Generation after generation of stars run their
course and billions of years go by.

Planets cannot form until many generations of stars
have expired and left behind vast quantities of enriched
dust. In the distant regions of the galaxy, stars are so
widely spaced that old stardust builds up very slowly.
In the central hub, stars are so closely packed that any
stray gas or dust is soon swallowed up by a nearby star.
It is within the spiral arms of a galaxy that conditions
are favorable for the birth of new stars and planets.

Thousands of stars are
born when giant clouds of
old stardust collapse.

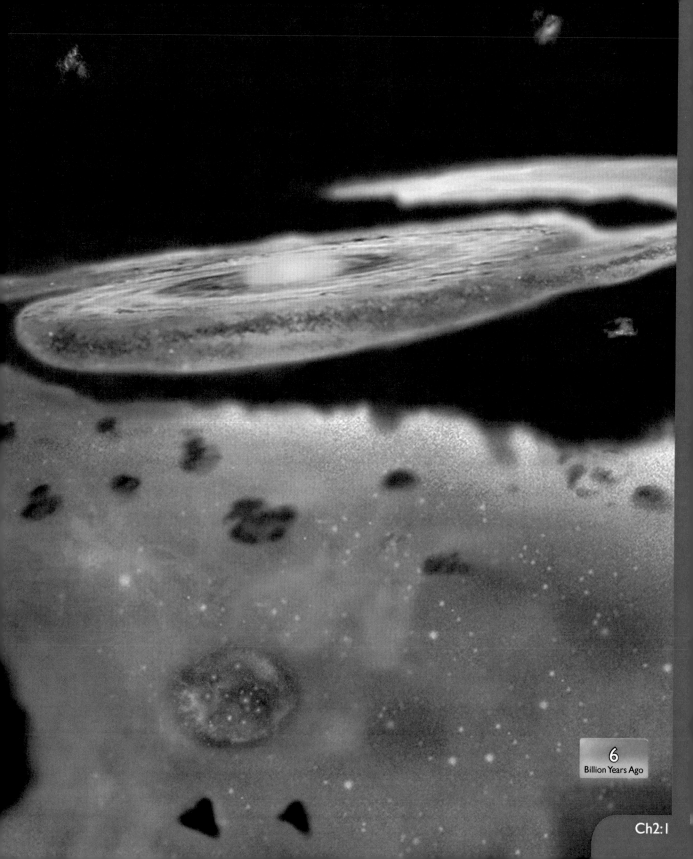

Once the cloud begins to collapse, many smaller, denser cloudlets form within it.

The cloud's gravity is weak but relentless. Once gravity gets the upper hand, the process of contraction proceeds and intensifies, and the cloud is transformed into a stellar nursery.

A cloud of old stardust can be triggered to collapse if hit by a shockwave.

As a shock wave impacts a giant cloud, it temporarily upsets the weak forces that have prevented the cloud from contracting under its own gravity.

5.2
Billion Years Ago

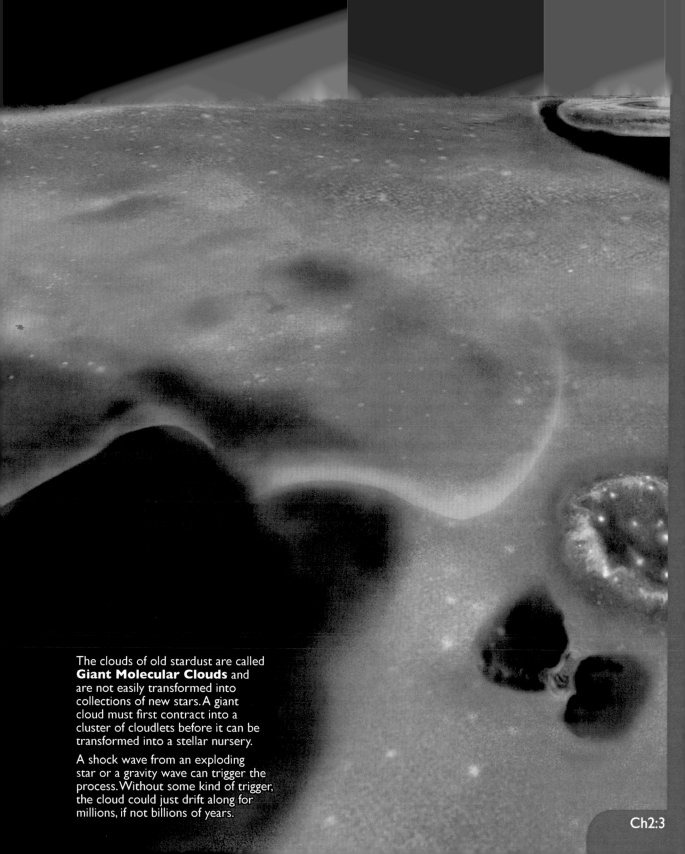

The clouds of old stardust are called
Giant Molecular Clouds and
are not easily transformed into
collections of new stars. A giant
cloud must first contract into a
cluster of cloudlets before it can be
transformed into a stellar nursery.

A shock wave from an exploding
star or a gravity wave can trigger the
process. Without some kind of trigger,
the cloud could just drift along for
millions, if not billions of years.

Each cloudlet can evolve to become
a hot spinning sphere that collapses
into a protostellar disc.

At the center of the disc, a
star is born.

The
temperature
within the
stellar disc is so
hot that most
materials are in
a gaseous form.

Only a few substances,
like iron and compounds
of silica, take a solid
form. Although these
solid grains are tiny, they
will not be pushed away
by the solar wind and
will remain behind and
become the building
blocks of the planets.

A star's nuclear furnace
produces light as well
as a radiant wind of
charged particles.

Stars are nuclear furnaces.

They synthesize medium-
sized elements like Carbon,
Oxygen, and Aluminum.

Nuclear reactions liberate energy,
causing stars to shine. The hydrogen
atoms that fuel the reactions weigh
more than the resultant helium atoms.
The difference in mass is converted to
energy in the form of sunshine. The sun
gets ever-so-slightly less massive
as it shines, in accordance with $E = mc^2$.

The solar disc is hottest near the sun and cooler farther out.

5
Billion Years Ago

The **solar wind** blows outward and
begins to push away the gas and dust that
still enshroud the nascent solar system.

Any theory about the solar system must be able to systematically describe it.

There have been several theories about the origin of the sun and Solar System. Any theory must explain the broad features of the system.

First, those features must be identified and described. The sun and all the objects in the solar system share a common sense of motion. The planets are arranged in a flat, frisbee-like plane aligned on the Sun's equator. The theory must also explain the compositional gradient of the planets with distance from the sun. The inner planets contain relatively large iron cores blanketed by aluminum silicate rock mantles, while those farther from the sun contain huge gaseous atmospheres of hydrogen and helium over rocky icy cores.

A scientific theory can have minor problems, but all major, broad-scale properties must be explained satisfactorily. Minor unresolved questions are tolerated under a watchful eye. Further research will bring new information that will either resolve the minor problems or cause them to widen into large fissures that eventually bring down the whole edifice.

The solar wind emanating from our young star acts like a snowplow, pushing the fog of gas that enshrouds it into a wall at its leading edge.

There is no liquid water. H_2O exists only as a gas or as a solid; as water vapor or as ice.

The solid particles that had been able to condense out of the hot haze aggregate into **planetesimals**.

The planetesimals in the inner solar system continue to grow larger in size and smaller in number as gravity pulls them together.

Planetesimals can be meters to kilometers in size. When a planetesimal grows large enough, its own gravity pulls its atoms toward its center and it becomes spherical.

The inner planetesimals are dry. They were too small and their gravity was too weak to incorporate the hydrogen gas when it was available. By the time they become large enough to hold onto vapors, there aren't any left.

When the front of the solar wind reaches the Frost Line, Jupiter, a massive planet, is exposed.

At the 'Frost Line,' the point at which water vapor becomes ice, there is a huge increase in the amount of solid material available.

Jupiter had already grown large by feeding on ice crystals, which gave it enough gravity to retain gases. The solar wind pushes the wall of gas right to it and Jupiter sucks it all in, becoming a truly immense planet.

The gas is composed mostly of hydrogen atoms and Jupiter gathers so much that it comes to consist mostly of hydrogen.

As the front of the solar wind moves farther outward, it moves into ever cooler regions where more of the gasses have condensed into solids. The increasing abundance of solid grains allows larger planetesimals to form with increasing distance from the sun.

Carbon is present as a solid in this region, as carbon dioxide and other carbon compounds freeze.

The front of the solar wind continues on past Jupiter, and Jupiter grabs most of the gas and dust as it passes by. As a result, the protoplanets outboard of Jupiter (Saturn, Uranus, and Neptune) will not grow as large.

Jupiter begins to upset the orbits of the planetesimals that formed near it.

Some of these fall into Jupiter while others sail through the inner solar system as they fall toward the Sun.

Once planetesimals reach large sizes, collision between them can be destructive, fragmenting rather than aggregating the bodies, depending on the speed and angle of the collision

Planetesimals that continue to increase in size become protoplanets. Fragments of smashed protoplanets are called **asteroids**. Small planetesimals that never get incorporated into larger bodies are also called asteroids

The rocky protoplanets of the inner solar system cool as they radiate their heat into space, but each impact heats them up anew

Some of the disrupted planetesimals are sent off on wild trajectories and leave the plane of the disc to wind up in the Oort Cloud, a faraway shell of debris surrounding the solar system

Proto-Earth is struck by another protoplanet whose orbit brings it just a little too close.

This event will create the **Moon**.

4.53
Billion Years Ago

The moon coalesces.

When the debris from this collision settles, the moon has formed. Scientists call the impacting protoplanet Theia, or sometimes Orpheus. Theia had been orbiting the Sun on an orbital path not far from that of Earth. The collision is not head-on but is a glancing blow.

The collision plows off a piece of Earth's mantle. The heat generated by the impact melts the chunk of mantle as it is pushed away. Theia is also vaporized and cast into space. The heaviest parts of the orbiting debris, the iron portions, fall back to Earth, increasing the size of Earth's core. The lighter portions reassemble into the moon.

During the great collision with Theia, some of the water on Earth is vaporized and lost to space. Luckily, asteroids will continue to impact the Earth, delivering more water in the form of ice. Earth might have already cooled off and had an ocean before the impact with Theia, but it is definitely made molten after impact. The continuing bombardment of asteroids will eventually increase the size of Earth by about 10%

The topography of space is an expression of gravity.

The Sun creates a massive gravitational well – a dent in the topography of space – around itself. The planets also make dents, which helps them to stay in orbit and keeps them from rolling down the gravitational gradient into the Sun.

A planet must orbit at a sufficient speed.

As a planet travels in its orbit, some of its momentum is directed away from the sun. Similarly, a rock swinging in circles at the end of a rope will fly off and away if the rope is released. The portion of the planet's vector of motion that is in a direction directly away from the sun must be sufficient to balance the tendency for the planet to roll down the gravitational gradient toward the sun.

The solar system has become segregated into different compositional zones.

The planets of the inner solar system are small and rocky with iron cores. The planets of the outer solar system have so much hydrogen incorporated within them that they are mostly hydrogen, despite also having rocky centers and iron cores.

The composition of the solar system is largely similar to that of the Universe, but the rarer elements in the solar system are concentrated in the solar disc.

Eventually only Mercury, Venus, Earth and Mars will remain in the inner Solar System but at this stage, the protoplanets are smaller and more numerous.

Asteroids carouse.

Planetesimals that have been dislodged from their once stable orbits out near Jupiter continue to fall toward the sun.

The asteroids and protoplanets sailing in from the outer regions carry frozen water, which they deliver to any of the protoplanets of the inner solar system they collide with.

Some of the disrupted planetesimals are sent off on wild trajectories and leave the plane of the disc to wind up in the Oort Cloud, a far away shell of debris surrounding the solar system.

No new protoplanets will be able to form in the gap between Mars and Jupiter because of Jupiter's immense gravity, however there is still some matter left in this area –we call it the asteroid belt.

Comets are asteroids composed mostly of ice with minor rocky parts and are sometimes referred to as 'dirty snowballs.'

Hydrogen is the most common element in the Universe because it condensed directly from the cooling energy in the aftermath of the Big Bang. It is the most common element in the solar system as well. Because hydrogen is such a small element, it makes a light gas that only a large planet has enough gravity to hold onto.

Oxygen is one of the next most abundant elements because it is made more easily in the nuclear furnaces of stars than are most other elements. Atoms larger than iron, which are created only in stellar explosions, are rare indeed.

Buoyancy governs the process of stratification as the Earth cools.

Although not much crust has formed at the surface, minerals are solidifying, mostly at depths far beneath the orange waves.

Iron sinks as silicates are buoyed upward.

The molten ocean of liquid rock and liquid iron separates like oil and vinegar out of a shaken salad dressing. The two liquids do not interact chemically.

Hadean Era
4.5
Billion Years Ago

Earth's atmosphere is so thick that we don't attempt to show it here. It contains steam, methane, carbon dioxide, and even some silicon dioxide from vaporized rock.

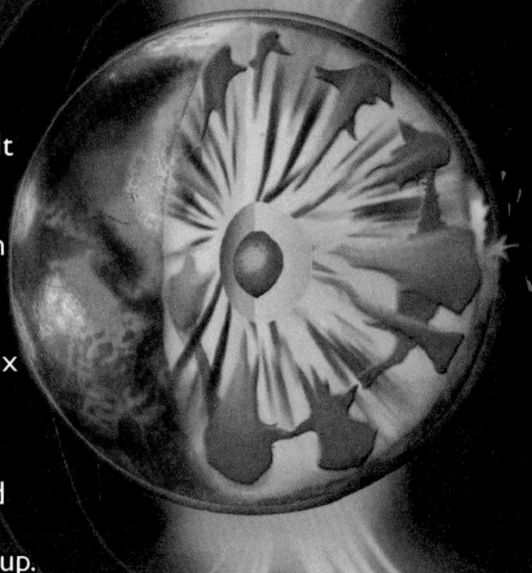

All of the atoms in the mix are each pulled toward the center of the Earth by gravity. The dense iron molecules sink downward rapidly. The less dense silicates are buoyed back up.

The iron molecules are iron oxide. The liquid rock molecules are composed principally of silicon and oxygen with some aluminum and other elements mixed in. Oxygen is an abundant atom on Earth and it is highly reactive, bonding easily with other atoms.

Gravity pulls on both of the liquids but only the iron rich liquid readily sinks. The descending streams of liquid iron (drawn here in green) encounter increasing pressure as they sink to deeper depths.

The pressure is the result of the atoms vibrating and bouncing around within the fluid; at greater depths the weight of the liquid above them confines the movement of the atoms and they are unable to easily bounce away from each other when they collide. The impact of their collisions increases with their confinement.

The pressure, at any given depth, acts in all directions. Lateral movements to the right or left cancel each other out and it is only the force of pressure in the vertical directions that dictates whether the liquid will sink or float. There is more pressure from below than from above.

Great plumes convect hotter magma from near the hot core up to the surface.

Heat always flows from hot to cold and never the other way. This is a law of **Thermodynamics.**

Currents of the molten magma flow because of the difference in temperature between the hot interior and the cooler surface above.

At the surface, some of the heat radiates out into space and the magma at the surface cools. Curtains of cooled magma sink back into the depths. As liquids cool, their molecules bounce around less energetically and therefore the molecules require less space.

The currents are also affected by the Earth's spin, as are ocean currents today. Surface currents veer to the right in the Northern hemisphere and to the left in the Southern Hemisphere. The currents are also influenced by the tides caused by the pull of the moon.

The dense iron liquid continues to descend to depths even where pressure is great because the downward pull of gravity is greater than the upward component of the pressure force.

The less dense silicate liquids are more susceptible to pressure because they have more surface area relative to their mass. Gravity acts on mass and pressure acts on surfaces. The upward component of the pressure force acting on their larger surface areas is greater than the downward pull of gravity.

Water and carbon compounds are still scarce on the young Earth.

Most of the incoming asteroids are from cooler regions and they continue to deliver these precious substances to our developing planet. The amount of water will soon increase to modern levels, remaining miniscule in relation to the whole Earth. We call Earth 'the water planet,' but in fact our oceans are just a thin veneer.

Some scientists have proposed that asteroids delivered not only water and carbon compounds (including amino acids), but also living cells of bacteria which seeded the Earth with life. The hypothesis that life evolved elsewhere and was transported to Earth is known as **Panspermia**.

Earth is almost completely comprised of just 4 kinds of atoms.

Earth consists almost entirely of just 4 elements: oxygen, iron, silicon, and magnesium These 4 elements constitute over 90% of the matter that makes up Earth. Of these, oxygen atoms are the most numerous. Most of us think of oxygen simply as the air we breathe, but it is also the major constituent of most rocks. Earth could aptly be called *The Oxygen Planet*.

The great variety of elements that interest humans, like carbon, copper, gold, mercury, and aluminum compose just a very small fraction of Earth, but they will become concentrated in the crust.

The Earth and the Moon form a double-planet system.

The moons of most planets are ornamental, but our moon has a radius that is more than 1/4 the size of the Earth's radius.

The Moon is in synchronous rotation with Earth; the same side of the moon always faces Earth.

The side of the moon facing Earth stays hotter than its far side.

The smaller moon cools off more quickly than the larger Earth.

White crystals are buoyant on the moon.

A crust of white crystals has grown like a shell, covering much of the surface of the moon, including almost the entirety of the far side. The crystals are calcium rich feldspar and although they are solid they are less dense than the magma below.

The moon will not be able to hold onto much of the water that is being delivered as ice by asteroids. The ices soon turn to water vapor and the moon doesn't have enough gravity to hold the gasses close. Because it lacks an iron core, it will not develop a strong magnetic field to shield its gases from the relentless solar wind.

Chapter 3: Oceans Fill, Life Arises, and Photosynthesis Creates Free Oxygen

Earth's **crust** finally solidifies. Hot spots of magma still erupt at the surface but they are separated by extensive pavements of rock.

As cooling continues, the skinned-over sections of primitive crust on Earth grow larger.

Although calcium feldspar was buoyant on the moon and created its whitish surface, these crystals are not buoyant in Earth's deeper magma oceans

Calcium feldspar minerals do not float to the surface of Earth's deep magma ocean. This is because the calcium feldspar crystals form at a deep depth and cannot easily make their way to the surface. Both pressure and temperature control the formation of solids (which form as crystals, also called minerals) within a cooling liquid. Flotation is controlled by a difference in density between the crystals and the magma, the viscosity of the magma (its ability to flow), and currents stirring up the magma. The composition of the residual magma changes as crystals are removed from it.

The aluminum found on Earth is located in the crust and mantle, mostly in the form of aluminum silicates. Due to its high affinity to oxygen, elemental or raw aluminum is rarely found on its own, instead it manifests as a silicate or oxide.

As a molten planet cools, its plumes diminish in size and increase in number. Hot spots become smaller but more numerous.

Earth's atmosphere is thick but the moon's has been pushed away by the solar wind.

As the temperature continues to drop, water vapor condenses out of the atmosphere and it rains.

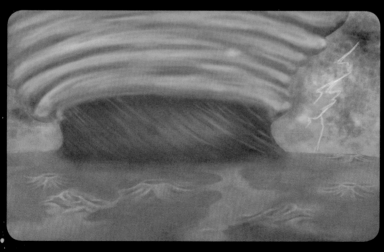

Some of the rain falls on red hot lava and steams back into the atmosphere, but some falls on cooler rocks and gathers into puddles.

It rains and it rains. Pools of water grow into shallow seas.

Hadean
4.4
Billion Years Ago

Sea level is rising.

The sea is green and the sky is red.

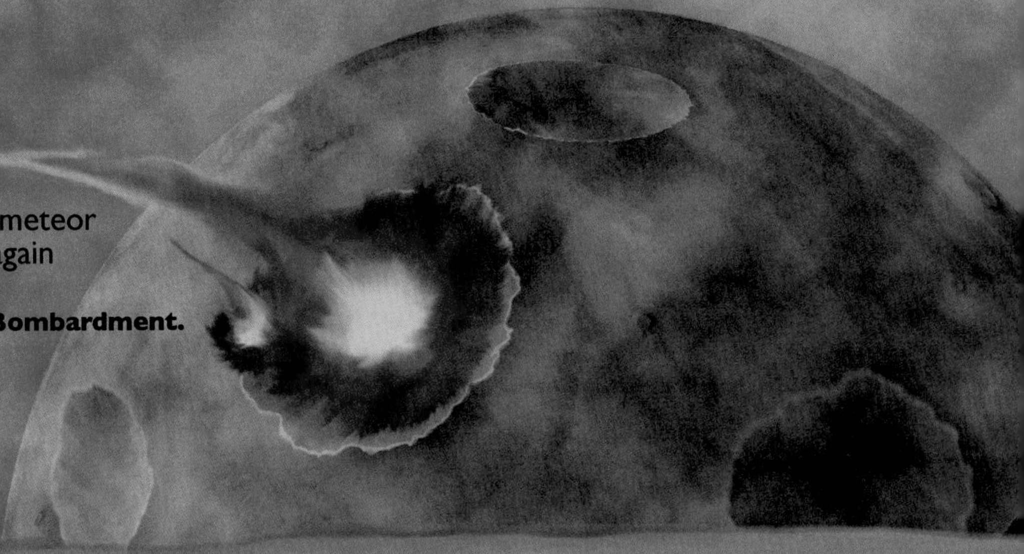

The frequency of meteor
strikes increases again
in a spike called
The Late Heavy Bombardment.

Although covered in water, Earth is still very hot.

Convection currents continue to bring heat
from the core and mantle to the surface and
new plumes of molten magma continue to
erupt in numerous places across the globe.
Some of the magma erupts from volcanos.
which reach the surface of the waters but m
Some of the magma erupts from volcanos.
which reach the surface but most of the
magma erupts out of cracks in the crust
that became submerged as the oceans fill.
At these deep sea vents, the sulphur, iron,
and manganese that had been dissolved
in the magma precipitates out. The
precipitating minerals build strange, pillar-
like chimneys around the hot gasses that
pour out.

Systems of complex molecules develop at the Deep Sea Vents.

One theory for the origin
of life is that it arises from
inanimate, prebiotic molecular
associations and systems in
a series of emergent steps.
Exactly when and in what order
these steps occur is a matter of
great debate.

Life requires an energy source
and the ability to make use of
it (metabolism), the ability to
replicate itself (i.e., RNA), and
the ability to keep itself separate
from the rest of the world (cell
wall). Once these three necessities
are met, natural selection will act
definitively on the system.

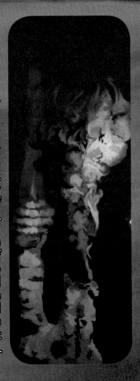

Atmospheric gases dissolve into the gathering ocean waters, and atmospheric pressure falls dramatically.

New rock types emerge.

The Earth's crust is not flat: there are higher areas and lower areas. The lowest areas are composed of basalt, which came out of the mantle through rifts as lava. Basalt is dense. After it cools off, it settles down and rides low on the mantle. Because it sits low on the surface of the Earth, it is generally covered by water as ocean floor. If there were no water, basalt flows would be low- lying, empty basins.

Most of the areas above sea level are made of less dense rock types that have a higher portion of silica and are infused with granite. A few very high volcanos do emerge above sea level to spew out basalt, but later, when they are no longer fed fresh magma, they will settle down into the mantle and submerge beneath the waves.

Granite emerges as the building block of continents.

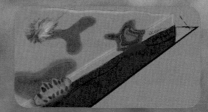

Most scientists think that granite is formed by the partial melting of basalt, the most typical volcanic rock. When a rock is heated, some of the minerals in it melt before others. If the melt portion repeatedly flows away, resolidifies, and is partially melted again, granite might eventually be produced from basalt. The granite is less dense than the rock it formed out of, is buoyant, and floats at a higher elevation.

Archean
3.8
Billion Years Ago

Megatides and relentless winds raise giant waves that pound the shores of the protocontinents.

The moon is still much closer to the Earth and pulls strong tides that shape the shorelines into shallow grades with sand spread over the great distance between the high and low water marks. The Earth still spins fast on its axis, so high tide follows low in just a few hours. The raging waves will soon soften the shoreline by breaking up the edges of continents and the sediment generated by this process will create continental shelves.

The Late Heavy Bombardment ends.

The intense bombardment of meteors is over when the leftover debris from the creation of the Solar System is finally incorporated into the planets or confined into relatively stable orbits in the asteroid belt.

It is the end of a geologic era as the Hadean gives way to the **Archean**.

Life emerges.

Single cells, bounded by a membrane, exist in the form of **bacteria.**

Platforms of granite-infused land merge to form **protocontinents.**

Living cells begin to modify the chemistry of the ocean.

The moon's gravity rhythmically rocks the massive tides back and forth, stabilizing the biorhythms of Earth's evolving creatures.

Colonies of photosynthesizing bacteria flourish in shallow shores.

Sediment inundates the shorelines of the continents. Created as the great tides erode coastlines and rain beats upon the rocky surface of the land, this load of debris softens the coastline environment. Beaches slope at a shallow grade and sandbars form offshore.

The bacteria colonies form mounds, called **Stromatolites,** which are composed of alternating layers of sand and biofilm. Twice a day, the tide washes in a fresh layer of sand (and nutrients) that covers the bacteria, which must now grow up through it in order to reach the sun.

The photosynthesizing bacteria use the energy of the Sun to recombine molecules to make their food and give off **free oxygen** as a byproduct.

Archean
3
Billion Years Ago

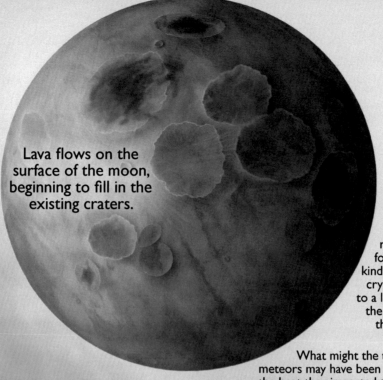

Lava flows on the surface of the moon, beginning to fill in the existing craters.

Why does the lava begin to flow now, so long after the craters formed? One hypothesis is that the mantle had stratified in a gravitationally unstable pattern; the first crystals to form and sink were magnesium-rich olivine crystals, which are less dense than the iron-rich olivine crystals that formed later. So with any kind of a trigger, the denser crystals on the top will fall to a lower level and displace the less dense crystals and the mantle will overturn.

What might the trigger be? Some of the meteors may have been deeply embedded, with the heat they imparted taking a while to remelt the mantle enough to allow it to overturn. Perhaps the mantle had never solidified because it was so well insulated by the white crust and a gap developed between it and the crust as the mantle cooled and contracted. Then, perhaps the crust and mantle made contact in one spot and magma flowed out into the craters of this area.

The moon's gravity rhythmically rocks massive mega-tides tides back and forth, stabilizing the biorhythms of Earth's evolving creatures.

Like modern plants, the bacteria use the energy in sunlight to rearrange the atoms from carbon dioxide and water into carbohydrate foods and carbon-based skeletal structures. They give off oxygen as a waste product.

Oxygen is highly reactive; atoms of oxygen combine readily with almost any other atoms they encounter. This makes oxygen toxic to most life forms. Free oxygen, however, is rare on the early Earth, where the same number of oxygen atoms are present but they are bonded in rock rather than present in the ocean waters or the atmosphere. The sky is a red shroud rich in CO_2. The ocean is green with unoxidized iron suspended in solution.

Sea level is high. With the LHB over, meteors have delivered their water and no longer create heat by their impacts, allowing the atmosphere to cool and more rain to fall.

It's not certain that stromatolites could have prospered on shorelines with large waves. If not, their habitat would have been restricted to coves and bays with protected shorelines, which would have been rare until shallow continental shelves were created by the erosive action of the great tides and previously giant waves.

The tides continue to diminish in intensity as the moon moves farther away. When the moon first formed, it was perhaps as close as three Earth diameters away. Today, it is 30 Earth diameters away and still receding.

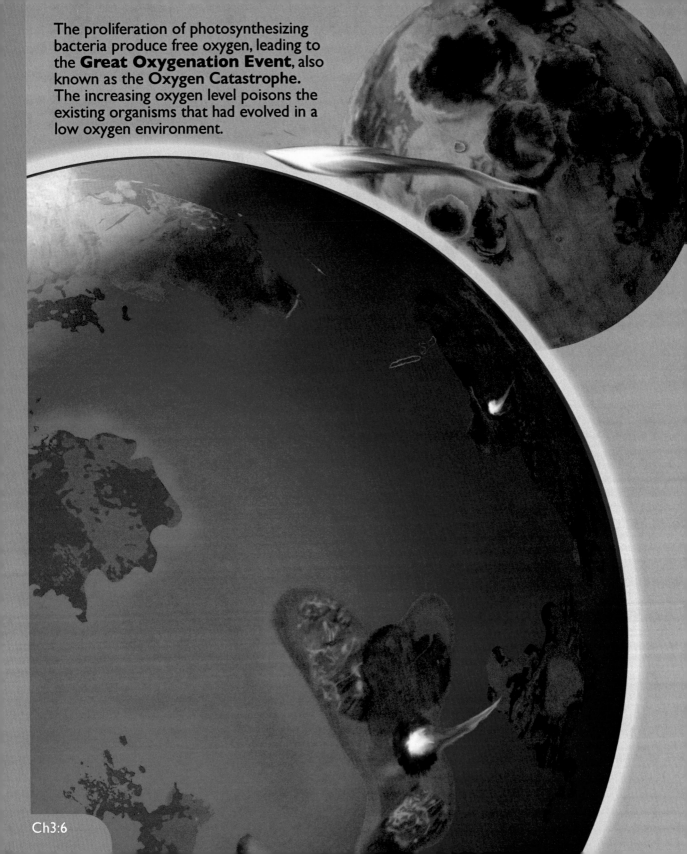

The proliferation of photosynthesizing bacteria produce free oxygen, leading to the **Great Oxygenation Event**, also known as the Oxygen Catastrophe. The increasing oxygen level poisons the existing organisms that had evolved in a low oxygen environment.

The moon looms large in the sky.

It is still close to Earth and Earth still spins fast on its axis. Day follows night, then day appears again in only 6 short hours.

A major extinction event occurs.

Most of the early life forms evolved in a low oxygen environment and cannot adapt fast enough to the change, and a **mass extinction** occurs.

A giant asteroid streams in and strikes the Australian and South African protocontinents.

The crust melts at the impact area. Some of the liquefied rock spatters into the atmosphere, away from the direction of the impact. It drifts in the wind, following the jet stream, and then settles back down as a deposit of sphericals - glassy beads of solidified silicates.

The sphericals contain iridium (which indicates an extraterrestrial source because Earth's supply of iridium, which is a dense element, long ago migrated toward the core). The amount of iridium implies that this asteroid is larger than the one that will later cause a mass extinction for the dinosaurs.

The similarity between the chemical signatures of the bedrock at the Southern tip of Africa and the western coast of Australia indicates that they were impacted by the same asteroid. These two land masses were likely connected, unless the asteroid broke apart just before impact.

The sea turns from green to blue.

Free oxygen reacts with the iron that is dissolved in the sea water. As the iron begins to rust, it falls out of solution.

Iron ore is deposited.

The many layers of rust accumulate into thick sedimentary sequences called banded iron formations. They will become the source of almost all the iron we mine today.

When most of the iron has rusted, free oxygen levels in the ocean increase, leading to the creation of many new mineral forms in addition to iron oxide.

Plate tectonics reshapes the configuration of the protocontinents.

Scientists debate just when plate tectonics starts working. Some think it started way back in the Archean as long as 4 billion years ago, but all agree that it is well underway by now.

Plate tectonics requires that cool crust sinks at subduction zones and new crust forms elsewhere, principally along rifts at the bottom of the ocean. Old, cool oceanic crust is dense and sinks down in subduction zones and it pulls the rest of the plate that it is part of along with it. At the other end of the plate, a rift develops and becomes a spreading center as lava fills the gap.

Where plumes are rising, the rock that is being transferred to shallower depths experiences a lessening of pressure and it melts in a process called 'pressure release melting.' Temperatures were higher when the rock was at deeper levels in the mantle, but it was confined to a solid state by higher pressures.

The first ice age occurs.

This also contributes to the extinction event.

Proterozoic
2
Billion Years Ago

Ice floats due to its unusual properties and the laws of fluid mechanics.

The physical properties of gases and liquids are the subject of fluid mechanics. The technical distinction between a solid and a fluid is that a solid will either resist or deform in response to an applied force, whereas a fluid will shear continuously. Both have definite volume, but only solids have definite shape. Gases have neither definite volume nor shape. They are much less dense than liquids, typically by a factor of a thousand. Differences of density between a solid and a fluid or between two fluids give rise to the phenomenon of buoyancy.

Frozen water is an unusual solid because it is less dense than the liquid form. Usually solids are denser than liquids.

A lighter-than-water solid is subject to an upward buoyancy force equal to the weight of the volume of water that the solid object displaces. The shape of the object does not affect the buoyant force, only its volume.

Because ice is only slightly less dense than water, only a small amount of the ice floats above the surface of the water.

The sky turns blue.

After all the iron in the oceans is oxidized, free oxygen starts to build up in the atmosphere.

Cells become more varied and complex.

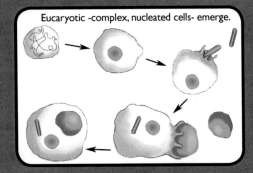

Eucaryotic -complex, nucleated cells- emerge.

Some cells evolve flagella and are able to swim and propel themselves.

Flagella provide propulsion.

Bacteria have evolved elongated structures, called flagella, that are rigid enough that when ions are passed along their length, the cell can achieve propulsion. Eucaryotic cells have evolved their own flagella, which are more complex. Eucaryotic flagella are composed of tubule structures that not only provide propulsion, but also communicate sensory information and can transport food into the cell body like a straw.

Theories exist that state that eucaryotic flagella originated as separate cells of different structures. These highly mobile helical cell structures, called spirochetes, may have created symbiotic relationships with cells that were less mobile, but far more efficient at energy production.

The distribution of the continents around the globe is always changing.

Sometimes the continents are evenly distributed across the planet, but at other times they collide and merge into larger conglomerations. Sometimes they all merge together into a single, giant supercontinent. A supercontinent, once assembled, persists until convection currents within the Earth's mantle rift it apart again. One complete round of assembly followed by disassembly is known as a **supercontinent cycle**.

All of the continents join together to form the supercontinent called Rodinia.

Rodinia assembles at 1 billion years ago but it, too, will break apart. The next supercontinent to assemble, Pangaea, is more likely to be familiar to the reader.

When continents collide, mountain ranges rise up between them at the suture zones. The mountains are primarily made from the sediments that had been lying on the continental shelves of each continent. These sediments are thrust upwards as the continents come together and the ocean that had been between them disappears. When a supercontinent forms, all of the new mountain ranges are of similar age.

The mountains that form on the edge of the North American continent are known as The Grenville Mountains.

Algae evolve that can exist on land, at least in moist areas such as shorelines. They form crusts and scums but the land is otherwise devoid of vegetation.

Proterozoic
1
Billion Years Ago

Proterozoic
1,000
Million Years Ago

One billion years is the same as one thousand million years.

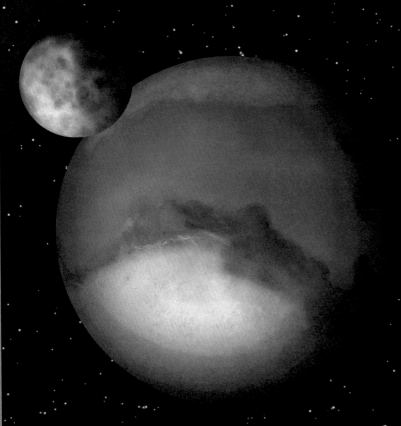

The great landmass of Rodinia drifts toward the south pole, creating the perfect platform for ice to accumulate.

Ice, the solid form of water, reflects sunlight rather than absorbing it as liquid water does.

The ice sheets advance and keep growing.

As more ice forms, ever more sunlight is reflected back out into space, in a self-reinforcing feedback loop.

The unique buoyant property of ice creates conditions in which life can survive.

Unlike most materials, water is less dense in its solid form. This allows ice to float on top of liquid water. Although the ice sheets are thick, and possibly extend all the way to the equator, some liquid water still circulates beneath them, allowing living organisms to survive.

Earth becomes entombed in an icy shell.

This episode, which geologists refer to as **Snowball Earth**, is one of the most extreme extinction events that the Earth has ever endured.

Proterozoic
700
Million Years Ago

Chapter 4: Complex Organisms Diversify and Insects Fly

The supercontinent Rodinia finally rifts apart, bringing heat up from the interior and allowing Earth to break out of its icy shell. Life survived the great freeze, and it suddenly flourishes in what geologists now call **The Garden of Ediacara.**

The supercontinent acted like a blanket, trapping heat from the interior. In turn, the heat caused the supercontinent to rift apart. Places already riddled with faults gave way first. The areas with the faults were underneath the mountain ranges that arose when the continents collided to form the supercontinent. Therefore, the supercontinent broke apart mostly along previous continental borders.

With some water still tied up in ice, sea levels are low. The seas between continents near the equator flourish with new, multicellular forms of life.

Many of the Ediacarin life forms are anchored to the sea floor. They wave in the water currents.

It is debated whether these life forms are plants or animals. Do they harbor photosynthesisng bacteria? Do they filter-feed on bacteria? Are they some sort of chemotroph? Fossils exist, but it is hard to discern the anatomy of these soft-bodied forms from the fossil evidence.

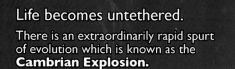

Life becomes untethered.

There is an extraordinarily rapid spurt of evolution which is known as the **Cambrian Explosion.**

Life continues to evolve. Animals with hard parts and complicated body plans emerge.

Anything goes - even clumsy methods of locomotion allow animals to filter-feed planktonic material in the water column. Other animals, higher on the food chain, evolve to feed on these life forms.

Cambrian
525
Million Years Ago

The earliest **land plants** evolve.

About 450 million years ago, the first plants colonize dry land. They are low-lying algae, mosses, and bryophytes like liverwort. Possessing no vascular systems, they can only live near the top of the water table. They rely on wind to spread their spores instead of water currents.

Although only centimeters in height, land plants lift their heads above the ground. It is not easy to transport water upward against gravity; land plants are finally able to grow taller as their vascular systems develop. Upright plants like Cooksonia (the earliest known vascular plant), are able to extend their spore producing organs higher into the wind than their predecessors.

Larger, more sophisticated predators evolve.

The **nautilus** uses buoyancy to adjust its height in the water column.

The nautilus is a mollusc that lives in the last segment of its long conical shell. Each of the other segments is separate and sealed but an internal tube runs through them all. When the compartments are filled with water the nautilus is neutrally buoyant at deep depths. When air moves through the tube and displaces the water in the compartments the creature rises to drift at shallow levels.

The nautilus can move like a rocket.

When the nautilus wants to move quickly it spits out compressed water in the direction opposite the way it wants to go. The water expelled was pressurized by being compressed into a smaller space by the action of the nautilus's muscles on the walls of the bladder that lines the chamber. The water rushes out of the bladder when it is allowed to escape because the water pressure of the surrounding ocean is less. The molecules of H2O that compose the liquid water that is vented are no longer confined and the average distance between the molecules increases as the previously compressed fluid is released. The nautilus is propelled quickly, if only for a short duration, in the direction opposite the blast. Isaac Newton codified this concept with 'every action has an equal and opposite reaction'.

The first **vertebrates** (animals with a backbone of articulating vertebrae, that protect a nerve or spinal column) keep evolving from their pre-Cambrian ancestors.

The first animals to venture from the sea onto land are the six-legged **Arthropods**.

Arthropods (the ancestors of insects) are among the first herbivores, and became agents of evolutionary selection for land plants. Early plant life reproduced via **spores**, which grew high up on special leaves called 'sporophylls.' The jaw and mandible anatomy of insects in the fossil record is consistent with a diet of these early plants.

The world's oldest known insect, *Rhyniognatha hirsti* lived in what is today known as Scotland. As far back as 400 mya, during the Silurian, North America and Europe were connected by a massive mountain range, the Grenville. Based on *Rhyniognatha*'s body structure, some scientists believe that it may have evolved primitive wings by this time.

The continents, which had been joined together in the super-continent Rodiania drift away from one another. Soon they will reach their most scattered arrangement and then eventuallu they will get stuck together once again to make a new super-continent. But for now the individual landmasses will be widely sperated continents,

Vertebrates radiate into a huge variety of fish forms.

Insects evolve proto-wings.

There are several popular theories for insect wing evolution.

One theory postulates that some insects evolved gills on their thorax as well as their abdomen, and used these for added propulsion in the water. If these insects spent any of their life out the water, these extra gill plates could have been used to steer during a fall while escaping predators. Evolution would have favored insects with the powerful muscles and large gill plates necessary to create lift, and flight would have eventually become a mode of transportation.

Another theory states that insect wings come from plates used for heating and cooling the body. The ability to warm up faster than a predator on a cold day could save an insect's life, and having a hinge to be able to orient its solar collectors toward the sun would expedite this process. At certain sizes, these platelets could become effective gliding surfaces, and with strong hinge muscles, flight would eventually evolve.

Silurian
430
Million Years Ago

Some of the vertebrate animals step out of the water and onto dry land.

They are called tetrapods and have a four-legged body plan that is quite familiar to us.

It takes a lot of strength to stand on dry land. Without the support of the water, a strong skeleton and muscles are required just to raise the head and support the internal organs.

Tetrapods emerge as some fish evolve sturdier fins, which they use to 'walk' about in the mud. This skill likely becomes more useful as fish in drying lagoons are able to waddle to the next lake or puddle and swim again.

These evolving fish develop lungs from their gills, then develop thicker skin, and their fins evolve into sturdier legs.

Plants grow ever taller as their vascular systems develop to keep their tops supplied with water.

These newly land-based animals must return to the water to breed.

The development of the **Tetrapod** from a fish ancestor is truly significant for humanity! Other fish species continue to diversify into other new fish species.

Devonian
375
Million Years Ago

Tectonic motion is causing the continents to converge again. A new super continent will soon form.

Vegetation grows tall.

Plants evolve that can produce lignin, a tough molecule that gives them the strength to stand up. Taller plants are able to gather more sunlight and therefore rapidly become prolific.

Insects fly.

The first flying insects appear in the fossil record around 320 mya, with 10 genera having fully functional wings.

The earliest winged insects are from the *Pterygota* subclass, now the most species-rich group of insects on Earth (around 60% of all described species).

Huge coal deposits form.

Leaf litter and vegetative debris pile up on an unprecedented scale. Microorganisms and fungi have not yet evolved to rapidly process the tough lignin, so vegetative matter accumulates without decomposing. This carbon-rich debris is buried and will eventually be turned into coal. Most of the coal that we burn today is from these deposits. They are so extensive that this geologic period is called the Carboniferous. Swamps flood the land. Shallow waters swallow the vegetative debris, further retarding its decomposition.

The atmosphere starts to become richer in oxygen because free oxygen is a by-product of photosynthesis and because the burial of debris sequesters carbon, removing it from the atmosphere where it would form carbon dioxide.

Carboniferous
330
Million Years Ago

Insects evolve two distinct body plans for flight.

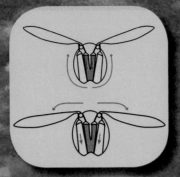

The earliest method for flying involves connecting each wing to a pair of muscles inside the sternum. One of the pair expands while the other contracts. They are directly connected at a pivot point and operate almost like a pulley system with one set controlling the upstroke while the other controls the downstroke. This is called **direct flight** and dates back to the first members of the Odonata (damselflies and dragonflies) and Blattodea (cockroaches and termites) families.

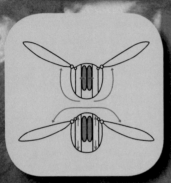

The second method is called **indirect flight**. With this body plan, the muscles are attached to the shell of the thorax, which contracts on the downstroke and expands on the upstroke. In this type of body plan, the muscles that specifically control the angle and pitch of the wing are generally connected directly to the wing itself. This combination of direct and indirect muscle-to-wing connection is much newer, and present in most extant insect species.

Some of the tetrapods evolve shelled eggs. These new animals are called **reptiles**.

Reptiles are free to stay on the land; they no longer have to return to water to breed.

The **amniotic egg** encloses a miniature ocean and a nutritious yolk sac for the developing embryo.

Temperatures fall and ice caps form at the poles, dropping sea levels.

As sea level drops, more land is exposed, creating more habitat for land-dwelling animals.

The enclosed egg, also called an amniotic egg, requires that fertilization take place within the female's body. While female fish and amphibians lay eggs in water and males deposit sperm over the eggs afterward, amniotes require penetrative sex to fertilize the eggs inside the body of the female before the eggs are laid.

High oxygen levels in the air facilitate the development of amniotes. The shell protects the embryo from drying out but can impede the exchange of gasses. It is easier for the carbon dioxide inside to diffuse out through pores in the shell and for the oxygen to flow in when oxygen levels are high. This is due to a higher concentration of each gas on opposite sides of the shell.

A continent can be seen approaching in the distance. The supercontinent **Pangaea** is forming.

As tectonic plates converge, the ocean crust between the plates is subducted and a belt of volcanos forms over the subduction zone.

Recent sequestering of massive amounts of CO_2 in the form of vegetative debris has created an oxygen-rich environment.

Oxygen levels reach their highest in Earth's history, about 30%. Today, oxygen makes up about 20% of the air.

This abundance of oxygen allows some flying insects to evolve giant sizes and energetic flight. High oxygen levels also make forests vulnerable to fires caused by lightning strikes.

Permian
290
Million Years Ago

The **Griffinfly** is large but maneuvers with precision.

The Griffinfly has a very similar body plan to extant dragonflies, but is only distantly related. Griffinflies have four powerful wings (some species possess wingspans over 2 feet wide), which they use for very precise aerial maneuvering in their hunt for other insects to prey upon, though they cannot walk very well.

The abundance of free oxygen in the air and the oceans plummets.

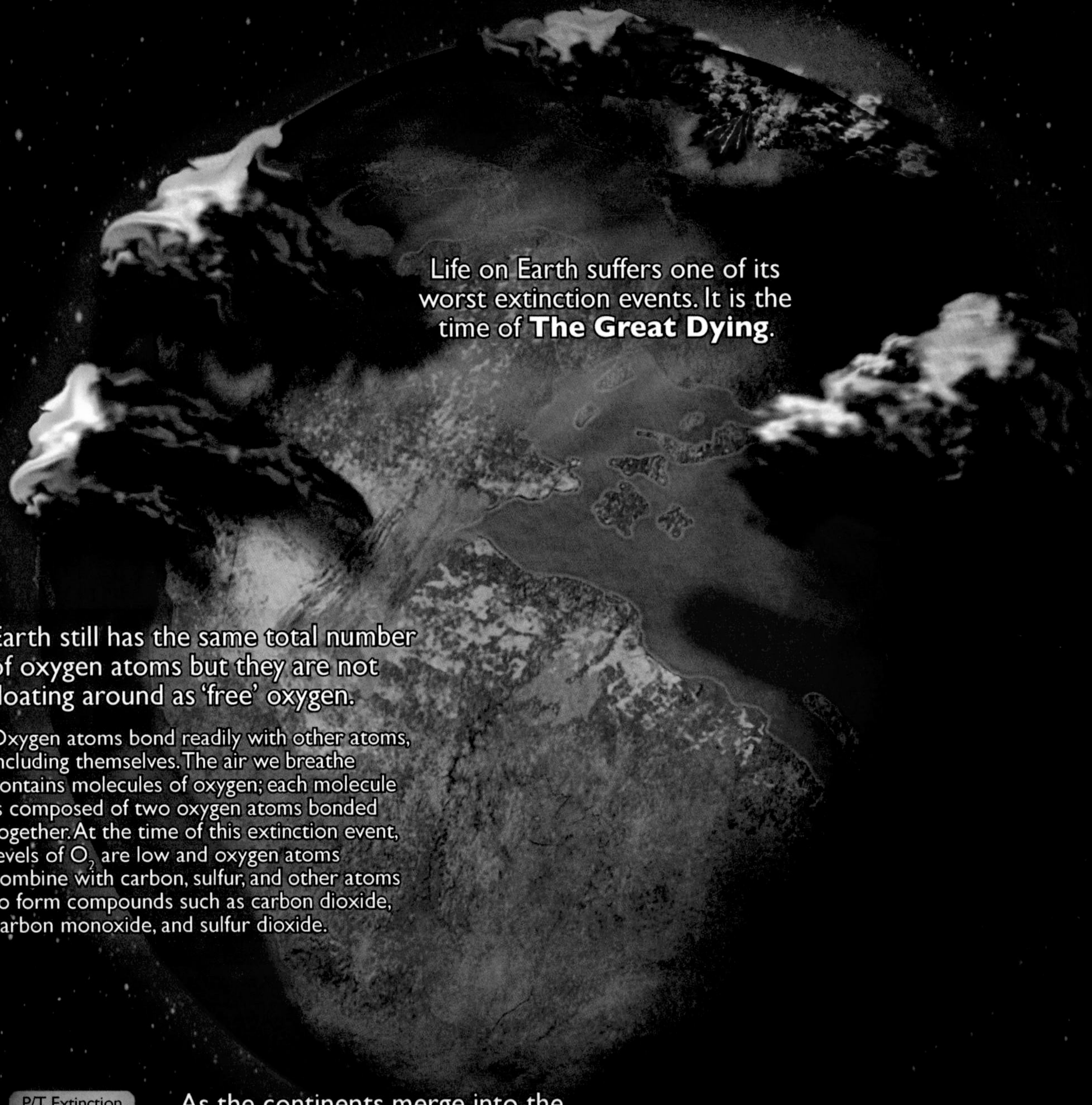

Life on Earth suffers one of its worst extinction events. It is the time of **The Great Dying**.

Earth still has the same total number of oxygen atoms but they are not floating around as 'free' oxygen.

Oxygen atoms bond readily with other atoms, including themselves. The air we breathe contains molecules of oxygen; each molecule is composed of two oxygen atoms bonded together. At the time of this extinction event, levels of O_2 are low and oxygen atoms combine with carbon, sulfur, and other atoms to form compounds such as carbon dioxide, carbon monoxide, and sulfur dioxide.

P/T Extinction
250
Million Years Ago

As the continents merge into the supercontinent **Pangaea**, another supercontinent cycle is completed.

This extinction event is probably caused by a perfect storm of several concurrent factors

Magmatic activity in Siberia causes air pollution.

Most scientists attribute the primary cause of this extinction event to effects from the extensive amount of lava pouring out in Siberia, which paves over an area the size of Western Europe. A plume of magma rising up from the mantle erupts underneath a continent. To make matters worse, it erupts under layers of peat and coal which release more toxic gasses that add to the load of sulphur dioxide and particulates, transforming the atmosphere into a suffocating shroud. These aerosols likely block sunlight and plunge the planet into freezing temperatures which also reduces the amount of coastline.

An asteroid may have struck.

It has been proposed that an asteroid struck, but no conclusive evidence of this has been found, despite much searching by scientists. Another version of the asteroid hypothesis is that the impact of a giant asteroid *caused* the eruption of the Siberian Traps. The culprit would have been giant and struck on the other side of the globe at the Wilkes Land Crater, also called the Wilkes Mass Concentration, which lies beneath the Antarctic ice sheet and is therefore hard to study. It is a 300 km wide area of unusually high density surrounded by concentric rings visible in satellite radar images. So far the date of this impact, if it was an impact, is not precise but most likely occurred between 500 and 100 mya.

Ocean currents change.

Earth's oceans become stagnant as ocean currents are disrupted by the new continental configuration. This starves the sea floor of oxygen, causing the dead sea life to accumulate rather than decompose. After a while, the deep ocean currents are reestablished and they churn up this anoxic load of biomass. As it rots, it sucks the oxygen out of surface waters, suffocating marine life.

Earth loses many of its coastal environments as the continents merge into the more compact supercontinent; a supercontinent has less perimeter than do multiple continents.

Anaerobic bacteria make a comeback.

Another hypothesis, championed by Peter Ward, is that anaerobic bacteria, once the dominant life forms on Earth, proliferate again, out-competing multicellular organisms when the oceans become anoxic.

About three quarters of terrestrial species go extinct.

Only about 3% of marine animal species survive.

land organisms

marine organisms

More than 75% of all land species become extinct.
Only 3% of marine species survive.

Chapter 5: Vertebrates Fly

In the new era, winged social insects will dominate the insect realm and tetrapods will achieve flight

Species that survived the catastrophe radiate and diversify into the wide range of recently vacated ecological niches, creating new ecosystems.

Species of flying insects are abundant.

Some of the most proficient insect flyers flourish and radiate into several new orders, including the precursors to what will become the social insects: wasps, bees, and ants.

Moths and butterflies are getting their start.

The supercontinent Pangaea begins to break up.

Cracks in the crust of the super continent widen into rifts. Molten rock flows episodically out of the rifts, as huge amounts of liquid rock erupt in the rift zone. The newly created pavement grows in extent as the rift continues to open. The continuing effusion of magma and the continual spreading apart will create the Atlantic Ocean.

North America begins to separate from South America and Africa.

As new crust is created in the rift, elsewhere on the planet, old crust sinks back into the mantle at a subduction zone.

Small reptiles jump around in the trees.

Pterosaurs evolve in the Late Triassic (approximately 228 mya. They are not dinosaurs but they do share a common ancestor.

The small hopping reptiles evolve progressively larger skin flaps under their arms to ease landing after catching an aerial meal or dropping from a tree limb to escape a predator.

Pterosaurs evolve and fly.

Pterosaurs are the first group of vertebrates to evolve true flight. Most species of pterosaur have wings with a high aspect ratio, meaning that they are long and narrow, which makes them excellent gliders. Wing loading refers to the ratio of body weight to overall wing surface area. Pterosaurs have lightweight bodies and big wings and so have a low wing loading value. High aspect wings and low wing loading allow them to thrive in coastal, mountainous, and plains environments.

Pterosaur wings are tensile.

The skin flap extending across the elbow from thumb to shoulder (the *propatagium*) is attached to a wrist bone. This bone, called the pteroid, enables them to fine-tune wing cambering.

Research suggests that pterosaurs could tighten or release different sections of the wing independently, allowing for differential cambering.

Dinosaurs are evolving.

Their hind legs are situated beneath their hips, giving them a more upright stance than their reptilian ancestors. This allows them to move on dry land with great speed and agility. They soon out-compete other reptiles on land.

Thermoregulation is essential. Animals must maintain their temperature within a narrow range; too cool causes sluggish chemical reactions, and too warm causes some proteins to begin to unravel. Dinosaurs evolve many energy-saving attributes.

Dinosaurs evolve **Feathers** for insulation.

Long, hair-like filamentary tubes are the first structures to evolve in the feather family. These filaments may be the predecessor of the rachis, the backbone of the feathers we know today. This morphotype of feather is so similar to filamentary structures found on pterosaur remains that it may have begun to evolve as far back as 240 mya, before the pterosaur line diverged.

Pterosaurs take off by leaping.

Pterosaurs face into the wind and launch themselves forward by rocking and pushing off their knuckles, like pole-vaulters.

Feathers are adapted for flight.

Feathers are adapted for flight by Theropod dinosaurs that are called birds. One of the earliest birds, Archaeopteryx, appears in what is now Germany. Other early emerging bird species are also found in the fossil record of China.

Feathers have multiple uses.

Dinosaurs of the Theropod line evolve with various configurations of feathers. Hypotheses for their uses include thermoregulation, the ability to run faster, to cover eggs during brooding, and as mating displays. Feathered arms and tails allow for greater speed and agility while skipping along trails and also for the ability to glide down from trees.

The ability to fly gives some pollinating insects an advantage. These pollinators prosper and build complex relationships with plants that prosper with them.

Angiosperms, land plants and trees that produce flowers and fruit, are evolving. Alongside them, insects like beetles and flies evolve mouthparts suited specifically to certain families of plants. This exclusivity causes parallel evolutionary changes in both the plants and the insects. As the insects' diet becomes less general and more attuned to individual plant families, the plants in turn adapt methods of better attracting and rewarding them. Pollen-producing and receiving organs of angiosperms evolve to best suit the body shapes of their biggest pollinators, maximizing their potential for reproduction.

Superorganisms evolve.

Superorganisms are colonies of individuals who have different roles, like forager, soldier, and queen. Reproduction is a role limited to few. Colonies contain thousands of members, but individuals are not autonomous and can only survive as part of the group. Insect species that evolve the trait of eusocialness will come to dominate the insect realm.

Termites are the first superorganisms.

Jurassic
170
Million Years Ago

Pterosaurs diversify into many different ecological niches and develop appropriate body plans.

Some species of pterosaur soar and traverse the sky at great heights with their high aspect ratio wings. Their narrow wings can be up to 15 meters long.

Species of forest-dwelling pterosaur have short stubby wings that are maneuverable in close quarters.

Feathers improve.

Developments, or morphotypes, include clusters of filamentary structures emanating from a common base, long pendulous structures with barbules at the end, and even structures that resemble modern feathers. Developments such as the rachis emerge. The helical structure of the rachis suggests that it could be the product of several filament structures twisting and fusing as they grow.

True follicles, the specialized openings from which feathers grow, are hard to document in the fossil record.

Barbules, tiny hook structures that hold the vanes of a feather together during flight, develop. These allow the feather to displace air. The dominant theory at the moment is that the follicle and barb structures evolved simultaneously.

Pennaceous feathers develop.

Pennaceous feathers, which are one of two types of modern feathers, develop approximately 160 mya. They are capable of specializations such as asymmetry and much stronger barbule formations, both of which are ideal for flight.

Some pterosaurs adapt to feed with baleen like teeth while standing in the water. They develop rudder-like tails.

Aquatic birds emerge.

Gansus yumenensis, an aquatic bird from western China, is one of the oldest known "true birds," a member of the *Ornithurae* group/clade. Similar to extant loons or diving ducks, *G. yumenensis* is capable of proficient flight, but has significant webbing between its toes. When comparing the pelvis shape to the length of hind limbs, scientists consider *G. yumenensis* capable of some degree of diving-hunting, probably using both wings and their webbed feet for propulsion. These birds have serrations in their bills, unlike other early bird species, which have teeth.

Flying in *Ground Effect* requires less effort.

In calm conditions, birds and pterosaurs can fly just above the surface of open waters. As the wings are pushed down, they push air downward. The deflection of the air downward causes an equal and opposite reaction and the bird's body moves upward. When flying more than a few wingspans above the ground, some of the air pushed downward by the wing escapes to the sides but close to a surface, more of the air that is pushed down by the wings increases the pressure below the wing.

Social insects evolve flight, lending them a second advantage.

Bees and ants follow termites in becoming eusocial organisms, living in colonies as superorganisms with roles determined by gene expression.

They co-evolve with many angiosperms, consuming, collecting, and spreading their pollen. Nectar is their reward for their pollinating efforts. Some plants evolve traits that cause their flowers to be brightly colored, signaling to pollinators where their rewards are. Bees are able to see ultraviolet light and some flowers evolve nectar guides that are only visible in UV. Flight allows the bees to reach flowers quickly.

Some insects evolve **holometabolism**.

Holometabolism, a particular evolutionary trait of some insects, is a form of development that includes complete metamorphosis with four distinct stages of life. It is likely that holometabolism was evolved by insects that occupy different niches within their environment at different stages of their lives. Larva and the adult insect never compete for food if the niches are separate. Holometabolism allows one insect to feed on several different types of prey over the course of its life. It also allows for the sustenance of some species whose larva do all of the feeding while the adults concentrate entirely on procreation. Holometabolic insects also have different predators throughout their life cycle. With the capability to fly limited to only some stages, a species is able to inhabit distinctly separated niches at different times in its life cycle.

Sails improve thermoregulation.

Spinosaurus is the only aquatic dinosaur to evolve.

Its sail can absorb the sun's heat, or it can be wetted to aid in venting heat away from the body.

Sea turtles evolving in the narrow sea between South America and Africa have only a short distance to go as they migrate back and forth from one shore to another.

A medium-sized asteroid strikes the Moon, creating the **Tycho Crater,** which is still clearly visible today.

India is an island continent that also contains Madagascar.

Pterosaurs utilize the updrafts at cliffs.

As winds push air masses into the obstruction of a cliff, air pressure rises and air flows upward.

Departing their nests at the top of a cliff, pterosaurs face outward into the wind. The wind moving over their wings generates lift. They are able to take off and fly into rising air currents to gain altitude. From high altitudes they can trade height for speed and traverse long distances. Later, they can flap their way back toward the cliffs and then find a rising current to carry them back upward without having to do much flapping.

Hollow (pneumatic) bones and strong flight muscles anchored to their deltopectoral crest make Pterosaurs capable of flapping flight, but the high aspect ratio of their wings implies that they probably preferred to soar.

Cretaceous
120
Million Years Ago

A plethora of marine reptiles that are neither dinosaurs nor fish hunt the seas.

Pterosaurs must compete with birds.

Seeds fly for dispersal.

The *Asteraceae* family, one of the largest families of flowering plants, emerges around 76 mya. This family will eventually achieve worldwide coverage and many members evolve advanced methods of seed dispersal. As pollinated flowers change to seed-bearing pods, a sheath of bristly material forms form beneath the pods. This wind catching apparatus remains attached to the seeds as they mature and break away from the plant. With strong winds, the seeds can drift far away from the host plant. Dispersal of seeds by the wind is known as anemochory by botanists.

Flowering trees prosper and multiply.

Flowering trees have leaves instead of needles and a different method of reproduction. Known as deciduous trees, they begin to supplant ferns and conifers as the dominant vegetation

Plants evolve fruit, enticing larger animals to snack. The fruit contains seeds, some of which pass through the digestive tracks of the animals intact and are then deposited far away from the plant. Just as the much smaller insects are rewarded with sugary nectar for cross-fertilizing seeds by transporting pollen from one plant to another, the larger animals are rewarded with fruit for transporting the seeds.

Flowering plants together with their pollinators and seed dispersers form a self-reinforcing symbiotic cycle. The pollinators and seed dispersers increase the ability of the plants to reproduce and spread into new territories, in turn benefitting from the proliferation of more plant life. The territories of the plants and their animal symbionts expand. Unfortunately for the plants, animals sometimes eat their leaves. Plants need their green leaves to catch sunlight for photosynthesis. Plants evolve various defense mechanisms, such as thorns, waxy coatings, and indigestible or toxic compounds, to discourage animals.

The *Asteraceae* family, one of the largest families of flowering plants, emerges around 76 mya. This family will eventually achieve worldwide coverage and many members evolve advanced methods of seed dispersal. As pollinated flowers change to seed-bearing pods, pappus is formed. Pappus are a specially modified version of the calyx (the often-green part of flowers that protects the petals), and remain attached to seeds as they mature. In many species, the pappus is feathery or made of bristles that can catch the wind, carrying the seeds far away from the host plant. Dispersal of seeds by the wind is known as anemochory by botanists.

Other species of flowering plants evolve methods that do not require flying animals for seed dispersal. Seed casings develop barbs that can hook themselves onto the coats or hides of passing animals, which then drop them far away.

Bees communicate with the waggle dance.

Bees develop complex dances through which they are able to communicate information such as direction, distance, and quality of new foraging grounds. The dancer aligns herself in the direction of the attraction, the vigor of the dance indicates its quality, and the duration of the dance indicates its distance away.

The social organization of insects that act as a eusocial colony is so successful that they soon have the dominant share of total insect biomass.

Pterosaurs still dominate some niches but birds, with their feathers and improvements in thermoregulation and respiration, gain an increasing presence.

Gliding saves effort.

Flapping allows birds to gain altitude and forward momentum, while gliding and soaring evolve to conserve energy. By angling the forward edge of their wings upward, birds gently deflect the air flowing around them downward, creating lift. In any flying body, the force of lift acts perpendicular to the plane of the lifting surface.

Both the top and bottom surfaces of the wing deflect air. Air currents moving under the wing are deflected by the solid surface of the wing itself, while air currents moving above are pulled along the top surface because of the "Coanda Effect." This phenomenon occurs when the air current clings to the surface of the wing as it passes over it.

Aquatic birds feed in new ways.

Ancestors of extant waterfowl develop multiple methods of feeding. The interior structure of waterfowl beaks allows for water to be drawn in from the tip of the bill and pumped out from the sides. A system of fine, hair-like structures that act like filters on the tongue and roof of the mouth catch particulate matter, such as minuscule shrimp. Additionally, according to the niches that these ancient waterfowl adapt to fill, they will develop other diets. Some will also hunt for fish or graze on vegetation.

Cretaceous
90
Million Years Ago

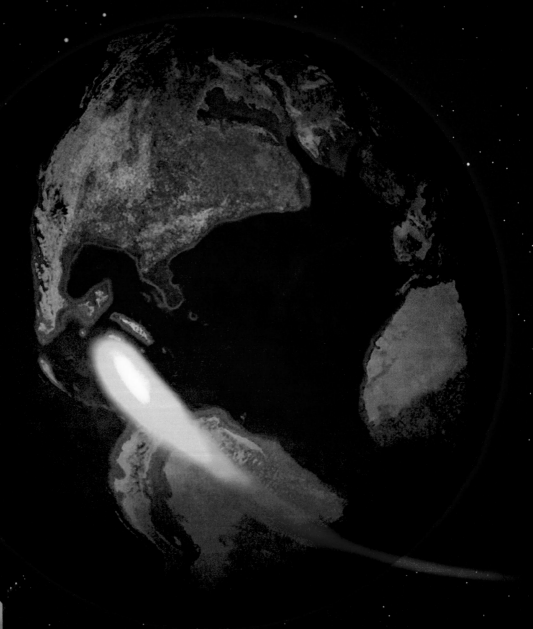

Unfortunately for the dinosaurs, a very large asteroid is heading toward Earth.

K/T Boundary
65
Million Years Ago

The asteroid strikes Mexico at an angle. North America is the first casualty, but the damage will soon be worldwide.

The heat of the impact melts the rock where it lands and flings molten glass sphericules across North America, setting forests aflame.

The Chixalub Crater created by this event can still be found on the Yucatan Peninsula of Mexico. The deposition of glass sphericules is arrayed outward from it, in a northerly direction.

The asteroid strikes a highly developed, complex ecosystem.

The asteroid hits just when life on Earth is flourishing. Dinosaurs fill the niches on every continent, while highly evolved mammals coexist at their feet. Flowers, which had become ever more beautiful to attract the beneficial animals that coevolved with them, are in full bloom. It is a beautiful world, but it is about to change abruptly.

Flowering plants will survive this extinction event and continue to evolve.

This closes the chapter of the dinosaur age.

Chapter 6: Mammals Embrace the New Era

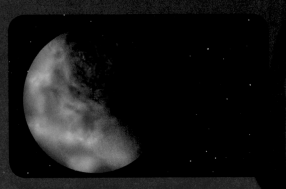

The asteroid that sails in causes so much destruction to the biosphere that all large land animals die. Only the small straggle into the new era.

The asteroid comes in at an angle and crashes into the sedimentary rocks of the Yucatan Peninsula of Mexico. Some of the kinetic energy of the asteroid is converted to heat when its motion is stopped, which liquefies the rocks at the impact site. Some of its energy is transferred to the now molten mush of silicon dioxide, which is pushed into the atmosphere as a spray of shiny sphericules. When these droplets of glass eventually rain down, they set the world's forests ablaze. These sphericules can still be found today in the sediments of North America; they fade in concentration with distance from the impact site, which is also still discernible.

Temperatures plummet in the weeks following the blast, as sunlight cannot penetrate the dust-filled atmosphere. Plants cannot perform photosynthesis. Freezing temperatures continue for months.

Mammals, the small, wily, burrowers that had been sidelined in the dinosaur age, suddenly find themselves survivors in a largely vacant world.

Their burrows protect them from the effects of the impactor's blast, the forest fires, and the low temperatures that follow. Their small size helps them survive because they require less food than larger animals, and their mammalian metabolism helps them maintain proper body temperature.

Present on every continent, mammals will soon diversify to fill the vacant niches; some will even take to the skies.

Mammals are a class of animals named for their sucking behavior.

Infant mammals drink the nutritious milk from their mother's mammary glands.

Birds survive the extinction event!

Until recently, scientists did not recognize that birds are dinosaurs. This extinction event, one of the 7 largest extinction episodes that Earth has endured, is referred to as the end of the dinosaur age. But the birds carry on!

Flight allows birds to move between any pockets in the landscape that were spared the brunt of the devastation.

Pterosaurs become extinct, reducing competition for the birds. Birds are becoming ever more evolved than their dinosaur ancestors, and will fill ecological niches where they find them.

Some bird species will evolve impressive wingspans capable of sustained flight over many hundreds of miles. Some will evolve stealth in slow flight. Beaks and bills will evolve to suit individual habitats and food sources. Their plumage coloring and feather types will evolve as needed.

Scavenging birds as well as the ancestors of ducks are particularly well suited to the new circumstances.

Scavengers have access to plenty of food in the dark days of the early aftermath. Ducks, which are robust and still fairly mobile, have the ability to limit heat loss from their legs in cold water because the arteries and veins of their legs run so close together that heat is scavenged from the arteries that supply blood to the feet, prewarming the blood as it returns to the body. Reducing the temperature of the blood to the feet minimizes the temperature difference between the feet and the water and so reduces heat transfer to the water.

Mammals fly.

With claws on the end of every digit, the oldest known **bat** ancestor hunts the night.

Bats, which are the only mammals to evolve true flight, also evolve the sophisticated instrumentation of echolocation. Scientists have long debated which came first, powered flight or the ability to navigate and locate prey with sonar. Scientists are in agreement that bats evolved as arboreal gliders, climbing trees and catching prey on the way down. Both traits evolved quickly, in less than 13 million years after the end of the dinosaur era, and were already fully developed in the limited number of bat fossil specimens that have been found.

Bats do not readily fossilize; their bodies are small and delicate and they typically lived in tropical climates where their remains decomposed quickly. In 2003, fossils of a transitional species, *Onychonycteris finneyi*, were found in the fine grained sedimentary rocks of the Green River Formation of Wyoming. This species had well-developed wings but lacked an enlarged cochlea, the spiral shaped cavity of the inner ear necessary for echolocation. Flight came first!

Paleogene
50
Million Years Ago

Birds speciate at an astonishing rate.

Birds are able to travel long distances in very short amounts of time, speeding their dispersal into all kinds of environments all over the world. As they encounter new biomes, they are well-equipped to fill local niches, which speeds their speciation. Their body plans, beak shapes, diets, flight patterns, and mating habits all shift and change to meet the rigors of their environment.

Monkeys make it to South America by raft.

Monkeys evolve in Africa, but by 36 mya they are present in South America as well. Unlike sea turtles, monkeys could not have swum - the continents are too far apart - so they probably floated over on rafts of vegetation.

Their thumbs are opposable and nails have replaced claws to allow for sensitive grasping of vines and branches.

They have forward facing eyes for stereoscopic vision, which allows them to accurately judge distances.

The allure of sweet fruit at the ends of branches tempts the daring and inquisitive primates to brave the danger of falling. They swing and scamper as they watch the pollinators fly with ease.

Primates develop a swinging form of locomotion. Their shoulders allow their upper arms to rotate in their sockets. Tails can serve as a counterweight or grasp onto branches for an additional anchor.

Eocene
40
Million Years Ago

Around 50 mya, the *Accipitridae* family, which includes all extant hawks, eagles, kites, harriers, and Old World vultures, arises. These species will go on to fill biosphere niches, on every continent except Antarctica. This family is extremely well suited for long bouts of soaring, expending very little energy flapping their wings in their search for food.

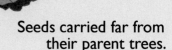

Flying squirrels glide.

Although they do not achieve true flight, flying squirrels have grown large skin flaps between their limbs, allowing for medium-distance gliding. A few hypotheses have been proposed to explain the differences between tree squirrels and those capable of gliding. The prominent theory is that flying squirrels evolved skin flaps to become more efficient arboreal foragers; they do not need to return to the forest floor before exploring a new tree but can simply leap from one tree to another. Gliding is an extremely efficient method of travel that requires minimal energy. It also allows them to quickly escape predators without risk of bodily harm upon impact.

Seeds carried far from their parent trees.

Samara structures carry seeds far from their parent trees. Some tree species, such as maples and elms, evolve methods of seed dispersal that harness the power of the wind to carry them to new growing grounds. Samaras are actually dried fruit hulls that are light and papery and grow around the tree's seeds. By catching the wind and pulling the nutlet away from the tree, seeds can travel long distances.

The **Hummingbird** family breaks away from the Swift family around 42 mya. These tiny, powerful fliers are a good example of animals coevolving with their food sources. Hummingbirds are mostly nectarivores, and the flowers they feed on coevolved to rely on them for pollination. The degree to which individual hummingbird species have evolved to pair with specific families of flowers means that not only are their beaks perfectly shaped for the flowers they visit, but also that many species of hummingbirds can cohabitate in a given environment without competing for food.

Oil forms in the Middle East.

The open seaway between Africa and Eurasia is closing.

The oil fields of the Middle East will soon form; the remains of planktonic organisms will accumulate in the drying waterway between Africa and Asia. When this debris is buried it will be transformed into oil. Whales will become trapped in the closing seaway. Their remains are found today in the Sahara.

The Himalayas rise as India converges with Asia.

India is a small separate continent that has been drifting northward at a fast rate. Eurasia is moving slowly southward.

Owls are hunting.

The oldest known owl ancestor is also one of the largest. With long slender bones, *Ogygoptynx wetmori* may be more than a meter tall. Scientists know that this species, which is found in Colorado, is at least 60 million years old, but may have even hunted the Cretaceous skies, surviving the extinction event that killed the non-avian dinosaurs.

Specialized feathers allow owls to hunt silently.

On the leading edge of their flight feathers, owls have specialized ridges in the rachis structures. These structures disrupt airflow over the wing, muffling the sound of flapping into a near-silent hum.

Owls have stereoscopic vision.

Stereoscopic vision improves navigation in three dimensions, helping the hunter to fly between branches and to judge the distance between its prey and the background. Most birds have eyes on the sides of their heads, giving them better peripheral vision, allowing them to look for predators from all angles. Owls must turn their heads to look sideways.

The Alps rise and the jet stream is diverted northward.

As Africa continues to converge with Eurasia, the Alps form. When the jet stream moves northward, the plains at mid latitudes cool down and dry out.

In Africa, tectonic uplift associated with the opening of the East African rift also contributes to jungles becoming savannah.

Mountains affect weather and airflow.

When an air mass encounters a mountain range, it must rise to cross it and it encounters cooler temperatures as it rises. As the air cools, clouds form and the moisture they hold condenses out as rain. The windward side of the mountain gets the rain and is more fertile than the leeward side.

The air mass descends over the mountain in a chaotic way, creating burbles and turbulence that can pull flying bodies dangerously close to the mountain.

Some species of animals adapt to the mountains by making a short but significant annual migration: altitudinal migration. In winter, they seek food and shelter in lower climes and move higher up the mountains in the warm season.

Miocene
25
Million Years Ago

A new, more energy efficient, kind of grass evolves.

The new kind of grass, called C4 grass because of the way it fixes carbon, uses the energy from bright sunlight more efficiently when temperatures are high.

All photosynthesizing plants take CO_2 from the air and break it apart using the energy of sunlight. Plants use the carbon part of the CO_2 to make sugars for their own energy use and to build their leaves, roots, and other structures. They release the oxygen atoms, which then latch onto one another, forming O_2 - free oxygen - which animals can inhale.

Grasses and some other plants that also evolve a C4 system will soon out-compete plants that still use the old C3 method, but only at low- to mid-latitudes, where the sunlight is intense and temperatures are high enough.

Grasses evolve and prosper, and the animals that graze on them evolve with them.

The grazers eat the grass but they also nurture it by fertilizing it with their manure. Soils increase in depth because grass excels at preventing the soil from washing away. Savannahs, open grasslands with occasional scattered trees, replace woodlands and produce ever more grass.

The landscape opens up as the symbiotic feedback loop continues.

Some of the mammal species evolve longer legs to move across the expanding savannas. Proto-horses make the switch from the low calorie shrubbery to the more nutritious grass and are able to reduce the relative size of their gut and to speed up their metabolism.

Some birds give up their ability to fly.

Flight is expensive. For all its rewards, there is a price to pay. In order to fly, all parts of the body must be optimized for this one goal and must work together as a finely-tuned whole.

For natural selection to have favored other traits over the ability to fly (by allowing birds with these other traits to survive and reproduce), the savings gained by not optimizing for flight must have been substantial.

Flightless birds or their fossilized remains are found in areas that had once been adjacent when the southern portion of Pangaea, known as Gondwana, was still assembled. Gondwana contained South America, Africa, and Australia. It seems natural to assume that because flightless bird species evolve on all of these continents, they must have had a flightless common ancestor dating from before the breakup of Gondwana.

However, recent genetic evidence suggests otherwise. It seems that some bird species evolved in a flightless direction on a few different occasions. Because flight is useful for finding food and mates, escaping predators, and migrating to more favorable climates, it really must be expensive.

Avians that lose their ability to fly still posses other tools and body plans that evolved in their flying ancestors. These include an efficient respiratory system, lightweight bones, and several kinds of feathers.

The ostrich is the most familiar flightless bird living today. Its legs are long, allowing it to run fast over open expanses, and it lives in a tough desert environment. The ostrich is tame compared with its early cousins.

Truly formidable flightless birds evolve in South America, .

Paleontologists refer to these lightweight, long legged, terrestrial avians that run down their prey and impale it on their hatchet-like beaks, as **Terror Birds**. On the isolated continent of South America, terror birds become the apex predator.

Volcanos pour out lava in what will become Central America.

The volcanos between North and South America pour out lava and erupt clouds of ash that build into new islands. Some species of animals move from island to island. Small animals can survive on rafts of debris when washed out to sea in storms. Islands give a resting place to birds that cannot fly long distances. But most large animals are still confined to either North or South America.

In North America, social carnivores that live in packs and hunt as a team are among the apex predators. The grey wolf coexists alongside the much larger dire wolf but they do not compete. The dire wolf is stout with short legs and a big head; it preys on large, lumbering game. The grey wolf is smarter, slimmer, and faster; it preys on the smaller game that the Dire wolf would have a hard time catching.

The Yellowstone Hotspot erupts.

The Yellowstone Hotspot erupts repeatedly. The North American tectonic plate is moving slowly southwestward and it is sliding over the stationary hotspot. At about 16 mya the hotspot pours out lava on the border between Oregon and Nevada. Major eruptions follow at 15 and 11 mya. Old calderas are buried under subsequent flows and the trail of flows extends to the northeast, forming what is called a hotspot track. The Castleford Crossing Eruption at 8.1 mya qualifies as a supereruption; it leaves a layer of basalt (solidified lava) 1.3 km thick.

As the tectonic plate moves along, the hotspot will eventually end up where it is today, under Yellowstone, Wyoming.

The hominin line branches away.

The hominin line of primates branches away from the hominid line at around 6 mya. The word Hominid refers to all Great Apes, alive or extinct. This includes Orangutans, Chimpanzees, Gorillas, and Humans, as well as all of their ancestors. Hominin, however, refers only to humans and our immediate ancestors. Today there is only one extant species of Hominin. Long before Homo sapiens will appear on the scene, however, many other hominins will have their day.

Surprise and speed enable some birds of prey
to hunt with deadly efficiency.

Some birds of prey, particularly falcons, can reach
incredible speeds by tucking in their wings midair and dropping onto their prey. This technique,
known as 'stooping,' either kills their prey
instantly or stuns them for easy retrieval.

Peregrine falcons have been known to exceed
speeds of 200 mph while stooping. These
high speeds could potentially damage their
physiology, but special adaptations, including
a third pair of translucent eyelids and a
protrusion over their nostrils, keep them safe
from rapid, drastic changes in pressure and
wind strength.

The new land bridge between the Americas changes ocean currents as well as ecosystems.

Pliocene
3.5
Million Years Ago

Animals travel overland between the continents, in the Great American Interchange.

There is some debate among scientists as to exactly when the land bridge blocks the ocean current and when it becomes a passable road for animals. The flow of water may have been hampered long before the bridge was completed and may, therefore, not be the primary cause of the ice age. The volcanism is episodic and early outpourings are hidden under younger layers, complicating the establishment of an exact date. Uplift can also raise previously deposited layers. Some animals may have been able to island hop or swim between the continents early on. The peak of animal species moving across and into the previously separate ecosystems is at 3 mya.

An Ice Age begins.

There have been 5 major ice ages on Earth. At other times, and during most of Earth's history, there haven't been any glaciers or permanent sheets of ice, even at the poles. The first ice age was caused by the Great Oxidation Event at 2.4 billion years ago and is called the Huronian. The Cryogenian, which included the formation of Snowball Earth, occurred 850 to 635 mya. Since the Cambrian Era, there have been 3 ice ages; the Andean-Saharan (460-435 mya), the Karoo (360-260 mya), and the Quarternary, which began 2.6 mya.

We are still in the Quaternary Ice Age. An ice age is any period of time when there is some seasonally permanent ice on the planet. An ice age has warmer and cooler periods within it, which are referred to as glacial periods and interglacial periods. We are currently in an interglacial period, known as the Holocene Epoch of the Quaternary Ice Age.

The Pleistocene is the first epoch of the Quaternary Period,

Some hominins are specialists and some are generalists.

Some hominins become specialists; they adapt to a limited range of resources. Some, like *Paranthropus boisei*, shown here, eat grass almost exclusively. *P. boisei* becomes extinct when the climate changes.

Generalists, such as **Homo habilis**, are adapted to make use of a wider range of resources. They can eat meat, fruits, nuts, insects, and more. They probably have bigger brains in order to process so much variety.

Bipedals can throw stones.

The earliest projectiles are most likely thrown stones. The path of an object moving through space over time is known as its trajectory. To hit a target, hunters must throw with trajectories that allow for the projectile's vertical drop due to gravity. The farther away the target, the greater the drop. Also, objects with faster velocities will drop less. A typical speed for a compact object thrown by hand is 38 m/s.

Hominins study birds in flight.

Hominins watch the birds fly, and it pays off. Birds can see over great distances and they see it when a large predator brings down a kill. They circle overhead as they wait for a chance to share the spoils.

The hominins race to the location, hoping to get there before all is consumed. Since they watch the birds so keenly, do they ever wonder how they fly?

Stone tools are used by the ancestors of modern humans.

Baskets and wood and bone tools are likely in use long before stone tools are developed, but these are not easily preserved and are not found in the archeological record.

The oldest stone tools yet discovered date to 3.3 mya.

Tools, whether of stone or wood, reduce the load placed on teeth. Tool use proceeds at a cultural pace, while teeth or other body parts can only evolve at a biological pace.

The hominin known as *Homo erectus* evolves 1.8 mya. They have enough imagination to tame fire and journey out of Africa in a wave of migration and expansion.

Homo erectus is the first Hominin in the human lineage to expand past the boundaries of Africa. They will reach Western Asia by 1.7 mya, Indonesia by 1.6 mya, and Spain by 1.4 mya.

The ability to cook food will transform not just the living arrangements and social habits of hominins, but their very anatomy.

Undisputed evidence for the widespread use and control of fire dates only to 125,000 years ago, but most scientists consider the evidence for the control of fire by *Homo erectus* 400,000 years ago to be convincing. A new hypothesis, advocated by Richard Wrangham in his book ***Catching Fire: How Cooking Made Us Human,*** places the date for the control of fire at almost 2 mya. More evidence will, we hope, eventually be found to pinpoint this date.

The Physics of Fire:

The fuel for the hominin's fires comes largely from plants. Carbon molecules are bonded together in living trees to make their woody trunks and branches. When the wood burns, the carbon-to-carbon bonds are broken and the freed carbon atoms then bond with oxygen atoms in the air. There is a difference in bond strength; it takes more energy to bond carbon to carbon than carbon to oxygen. This energy difference is released as heat and light.

Fires don't start by themselves; it takes some activation energy to start them. That energy can be supplied by a lightning strike, a spark from flint, the heat from sticks that are rapidly rubbed together, or with coals from a previous fire. The activation energy is required to break the first carbon-to-carbon bonds. Once the process is started, it proceeds on its own.

If tree trunks rot, rather than burn, the process is somewhat similar. Microorganisms and fungi break the carbon-to-carbon bonds, freeing the carbon which then combines with oxygen in the air. In either case, fire or decomposition, the end result is the same; the carbon that made up the tree trunk is returned to the atmosphere as carbon dioxide.

There is a carbon monoxide substage in the combustion process. The carbon-carbon bonds of wood are turned into carbon-oxygen bonds before picking up another oxygen atom. If the combustion process is incomplete, and is arrested at the carbon-to-single-oxygen atom stage, people near the fire can be poisoned.

Air really is a substance; trees form their bulk from it.

To make their trunks, living trees get the carbon from air. Trees take in carbon dioxide (CO_2) and release oxygen (O_2). They use the energy from sunlight, in the complicated process of photosynthesis, to re-arrange the bonds between atoms. The oxygen in the molecules of CO_2 is released into the atmosphere as O_2. This diatomic version of oxygen is also called free oxygen or even just oxygen; it is the part of the air that animals use in their respiration.

Ocean currents and wind patterns shifted in response to the formation of the land bridge.

The flightless Terror Birds become extinct.

The formation of the Panama Land bridge leads to a competition between the apex predators of North and South America. The solitary superstar birds are no match for the wolves, the socially organized pack predators, even though no individual wolf is as formidable as a Terror Bird.

Terror birds make it as far north as Texas and Florida but do not prosper long as the social carnivores there soon out-compete them.

Even after the land bridge had formed, the terror birds could not travel north through the dense vegetation of Central America until the volcanos had belched out enough ash – some hundreds of feet of it – to smother the jungle and pave a path for them.

Other northern predators, like bears and sabre-toothed cats, also made their way southward.

Species who traversed the bridge changed the ecosystem of the land they entered. The changes to North America are minor but many South American species go extinct.

Many of the South American species had been highly specialized, perhaps because there are more isolated environments in South America and fewer in North America, which is more easily traversable. The specialists are hunted down or out-competed by the generalists that come from the north. The opossum is among the few that gains new territory by moving north.

The use of fire transforms Hominin behavior and anatomy.

Primates usually sleep in trees rather than on the ground. All other primates are better at climbing than hominins and sleep in high, safe places like cliff sides, tree branches, or holes in tree trunks. Based on their physiology, *Homo erectus* probably did not climb trees any better than modern humans do. This suggests that *H. erectus* primarily slept on the ground, but the African woodlands (and the savannahs that are supplanting them) are dangerous places, with all manner of large predators. The control of fire allows *H. erectus* to come down out of the trees, by providing protection from predators overnight.

The emergence of *H. erectus* is perhaps the biggest evolutionary leap in human ancestry. H. erectus is larger than its predecessors, and has smaller teeth, a narrower pelvis, a less flared rib cage, redesigned shoulders, and a much larger brain. With the shift to dwelling on the ground, climbing-specific adaptations of the arm, shoulder, and torso are lost. Arboreal life favors smaller body plans and the switch to the ground frees *H. erectus* to grow in size.

Cooked food requires less chewing for digestion, and provides far more energy than raw food. It also allows more kinds of foods to be eaten. Cooked food provides the fuel for the increase in size of the body and brain of *H. Erectus*. The advent of cooked food also reshapes the species by favoring those individuals with smaller digestive systems and smaller teeth; larger guts and big teeth are no longer necessary, and reducing their sizes saves calories and increases agility.

Fire, although a dangerous and frightening element, provides warmth, cooked food, and safety from predators. Cooking renders food easier to eat and digest. This helps to make the large brains of the Hominins worth the calories required.

In the evenings, Hominins gather around campfires for warmth and safety. Together they listen to the spit and crackle of the fire, and to one another. Language begins to emerge.

Pleistocene
1
Million Years Ago

1,000,000
Years Ago

At a cave in China, *Homo erectus* continues to use fire.

500,000 Years Ago

Hundreds of fossilized bones and skulls and some complete skeletons of *H.erectus* have been found in Africa and throughout Europe and Asia.

Charcoal, artifacts, and the bones and skulls of Peking Man are preserved inside the Zhoukou Cave near Beijing. Some of the skulls bear cut marks and scratches that were originally interpreted by Western scientists to be evidence of cannibalism, much to the dismay of their Chinese counterparts. Years later, after forensic techniques were improved, the marks were proven to have been made by hyenas. Hyenas are scavengers and likely didn't kill the hominins but simply dragged parts of their already dead bodies into the cave to eat.

There is much debate as to how Peking Man lived. Evidence of fire and stone tool use in the cave abounds but the ash layers are somewhat scattered and a debate rages as to whether Peking man cooked over permanent hearths in the cave or used fire in the cave only occasionally.

When tree trunks fall into surface waters, the logs float.

All trees are made principally of chains of carbon atoms that are arrayed in a pattern that is less dense than water. Some types of wood are less dense than others and woods like pine float higher at the surface than hardwoods such as oak. Logs that float higher and bobble around with more of the log riding above the water line can support the weight of a human without becoming completely submerged.

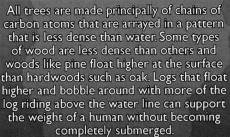

Rafts, platforms made from many logs lashed together, can support heavier loads.

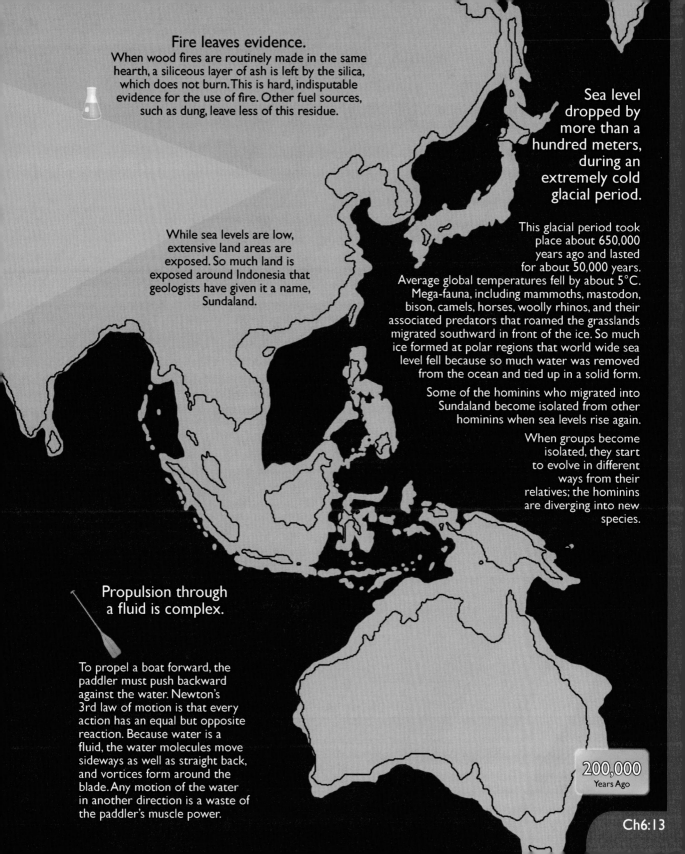

Fire leaves evidence.
When wood fires are routinely made in the same hearth, a siliceous layer of ash is left by the silica, which does not burn. This is hard, indisputable evidence for the use of fire. Other fuel sources, such as dung, leave less of this residue.

Sea level dropped by more than a hundred meters, during an extremely cold glacial period.

This glacial period took place about 650,000 years ago and lasted for about 50,000 years. Average global temperatures fell by about 5°C. Mega-fauna, including mammoths, mastodon, bison, camels, horses, woolly rhinos, and their associated predators that roamed the grasslands migrated southward in front of the ice. So much ice formed at polar regions that world wide sea level fell because so much water was removed from the ocean and tied up in a solid form.

While sea levels are low, extensive land areas are exposed. So much land is exposed around Indonesia that geologists have given it a name, Sundaland.

Some of the hominins who migrated into Sundaland become isolated from other hominins when sea levels rise again.

When groups become isolated, they start to evolve in different ways from their relatives; the hominins are diverging into new species.

Propulsion through a fluid is complex.

To propel a boat forward, the paddler must push backward against the water. Newton's 3rd law of motion is that every action has an equal but opposite reaction. Because water is a fluid, the water molecules move sideways as well as straight back, and vortices form around the blade. Any motion of the water in another direction is a waste of the paddler's muscle power.

200,000 Years Ago

Anatomically modern humans emerge in Africa about 200,000 years ago.

There is wide consensus among scientists that *Homo sapiens* evolved in Sub-Saharan Africa. Estimates of when vary from 200,000 to 125,000 years ago. This new breed of bipedal primate will soon out-compete all others. Some of these humans will soon journey out of Africa in a new wave of expansion.

The humans develop a new hunting technique.

Humans can tolerate heat better than many other animals. With little hair to trap heat and sweat glands that allow for evaporative cooling, humans can run down furry game like antelope by outlasting them in the heat of the midday sun, while other hunters, like lions, seek respite in the shade.

A continuous supply of water must be available to replenish the water lost through sweat, but the water can be carried in a container made from a gourd, egg shell, or animal-hide pouch.

Clothing is developed.

This is a step along the way to textiles, sail cloth and eventually skins for aircraft.

170,000 years ago, the body louse diverges from the head louse and becomes a separate species. While head lice can live in hair, body lice can only attach their eggs to the fibers of clothing. This speciation supports the hypothesis that clothing was adopted well before humans journeyed out of Africa.

The climate in Africa is in a state of flux.

At this time, the climate frequently alternates between wet and dry, but *H. sapiens* adapts well.

The Earth, like a spinning top, wobbles on its axis and completes one cycle in 20,000 years. It is just a minor wobble, but if it coincides with other factors, it can trigger rhythmic climactic changes. The climate of the whole planet went through profound changes during the rise of the mammals.

The creation of the Himalayas and then the Alps changed global wind patterns. The formation of the Panama land bridge fundamentally changed ocean currents and initiated the deep water conveyer system. The 20,000 year wobble cycle sometimes coincides with other factors and a tipping point is reached, causing the Sahara to become green and lush again.

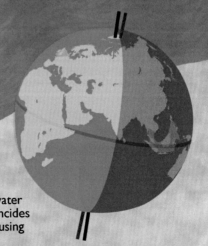

Glaciers grow in the Arctic and Antarctica.

This glacial period starts about 110,000 years ago and is just one of the pulses of the most recent ice age, which began about 2.6 mya and continues today. During an ice age, there is always ice at the high latitudes of the poles, even in summer.

Although the last glacial period is commonly referred to as an 'ice age,' the scientific definition of an ice age is any period of time when there is some seasonally permanent ice on the planet. An ice age has warmer and cooler periods within it which are referred to as glacial periods and interglacial periods. We are currently in an interglacial period, known as the Holocene of the Quaternary Ice Age.

Humans follow topography.

The graben valley that develops as the East African Rift opens up is a low-lying natural avenue. Another natural migration route is the shoreline of the coast. Shellfish and other ocean resources beckon them ever farther.

Birds sense the magnetosphere.

Birds migrate using a combination of specially honed senses. Scientists think that birds use both sight and taste to detect the magnetosphere.

While it is true that many birds have been known to use the sun as a compass to point them in their intended direction, they use other tools as well.

Magnetite crystals affixed to the trigeminal nerve in their beaks allow birds to 'taste' the strength of the magnetosphere as they fly. Additionally, specialized photoreceptors in one eye are sensitive to certain pigments in the presence of long magnetic wavelengths. These photoreceptors essentially allow the bird to 'see' the magnetosphere. Between these two senses, individuals are able to learn the particular 'taste' and look of the magnetic field along their migration route, allowing them to recreate the route on a yearly basis.

The individual importance of these two specialized senses in birds has been tested and debated by scientists. Some believe that migrating birds use one sense more than the other, or use one exclusively; some believe that it depends on the species. Regardless, it seems most likely that birds use some combination of the two tools they have evolved seemingly in tandem.

As they journey out of Africa, *Homo sapiens* encounter some of the descendants of earlier waves of hominin migrants, such as *Homo neanderthalensis*.

Many different species or subspecies of hominins had evolved. They had sometimes evolved in isolation (either by geography or by inhabiting a specific niche) and at other times interbred with other subspecies. Some had prospered and some had become extinct. Only Neanderthals, Denisovans, Florensis, and perhaps a few other hominin species or subspecies still exist at this time.

Many of the routes follow coastlines.

70,000
Years Ago

Mount Toba, a super volcano, erupts in Sumatra, causing a global volcanic winter lasting about a decade. Human populations decline.

Arrows may be in use.

Evidence of important technological advances is found in the Sibudu cave in South Africa, including the oldest instance of possible bone arrowheads, dating back to around 61,000 years ago. There is no evidence of a bow but wooden bows are not easily preserved. However the supposed arrowheads might have been some other kind of tool.

Humans journey to Australia, presumably by raft.

Sea level was lower than it is today but Australia would still not have been visible, even after a few days of rafting. Perhaps the voyagers deduced that there was a land beyond after watching migrating marine life or perhaps they were just accidently swept out to sea.

Australia experiences a wet period between 60,000 and 40,000 years ago and is humid and green when humans arrive.

Lush Australia is populated by giant animals.

The fauna of Australia has not coevolved with any bipedal apes, such as *H. erectus*. The giant animals, known as megafauna, are easy prey and soon go extinct. Once the symbiotic relationship of the fauna fertilizing the grasslands that feed them is broken, much of the land becomes desert.

Boomerangs incorporate the first human built airfoils.

Boomerangs spin around an axis perpendicular to the direction of flight.

The first boomerangs are shaped like rotating wings and are used in hunting. They are heavier and not as curved as the returning variety that will be developed later. The arms are not completely flat, but are shaped so that lift is generated, offsetting the weight of the boomerang and allowing it to travel long distances.

Boomerangs are used in Eurasia as well as Australia. A 30,000-year-old boomerang made of mammoth tusk has been found in Poland. They will eventually be used in the Americas, in Southern India, and in Egypt.

Returning boomerangs are much lighter than hunting boomerangs, which do not return. They are likely invented as people experiment with ways to improve hunting boomerangs. Aside from being a curiosity, they facilitate practice of throwing. They may also have been used to divert flying flocks of ducks in order to drive them into hunters waiting nearby.

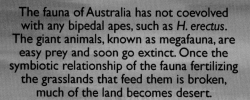

A returning boomerang returns because of the gyroscopic precession of its spin axis. It must be thrown almost vertically, with enough energy to have high angular momentum. The amount of lift produced by each wing varies as it rotates. During the first half of its rotation, the wing spins in the same direction as the flight path, but during the second half of its rotation, it spins opposite the direction of travel. The wing reaches a higher airspeed when the spin direction is along the flight path, and generates more lift during this interval. This effect causes the plane of rotation of the boomerang to tilt, thus allowing its flight path to change.

Humans journey into Europe and encounter the Neanderthals already living there. The two subspecies will coexist for thousands of years.

The DNA of all peoples today – except those from sub-Saharan Africa – contains 1 to 6% DNA from other human subspecies. Europeans have about 3% Neanderthal DNA. Farther to the east, other migrating humans encounter the Denisovans. Some genetic transfer happens and the group migrating on to Taiwan and Melanesia has about 6% Denisovan DNA in their genome. Those who go on to other parts of Asia have about 3%.

Neanderthals are better adapted for cold temperatures by having more body mass and shorter limbs; this gives them a higher volume-to-surface area ratio.

Clothing and blankets are made from animal skins.

Neanderthals prepare the hides of deer and other animals using scrapers made of flaked stone. Holes are pierced with awls and skins are lashed together with strips of hide.

While the climate is still cooling and the ice age has not yet reached its peak, the intrepid humans are encroaching deep into the range of the Neanderthals.

Neanderthals go extinct about 30,000 years ago.

On a cave wall in Spain, the stencilled outlines of hands are still visible. It dates to 30,000 years ago and may have been made by Neanderthals.

Neanderthal stone tools are assembled with handles fastened with a gluey pitch manufactured by heating birch bark without allowing it to burn. Analysis of artifacts shows that they contain pigments that might have been used for ornamentation.

Pleistocene
40,000
Years Ago

Flax makes strong, fibrous thread.

Fibers of wild flax, a reedy plant with extremely long, tough, thread like fibers are used either for sewing garments or hafting tools. Fragments of twisted and dyed flax have been found in the Dzudzuana Cave in the foothills of the Caucasus Mountains of Georgia, that are about 30,000 old.

Matts and baskets are woven.

Matts, baskets and roofing materials have been woven for thousands of years but are seldom preserved in the archeological record. The first materials to be used were likely reeds and vines. Eventually yarn and string are made from flax, wool and other fibrous plant and animal products.

Fitted clothing is fashioned.

Figurines found at the 20,000 year old archeological site of Buret in Siberia show humans wearing close fitting, hooded garments.

Pottery is created.

Early potters use the pinching and coiling methods to make clay vessels, which they bake in campfires.

Air bubbles, that can be present in clay, must be removed by kneading or wedging, lest the air expand more than the clay, causing it to crack. Sharp edges and corners are rounded because corners heat unevenly which can also lead to cracking during the firing process.

Pottery from Jiangxi, China dates to 20,000 years ago.

Relatively few people migrate across the Bering Land Bridge, as evidenced by the fact that there are only 5 genetic haplo groups among all Native Americans today.

The ice reaches its furthest extent.

The peak of the ice age, the Last Glacial Maximum, occurs sometime between 26,000 and 19,000 years ago.

Low sea level exposes the Bering land bridge between Asia and Alaska. There is only so much water on the planet and when much of it is tied up in ice, sea levels drop. Additionally, cooler ocean waters are less voluminous due to less thermal expansion.

Humans journey from Asia across the Bering land bridge into Alaska.

Bison also make the trip from Asia. Horses, which had evolved in North America, go the other way, westward across the bridge into Asia, as do the Gray Wolf and the camel.

At this time, the open land corridor between the vast continental **Laurentide Ice Sheet** and the smaller Cordilleran Sheet is overgrown with ice, so people probably follow the coast and use boats. Some scientists propose that two separate migrations occur, one through the land corridor and one by sea.

The American continent is home to huge animals including mammoths and mastodons the size of school busses. The megafauna are naive and plentiful and Clovis Point spear technology is soon developed.

It is the beginning of the end for the large direwolf as the megafauna that was the specialization of the species dwindle in numbers.

As the climate changes and the glaciers retreat, large mammals around the globe become extinct. In some cases, the timing of the die-off is suspiciously close to the arrival of the humans.

Fast flying arrows aid hunters.

The potential energy of a drawn bow is similar to the energy stored in a spring. When released, a light-weight arrow accelerates to speeds of about 76 meters per second. Thrown objects are only half as fast, and are more difficult to aim. Speed has advantages. Prey react to the sound of the bow being released. Sound travels at 343 m/s in air. Lighter arrows have greater velocities than heavy ones, given the same force applied by the bow. A faster moving projectile spends less time in the air and is less influenced by wind.

Humans journey into all of the Americas.

Glaciers are melting and receding to polar latitudes.

The Pleistocene Epoch ends around 11,700 years ago. All across the globe, the climate is changing; the Fertile Crescent becomes optimal for humans.

Ice had been a barrier to travel both for animals and for humans. Some of the largest mammals were adapted to be near the edge of the ice; some of these species adapt and some become extinct. Hunting by humans while the animals are losing habitat might have exacerbated the extinction process. Another climactic change is the regreening and the later redesertification of the Sahara. Additionally, the explosive growth of human populations and their activities might have led to further climactic changes.

As the ice recedes, monarchs fly farther.

As temperatures in North America begin to drop in September and October, the annual migration of the Monarch butterfly begins. Populations in southern Canada and the U.S. head south toward their winter grounds in central Mexico. This spectacular migration takes longer than any one butterfly's lifetime, so no single individual will fly the entire circuit.

As they migrate southward, Monarchs enter a semidormant physiological state called 'diapause.' Diapause causes the butterflies to store an unusually high amount of carbohydrates, fats, and proteins to fuel their long migration. This allows migrating monarchs to live well past their normal life expectancies and cross vast expanses of land.

While similar to other types of animal dormancy (such as hibernation or torpor), diapause begins and ends with very specific environmental conditions. When the environmental stimuli that initiate diapause are present, the monarch will remain in this state until it has reached its destination, where the conditions exist that trigger the monarch to cease diapause.

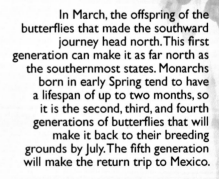

In March, the offspring of the butterflies that made the southward journey head north. This first generation can make it as far north as the southernmost states. Monarchs born in early Spring tend to have a lifespan of up to two months, so it is the second, third, and fourth generations of butterflies that will make it back to their breeding grounds by July. The fifth generation will make the return trip to Mexico.

It is possible that this instinct to migrate developed during the recession of the last Ice Age. Some scientists believe that stationary populations of monarchs around the world found habitat that didn't necessitate migration and thus lost the instinct to do so. This theory puts migration first and the homebody populations as secondary.

Hunting and gathering become more like **tending the wild**, also called 'wild crafting.'

In different places, different species of plants and animals are chosen. Many factors drive the process, as humans develop new methods of feeding themselves and begin to reshape ecosystems. Some of the factors involved include climate change, changes in animal populations, growth of human populations, and changes in human social organization.

People living in the temperate latitudes of Southwest Asia find themselves surrounded by bountiful resources.

They inadvertently cultivate fruits, nuts, and other plant foods just by picking them and dispersing the seeds along trails and in garbage heaps.

The bountiful swath of land known as the Fertile Crescent extends from the Nile River Valley to the Tigris and Euphrates. People harvest wild wheat and rye, which grow on hillsides.

The Sahara Desert becomes green again as the African Humid Period begins.

Lake beds that have long been dried up fill with water, and existing lakes in the rift zone grow larger and interconnect.

The **African Humid Period** is an interval from 14,000 to 4,000 BCE when Africa is much wetter. This is due to changes in climate caused by the wobbling of Earth on its axis. Ironically, it is when the axial tilt exposes the Southern Hemisphere to more solar radiation that the prevailing winds shift northward and bring more rain to Africa.

As humans hunt and gather and interact with plants and animals, they create selection pressures that cause the plants and animals to adapt to the human presence.

Hunter gatherers do not wander around on ever changing routes but rather they 'tend the wild.' They know from experience when nuts and berries ripen in certain places and when animals migrate and where they congregate.

Pottery improves.

Pottery is in widespread use. Potters sometimes rub the outside of the clay vessels with sand, crushed pottery fragments or shells to make them more impervious to water.

Gourds are also still used as containers and are one of the first plants to be domesticated.

Animals are tended..

Sheep and goats abound and people soon learn to protect the herd from predators as well as hunt them. They herd these still wild animals to lush pastures and to blind valleys where they confine them to be hunted and harvested when convenient.

Although humans prey on these animals, it is a mutually beneficial relationship. Humans learn that taxing the herd too heavily will result in less production, so they never take too many animals at once.

Pleistocene
12,000
Years Ago

Equivalent to

Neolithic
10,000
BCE

Felt is perhaps the oldest human-made textile.

By combining hot water with layers of sheared animal hairs, a thick mat of sturdy fibers is created. Through agitation and fulling, the fibers of the textile are joined and a sturdy, water resistant material called **felt** is formed.

Wild crafting gradually becomes **true agriculture**.

True agriculture begins first in the Fertile Crescent, around 11,500 years ago which is 9,500 BCE.

Wheat and other cereal crops are deliberately cultivated in the Fertile Crescent by around 8,000 BCE. Humans who had long hunted grazing animals become grass eaters themselves with the onset of agriculture and the growing of wheat, rice, and rye.

Some foods store better than others. Wheat is one of the best and will eventually become a **treasure crop**.

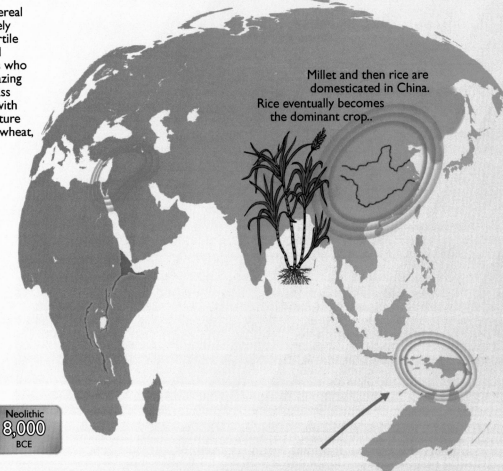

Millet and then rice are domesticated in China. Rice eventually becomes the dominant crop..

Holocene
10,000
Years Ago

Equivalent to

Neolithic
8,000
BCE

On the island of New Guinea, another agricultural society emerges independently. People learn to gather sugar cane, bananas, and some root crops which they begin to cultivate. These crops grow well but do not store well. People leave the fruits on the trees and the root crops in the ground until they are needed for consumption.

The bow and arrow are definitely in use by now.

The Holmegaard Bows, which are the oldest preserved bows, are left in a swamp in Denmark 8,000 years ago, .

Arrow heads are more easily preserved than bows but what appears to be an arrow head might have been used as a dart or some other tool. The earliest arrowheads may be as old as 61,000 years.

Arrows are fletched by attaching feathers to arrow shafts with birch tar as early as 10,000 BCE.

Shiny metals entice humans.

Gold, copper and silver are found in nature in pure states although only in small quantities. Most metals do not exist in nature in a native form, uncombined with other elements. Gold nuggets are found in stream beds and native copper is found in seams of rock. Gold is extremely resistant to corrosion and maintains its luster and color. The surface of a chunk of copper will combine with oxygen in the air and turn green but that oxidized layer will protect deeper layers of the metal from further corrosion.

When humans handle these curious objects they eventually learn that they are malleable and can be shaped.

They don't know that these substances are homogenous; a nugget of gold contains only gold atoms. And of course, they don't know that their appearance in the same column of the periodic table is a reflection of their similarities. They don't know that copper, the least dense of these substances, has fewer protons in its nucleus and correspondingly fewer electrons that orbit it arrayed in 4 shells and that silver has 5 orbital shells and that gold has 6.

The climate warms as the Holocene Climatic Optimum begins.

The Holocene Climactic Optimum is a warm period that begins about 7,000 BCE and lasts for 4,000 years.

Humans cultivate flax.

The long tough fibers of the wild flax plant have long been used to make thread and cord. It also yields seeds that contain a highly nutritious oil, and its fibers are also used to make textiles. Cultivation of flax begins around 8,000 BCE.

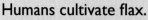

Neolithic
7,000
BCE

Camps become villages as crops are cultivated.

Living quarters improve as tools evolve, leading to the specialization of jobs. Hunting and gathering continues alongside agricultural development. This is likely a time of relative peace, prosperity and egalitarianism.

Boats are constructed

Reed boats are constructed 7500 years ago in Kuwait. Some of the earliest ships to be seaworthy are made of reeds. Some reed boat designs have masts, cabins on their decks, and maneuverable rudders. Bitumen is often used to seal the exterior of the hull. Sealed boats displace more water than log rafts. Their useful load (payload) is the weight of the amount of water displaced minus the weight of the boat itself.

Bits of yarn are made into fabric.

Nålebinding, also known as needle-binding or knotless netting, is a one-needle practice of creating dense, sturdy fabrics which predates knitting and crocheting by perhaps thousands of years. It lends itself well to the joining together of many shorter lengths of yarn because it requires the weaver to pull the entire trailing length of yarn through the current loop. The oldest fragment of cloth that survives in the archeological record dates to 6,500 BCE.

Neolithic
6,000
BCE

More animals are domesticated.

Domesticated animals begin to change in unexpected ways. Genes often influence more than one aspect of behavior or anatomy, so dogs that were selected for tameness, for example, also have floppier ears and shorter snouts.

Animals are no longer used just for meat, milk, wool, sinew, and other by-products. They are beginning to be harnessed and used for their muscle power. Cattle are proving to significantly enhance village life by providing large quantities of milk as well as by dragging heavy loads.

Copper tools are made.

Copper is malleable and easy to shape, not just into ornaments but also into tools. It holds a sharp edge and can be fashioned more easily than stone. Stone tools are extremely sharp but they are also brittle. Copper is more durable.

Smelting increases the supply of copper.

Rocks containing copper are much more abundant than copper in the pure state. Copper ores, like malachite, are easy to recognize by their blue green hues. By breaking these ore rocks and heating them, the copper is separated out in a process known as smelting. Fortuitously charcoal happened to be present during the melting process because a reducing agent must be available to combine with the oxidized impurities in the ore. A site in Serbia confirms that copper is smelted by 5,000 BCE.

Dragons fly in Chinese legends.

In contrast to Western cultures, which portray the dragon as an evil creature, Chinese imagery depicts it as a symbol of auspicious power. The dragon rules water, rain, and weather and plays an important role in the growth of crops.

Although occasionally depicted with small wings or feathers on their legs, their ability to fly is mystical and does not come from these physical attributes.

The potters wheel revolutionizes production.

The potters wheel is invented in Mesopotamia between 6,000-4,000 BCE. It will revolutionize the production of pottery. The wheel is probably invented by potters who use it like a lazy-susan.

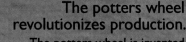

Some continents are more amenable to the spread of agriculture.

The geometry and orientation of continents make some more amenable to the spread of agriculture than others. This is one of the premises of Jared Diamond's book *Guns, Germs, and Steel*.

Africa spans from north to south. Although people in Sub-Saharan Africa can journey from one region to the next, they change latitude as they travel. Crops from one area may not be viable in the next, or may require several generations to adjust to the new daylight regimen. This is true for the Americas as well.

As humans journey across Eurasia, which spans east to west, they remain at the same latitude. The seeds they carry with them will be exposed to the same amount of daylight in the new land, which increases the likelihood of germination and growth. The skills and methods previously developed will continue to be viable.

Some continents have more species of animals that can be domesticated. Most domesticatable animals originate in the Old World, while few come from Africa or the Americas.

Agriculture originates independently in a few locations, and then spreads.

Yarn is woven into fabric.

The weaver divides the strands of yarn into two sets which will be interlaced at right angles to each other. One set, called the warp, is arrayed on a hand held loom, pulled taught and fastened. The other yarn, called the weft, is woven under and over alternating strands of the warp.

Warp-weighted looms are used.

Warp-weighted looms produce large pieces of textiles far faster than hand-crafted methods. The loom itself is made of a simple frame that can be leaned against a wall or other surface, with the vertical or warp threads tied in bundles and weighed down by stone loom weights. These weights keep the warp threads taut as the weaver uses a shuttle to pass the weft (or horizontal) threads through and between the warp threads. Because the loom's frame structure holds the fabric upright, the weaver is able to move from side to side of the fabric they are making.

The African Sahara is still green and humid, or at least comparable to a savannah, until about 5,000 BCE.

Although the Sahara is slowly becoming arid, ample evidence of a green and humid period exists, including archeological remains of numerous human encampments around (now dried up) lakes.

Written tallies are kept.

People have been keeping track of amounts using tokens kept in clay jars. They begin to use tally marks drawn in wet clay which will lead to cuneiform.

Bronze is occasionally created.

An alloy is a combination of metals. Bronze is an alloy of mostly of copper with small amounts of other metals. Copper ores in the area of the first smelters occasionally also contain arsenic. Arsenic is also a metal but it is highly toxic especially during the refining process. The resulting bronze alloy is stronger and harder than copper.

Wheeled carts evolve from a series of improvements to sledges placed on rollers.

The invention of the wheel could have proceeded in a stepwise fashion. Loads are carried by putting them on runners (this is called a sledge) or by putting a roller underneath. Both methods are combined as a sledge is placed on a roller. With use, the sledge cuts a groove in the roller. The groove helps keep the sledge from slipping off. People notice that deeper grooves make it easier to push the load, like shifting down a gear. Soon the inner part of the roller is hewn away at the start. Finally, the wheels and axles are made as a separate pieces and assembled with bushings or pins. Four-wheeled carts follow soon after.

The invention of the wheel comes late to humanity's tool chest. First, we invent boats, baskets, the sewing needle, woven cloth, rope, and even the flute before figuring out the wheel. The wheel represents a leap in imagination as there are few analogs in nature for humans to draw upon.

Hydraulic Civilizations develop. These empires are centered on rivers.

The Nile River Valley is ideally structured for humans. The wind usually blows in a direction opposite to that of the current. Boats and barges can drift downstream and then be sailed back. In order to float bow-first downstream, floats of reeds were tethered to the front and back of the boat. The buoyant float in front helped to keep the bow pointed in the direction of flow of the current, while the heavier aft float created enough drag to keep the back of the boat aligned.

Shipwrights use the shell-first technique.

This method of shipbuilding requires no interior frame for the ship and instead relies on the strength of the connection between each of the hull's planks to keep its shape. The first shell-first boats were made of lengths of planking woven or sewn together with lashings.

This technique will be superseded by the innovation of the mortise and tenon method of joining planks, in which a tenon, or tongue of wood, is fitted into a shaped hole called a mortise in an abutting plank. A wooden plug is often driven through the now-hidden tenon tongue to further hold the planks together. In ancient Egypt, papyrus bundles were used to fill seams.

Silk is produced.

Around 4,000 BCE, silk production begins in China. Silk has a high strength to weight ratio. It will eventually be used in parachutes.

The Sahara is once again becoming a desert.

At around 3,900 BCE, rapid desertification quickly ensues in the Sahara, and people are forced to migrate into river valleys.

Bronze Age
3,500
BCE

Hydraulic Civilizations develop all around the world. The major Hydraulic Civilizations are the Tigris and Euphrates, the Nile, and the Indus. Hydraulic civilizations will eventually arise on the banks of the Ganges, the Yellow and - much later - the Mississippi.

The earliest sails catch the wind from behind and push a vessel directly downwind. Later, boats use sails that are capable of sailing slightly off the wind but this requires a keel to hold the boat's course in the water, else the boat will just slip and slide around and only go directly downwind anyway. Although early sails are not true airfoils, these early boats still use the wind to 'fly' across the air/water interface.

Copper is cast.

Casting is a metallurgical process that uses molds to create metal objects. Molten metal is poured into a mold and allowed to cool. The resulting object can be further worked or finished. The use of casting reduces the amount of time and work required to make many copies of the same object, such as axe heads or food storage vessels.

Bronze made with tin is practical.

Tin replaces arsenic, making the smelting process less toxic and easier to control. Tin bronze is also far stronger than other bronze alloys.

Horses are used to pull carts.

Horses may have been ridden by people of the Botai culture of Kazakhstan as early as 3,500 BCE. The Botai had neither cattle nor sheep and might have ridden horses in the course of hunting.

Wheeled vehicles are in existence by 3200.

Cotton is used.

Cotton is a useful fiber of almost pure cellulose that encases the seeds of a shrub indigenous to the Americas, India, and Africa. The fluffy capsule gets caught in the wind, aiding in the dispersal of the seeds.

Cotton is cultivated in the Americas by 3000 BCE and in the Indus Valley by 2500 BCE.

Bureaucracy is born.

With increased food production, the division of labor, and the ability to keep records, the administration of large-scale projects becomes possible. This leads to more class distinctions and inequalities and to the development of bureaucracy. When societies are too large for the king to personally administrate all details, agents of the king are appointed. These agents must bear regalia to prove their authenticity and they must be able to document that they fulfilled their tasks, for example how much tax they collected.

Cities merge into larger empires as populations continue to expand and administration becomes more sophisticated. The two great kingdoms on the Nile, upper and lower Egypt, become united in one supersized realm and a small elite is able to dominate the entire society.

The Pharaoh, Djoser, of the Third Dynasty, is depicted as ruling over the "Nine Bows." This allegorical reference to the historical enemies of Egypt indicates that the bow and arrow are used as tools of war.

The Pyramids rise.

These monuments are apt symbols of social hierarchy and the new religions that arise to justify the existence of a wealthy and powerful elite.

Mathematics improves, from keeping track of quantities of goods and debts owed to calculating the volume of simple shapes like pyramids.

Granaries, places to store grain to keep it safe from weather, insects, and mice, may have led to small pyramids. The first granaries were stone-lined holes in the ground protected by a roof. Pyramids may have been built on top of them by expanding the holes and building a room above that may have been occupied by a guard or priest. By about 2500 BCE, large pyramids are built, showing off the wealth and power of the elite.

Egyptian formulas are approximate.

The formulas that show how the Egyptians calculated the volume of the pyramids are transcribed in a papyrus, now known as the Egyptian Moscow Papyrus, dating perhaps to 1800 BCE. The formulas are roughly accurate, although they are not derived by deductive reasoning. Other formulas on the papyrus include calculations for the length of a ship's mast, the volume of a basket, and the amount of grain required to make bread and beer. Some of these are more accurate than others and all were likely arrived at by trial and error.

A positional numbering system allows for multiplication.

The Babylonians invent a positional number system that uses 60 as a base. The system in use today is positional but uses a base of 10. The base 10 system has a one's place, a ten's place, a hundred's place, etc., and units in each place or column have a value 10 times greater than those in the previous column. In the Babylonian system, the first column has room for 60 items (rather than 10), as does the next, giving it a one's place, a sixty's place, and a 3600's place. Units in each column are worth 60 times more than those in the previous. Relics of this system survive; we have 60 seconds in minute and 60 minutes in an hour and we calculate degrees of latitude and longitude by dividing the sphere of the earth into 360 degrees. The Babylonians also make astronomical observations and a calendar.

2,000 BCE

The Phoenicians become proficient sailors and create a vast maritime trading empire.

The Philistines, who use ships in the Mediterranean to raid coastal towns, are supplanted by the Phoenicians, Canaanites from present-day Lebanon and Syria, who establish sophisticated maritime trade routes linking a network of city-states across the Mediterranean.

Giant bronzes are cast in China.

The Bronze Age begins in China by 1700 BCE. During the Shang Dynasty ceremonial vessels are manufactured. Sophisticated pottery, including fine glazed stoneware as early as 1400 BCE was already being created on a large scale, with high temperature kilns and molds for pottery. This technology is adapted for casting bronze. Huge pieces with exquisite details and designs are created. They become symbols of religious authority and the power of the ruler to organize a vast workforce in sophisticated ways. Many people are required to dig and transport the ore, operate smelters and build the giant kilns to cast these works.

Ideas can be stronger than technology.

The Hebrews are remembered for religion, rather than technology or conquests. Abraham (sometime between 2000 and 1550 BCE) is a pastoralist who is motivated to move away from his more powerful, agriculturalist neighbors. He leads his people to a less densely populated land.

The Indus River Civilization migrates.

In India and what is now Pakistan, the civilizations that had sprung up along the Indus River are abandoned and people move to the valley of the Ganges River, between 1,800 and 1,700 BCE. Overuse, salinization, or climate change are all probable causes.

Religions and law develop and change as societies try to adjust to the new conditions of civilization.

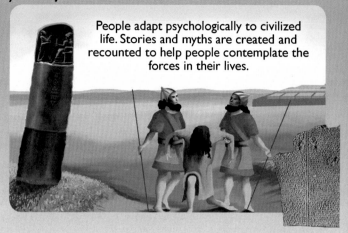

People adapt psychologically to civilized life. Stories and myths are created and recounted to help people contemplate the forces in their lives.

The Bronze Age is facilitated by trading networks.

Bronze is made primarily of copper, with about 15% tin added. Ores of copper and tin rarely occur together and an extensive trading network has to be in place for any significant amount of bronze to be produced. For example, evidence of tin ore from Cornwall, England will be found in bronze smelted on the eastern shores of the Mediterranean.

Named for the purple dye they become famous for exporting (*phoînix*), the Phoenicians are advanced shipbuilders who establish rule by controlling the shipping routes and supply of goods that crisscross the Mediterranean. In addition to goods and shipbuilding innovations, the Phoenicians carry with them the phonetic alphabet, which will facilitate efficient communication within their empire and will influence the Greeks and Romans, leading to the emergence of Latin.

Their early merchant ships use a single square sail, supported by a single sturdy mast and two curved horizontally arranged beams called the yard (upper) and boom (lower). The hulls are rounded and provide far more cargo space than previous ship designs. Rowers stand at long oars on either side of the vessel, allowing for more precise turning in unfavorable winds, and for steady speeds, even in inclement weather. War ships are similar, but with two banks of rowers on either side of the vessel and reinforced prows for puncturing the hulls of enemy ships.

The Phoenician sphere of influence continues to expand.

Phoenician colonies are built along the Mediterranean coastline to facilitate long distance trade. Perhaps the most famous of these is Carthage, built around a natural harbor on the Northeast coast of modern-day Tunisia. These colonies serve as way-stations for ships traveling along established shipping lanes.

Phoenician shipbuilding advances.

Newer hull designs reduce the amount of drag on the ship sailing through the water. Sails are made more durable with quilting and the addition of leather strapping sewn in a lattice pattern. The boom arm is done away with and the prow is further reinforced.

The Bronze Age suddenly collapses.

At about 1200 BCE the Bronze Age ends. In less than half a century, war and intense violence destroys many of the large cities in the eastern Mediterranean area. The empires of the Egyptians and the Hittites as well as the palace economies of the Aegean, the Amorite city states and many others disintegrate into chaos and trade routes are disrupted.

War wore out the superpowers.

In the power vacuum left by the Hittites and Egyptians, survivors will eventually form several small societies, none of which is strong enough to gain control of all the others. Between 1150 and 700 BCE, numerous small states emerge.

The iron age begins.

Iron requires much higher temperatures to smelt but does not rely on scare resources that require extensive trading networks.

Solomon's Temple is built in Jerusalem.

In Solomon's temple, a monument to monotheism, only one supernatural being will be worshipped. All of nature and humanity are of his making and subject to his control; there will be no god of thunder or wind, no god of fertility or war. No other supernatural beings, winged or otherwise, will be worshipped or depicted.

Daedalus and Icarus fly, in myth.

Daedalus is a master craftsman who designs masts and sails for King Minos on the island of Crete. He builds a labyrinth so the king can imprison the Minotaur, a creature half human and half bull. Later, Daedalus has a falling out with the king and is himself imprisoned in the maze. Although the clever inventor escapes the labyrinth, he must also devise a way to escape from the island. He and his son Icarus jump from a tower with wings to which feathers are attached with string and wax.

Daedalus warns Icarus to fly neither too high nor too low. If he gets too close to the sun, the wax will melt; too close to the water and the wings will get wet. Icarus becomes enthralled during the flight and, forgetting practical concerns, soars upward; his wings come apart and he falls to his death.

The myth is often used to illustrate hubris, a lack of humility that offends the Gods or results in a downfall. The earliest reference to Daedalus is by Homer, the poet most famous for his compilation of *The Illiad* and *The Odyssey*.

1000
BCE

According to the Hebrew Bible, Solomon's Temple houses The Arc of the Covenant and is built on the site known today as the Temple Mount.

Hard evidence for the existence of the temple is slim because political sensitivities discourage archeological excavations.

Evidence for the temple comes from the Hebrew Bible, also called *The Torah* or *The Old Testament*. Kings 6:1 states that construction of the temple begins in the fourth year of Solomon's reign over Israel, which most modern scholars agree occurred between 970 and 931 BCE.

The Assyrians were one of the few mid sized states to survive the collapse. They become dominant after 900 BCE. and cruelly punish vanquished states and glorify the horror they inflict in art. They rule by terror and strength of numbers.

The Austronesians sail forth.

On the island of Taiwan, the fishing and farming Austronesian people feel the pressure of population growth. They begin a string of migrations to the Philippines, the islands of the Celebes, Borneo, and Indonesia. On some islands, they are the first inhabitants while in other places they mix with local populations. Distinct dialects of Austronesian develop.

These explorations are undertaken before the invention of the compass. Navigational knowledge is passed on in the form of stories and song. Knowledge of winds, currents, wave patterns and landmarks against a background of stars informs this narrative. Navigators hold high statuses within their communities.

Canals facilitate transport in China.

The Yellow and Yangtze rivers in China, which flow from west to east, provide efficient transportation for goods. The Chinese begin to build canals to connect the rivers and provide waterways for transportation of goods to the north and south.

Winged beasts are displayed at the palace of Sargon 11.

Greek philosophers get started.

Thales of Miletus (625-547 BCE) is an early Greek philosopher. He philosophizes that water is an essential substance and that life emerged by spontaneous generation from natural materials, rather than from a supernatural source. A well-traveled polymath, he calculates distances, including the height of the Pyramids of Giza, by using trigonometry and measuring shadows. He uses a similar technique to calculate the distance from the shore to ships at sea.

King Bladud tries to fly.

According to legend, the Celtic King Bladud attempts to fly with wings attached to his arms around 843 BCE. He crashes into a temple and is killed. The temple was built on a sacred site that many other structures will eventually be built upon, including Westminster Abbey. Bladud is the father of King Leir on whom Shakespear's fictional King Lear will be based.

Solomon's Temple is destroyed.

The city walls of Jerusalem are finally breached after a 30 month siege by the Babylonian king Nebuchadnezzar. The temple and most of the city are burned to the ground, according to Kings 2:25.

Cyrus shows peace to be profitable.

Tired of chaos and violence, Cyrus The Great show justice to be a powerful organizing tool.

Cyrus unites a great empire centered in Persia (Iran). He outlaws slavery and allows freedom of worship. His laws are transcribed on clay cylinders that can be rolled across slabs of wet clay to mass produce tablets.

He conquers Babylon in 539 BCE, and allows peoples who had been forced to emigrate there to return to their homelands. Among them are Jews, whom he not only allows to leave but also provides with money for the rebuilding of their temple.

Sun Tzu writes *The Art of War*.

This classic Chinese text on military strategy and tactics is widely read in the Warring States Period. It describes effective use of terrain, deception, and explains how to boost or weaken morale, and a host of other topics.

Taoism and Confucianism emerge in China.

Confucianism seeks harmony by individuals respecting the social hierarchies and officials acting with morality. Taoism emphasizes harmony with the alternating aspects of the natural world not through rigid rules but with simplicity and compassion.

Athens cultivates democracy.

Democracy begins in Athens in 501 BCE and cultivates a dynamic level of personal involvement, although it is only open to the elite. The Athenians fight valiantly and cleverly to repel an invasion from Persia. For this they earn respect and trust from other Greek city states and become custodians of the war chest that all agree to pay into, in order to have the resources to repel any subsequent invasion.

Philosophers define the nature of matter.

Empedocles, born about 490 BCE, defines the essential substances which make up all things as earth, fire, air, and water. The substances are not changeable but they can be combined or separated by the actions of the forces of love and strife respectively.

A later scholar, Democritus, writes about the existence of atoms - very small particles that join together in different combinations to make different materials. Born around 470 BCE in the northern part of the Greek world in the city state of Abdera, he inherits his father's fortune and uses the money to travel to Egypt and parts of Asia. He is able to afford books and as one of the most well-traveled people of his day, to meet other scholars.

Spaces in and between atoms allow motion.

According to Democritus, atoms have different characteristics. Iron atoms are hard and have some kind of mechanical attachment points like hooks and eyes that allow them to form solid blocks, while water atoms are smooth and slippery. Salt atoms are sharp, which accounts for their prickly taste. Empty space within and between atoms allows them to flow as liquids.

The foundation of science solidifies.

Greek philosophers think about how we know what we know, how much we trust our senses, etc. This thinking about thinking, called epistemology, provides an internal critique, a check to which ideas will be subjected.

Many philosophers, including Plato, subscribe to the method of deducing the origins of things backwards from what use or function they serve today. This is called teleology; the Greek word telos means end or purpose.

Democritus and his fellow 'atomists' attempt to build up an explanation of the world by mechanistic causes rather than by teleology. He also has an ability to laugh at the foibles of humans even including philosophers. His ideas attain only moderate popularity.

The Earth is a sphere.

This idea is well known by Aristotle's time. Four facts support it; Earth casts a circular shadow onto the moon during an eclipse (if it were a flat disc it would cast an oval shadow); as a ship sails over the horizon a clear day the lower portion of its hull disappears while the rest of the ship is still clearly visible; the angle between the pole star and the horizon increases as a traveler moves northward; stones and other pieces of the earth, as they fall naturally toward its center, press it into a round form.

Mathematics connects nature and architecture.

Mathematics is appreciated for its beauty. Patterns and proportions in nature are discovered and expressed in art and architecture.

Although hampered by their non-positional numbering system, the Greeks excel in math, especially geometry. The limitations of their number system (more like Roman numerals than the Arabic numerals we use today) push them to explore the logic behind the relationships of shapes and to discover such things as the Pythagorean Theorem which describes the lengths of the sides of a right triangle. #

The Golden Ratio, which is commonly found in nature in relationships like the size of a tree limb to its sub-limbs, is discovered. This proportion of height to width is aesthetically pleasing and resonates in the human mind. It becomes the standard proportion used in architecture - for instance, it is used to choose the shapes and placement of windows and doors in designing the facades of buildings.

Greed leads to war and folly.

After decades as the preeminent Greek city-state, the Athenians use the common defense fund to finance their own monuments. When some of the other city states tire of paying into the fund, Athens prepares to make war against them. The Peloponnesian War begins in 431 BCE and ends with the Athenian surrender to Sparta. Athens will eventually be relieved of Spartan rule and science and the arts will again flourish but Athens will never regain its former glory.

Aristotle's laws of motion are flawed.

According to Aristotle, heavenly objects and earthly objects are governed by a different physical laws of motion. Heavenly objects, like the planets, by their intrinsic nature move continuously on circular paths. Earthly objects; which are composed of earth, air, fire and or water, naturally come to rest when they reach their proper place within the terrestrial environment.

According to this theory, no force is necessary to propel the planets in their orbits and no force is necessary to roll a stone downhill. But force is required to move a stone uphill because the proper place for a stone is as close to the center of the earth as it can get. Likewise, when a swimmer exhales air it naturally bubbles upward back to its proper place in the atmosphere. When a stone is thrown, the force exerted by the thrower acts on the stone in an unnatural and violent way but as soon as this force is used up, the rock drops in a straight line downward back to its natural place at rest on the ground.

Alexander unites an empire.

Alexander, tutored by Aristotle as a youth, inherits the kingdom of Macedon, a region of northern Greece. He soon conquers other areas of Greece and then Egypt and Persia in an empire that stretches to India. Although he will die at an early age and the empire fragment, Greek will remain the lingua franca for centuries and ideas will spread from Greece and from Asia through a network of trade routes facilitated by common coinage.

Rudimentary compasses are in use.

When a lodestone is suspended so that it can swing freely, it always points in a particular direction. Lodestones are shards of rock composed of the naturally magnetic mineral known as magnetite. During the Han Dynasty, compasses are used to plan buildings, tell fortunes, and harmonize building interiors in accordance with feng shui.

A comet is recorded.

Comets, dirty snowballs of rock and ice that are dislodged from their orbits far out in the solar system, fall toward the sun. Some comets fall into the sun but many establish new, highly eccentric orbits and will periodically travel by Earth. Halley's comet, recorded by a Chinese historian in 240 BCE, has a 75 year periodicity.

Ctesibius founds pneumatics.

Ctesibius (285-222 BCE) makes a water clock and writes a treatise on compressed air.

The Archimedes screw transports water.

Archimedes, enthralled with patterns of circles and spirals, creates a pumping device that employs a hand-cranked screw propeller to lift water in a pipe. The device is used for bailing out boats and irrigating crops.

Archimedes describes buoyancy.

Objects that float in water displace a volume of water that weighs an amount equal to the weight of the object.

Wind moves water in India.

The *Arthashastra* is a complex treatise on economics, politics, resource management, state-building, and military strategy authored by Chanakya in India's Maurya Empire. The Sanskrit text alludes to an irrigation machine which harnesses the wind to move water. (Ch6.6)

A windmill is built in Persia.

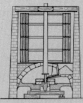

Bundles of reeds are attached as sails to spin a horizontal wheel, which turns a vertical shaft to which a grinding stone is attached. Built circa 200 BCE, these mills can be 10 meters high.

The Roman Republic expands.

The city-state of Rome had deposed its king in favor of a government of limited democracy in 509 BCE. The votes of men from the aristocracy are given far more weight than the votes of male peasants. Consuls are elected to one year terms and are advised by a senate. The system evolves dynamically to resolve ongoing tensions between the social classes. As Rome conquers neighboring areas, the vanquished are sometimes made citizens which eases the ability of the republic to administrate the new areas.

Archimedes describes many phenomena.

He explains the mechanics of levers and pulleys and the principle of buoyancy and contributes to mathematics. In his day, he is famous for his improvements to weapons used to defend the Greek city state of Syracuse (in Sicily) against the Roman invasion of 212 BCE.

Steam powers a turbine.

Powered by expanding gases, a chamber spins around an axis. Invented by Hero of Alexandria in the first century BCE, the aeolipile, demonstrates that torque can be produced by steam but it is unlikely that the device is employed to do any useful work. As a cauldron of water is heated, molecules of H_2O leave the liquid water as a gasseos vapor and flow up into the chamber. Pressure builds in the chamber not only because more molecules keep entering the chamber but also because the atoms that compose the molecules of water vapor are hot. When atoms absorb heat their electrons move into orbits that are further away from the nucleus and they vibrate faster. When the hot molecules collide with each other they bounce off at high speeds and if they cannot take up more space the pressure builds. Like a rocket motor, the pressure is released through carefully positioned outlet pipes and as the steam shoots out the chamber spins.

Hero also creates a wind-powered organ.

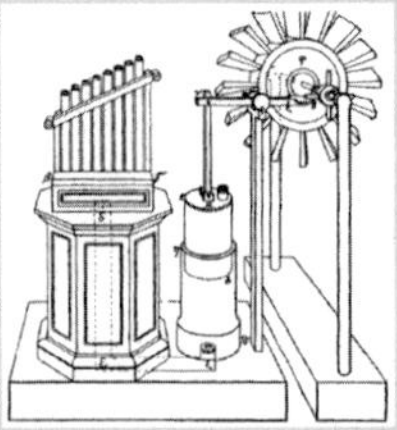

The instrument has a wheel with paddles arrayed perpendicular to its axis which spin the wheel in the wind. The energy of this movement is transferred to bellows in the organ by means of a pump whose arm pivots up and down like that of an oil derrick.

Aluminum is hinted at.

Alum is a salty compound which contains aluminum and has astringent properties. It is used to bind dye to cloth and in medicine to bind wounds. But metallic aluminum will not be separated and refined from the ores in which it is found until the modern era.

Bird migration is contemplated.

Thinkers such as Aristotle and Pliny the Elder observe species such as cranes and understand their migratory nature. Smaller species of birds are perhaps harder to track, and it is believed that swallows and other species hibernate during the cold months. In fact, some believe that these species pass the winter months in a torpid state while submerged in lakes and ponds.

The Roman Empire expands to include all the shores of the Mediterranean Sea.

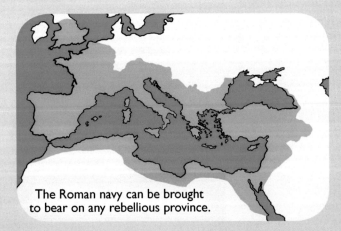

The Roman navy can be brought to bear on any rebellious province.

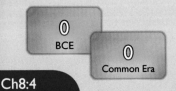

0
BCE

0
Common Era

Jesus preaches a gospel of equality.

That Jesus is a carpenter and not a member of the elite further drives home the message that salvation is for anyone. The idea that all people are equal in the eyes of God is a welcome respite from the rigid social class system of the Romans.

Oral histories from the disciples of Jesus will be told and retold. They will be of interest to many within the empire and these stories and other religious and philosophical ideas will travel, along with goods and soldiers over Roman trade routes. The new testament will be transcribe from these accounts, stories and legends in about 70 AD.

Austronesians sail across the Bay of Bengal to Sri Lanka.

The monsoon season trade winds are discovered.

The monsoon trade winds provide a more direct route for sailing from the mouth of the Red Sea to the coast of India. A return route is also provided, but sailors must wait until the winds change with the seasons and flow the other way. No longer must ships sail North and then East and South along the coastline.

The Greco-Egyptian astronomer, Ptolemy, creates a model that portrays the orbits of the planets around the Earth.

He portrays the universe as a set of nested spheres centered around the Earth. This **geocentric** model will be the most accepted model for many centuries. It successfully predicts the future positions of the visible planets, for example where will Mars be seen in the sky next April. However, it is cumbersome to use. In order for this model, that puts the earth at the center, to function, each planet must make sub-orbits, called epicycles.

Ptolemy accepts the current knowledge that the Earth is spherical. He estimates the distance to the sun as 1,210 Earth radii and the distance to the stars at 20,000 Earth radii. He creates star charts that show when certain stars will appear on the horizon. In addition to astronomy, Ptolemy makes contributes to geography and cartography.

Christianity becomes the official religion of Rome.

Emperor Constantine embraces Christianity in 313 CE.

The eastern portion of the empire will endure. It remains Christian, with a headquarters in Constantinople, and becomes known as the Byzantine Empire.

Miniature hot air balloons fly.

In China, sky lanterns (also known as Kongming Lanterns) are used for play or as part of the Spring Festival. According to legends, sky lanterns are invented in the Warring States Period of the 3rd century BCE, but are later attributed to the sage and military strategist Zhuge Liang (181-234 CE), whose courtesy name was Kongming. Fables say that he used the lanterns to pass messages and orders to his army. Sky lanterns have also been used to notify survivors when an attacking army is gone. The sky lantern is used today in many Asian countries to celebrate festivals and holidays.

Stirrups increase the utility of horses.

The invention of stirrups improves the utility of horseback riding. Among the oldest evidence for this invention is a pair of primitive stirrups from a Jin Dynasty tomb, dated 322 CE.

 As a balloon rises, it displaces the air above it sideways and wedges itself upward. The higher pressure air closes in below the balloon, pushing it upward.

The Gupta Empire ushers in a golden age for India.

Scholars come from as far away as Tibet, China, Persia, and Greece to Nalanda University in Bihar.

The Roman Empire cannot stay unified and divides into eastern and western portions.

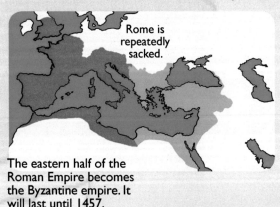

Rome is repeatedly sacked.

The eastern half of the Roman Empire becomes the Byzantine empire. It will last until 1457.

Gupta chemists crystallize sugar and separate it from cane, allowing for compact storage.

500
CE

The Polynesians sail on and reach Hawaii.

Sometime between 300 and 800 CE people of Polynesian descent settle Hawaii and then Easter Island a few centuries later. They carry the suite of plants used in their agricultural system as well as semi-domesticated pigs.

The outrigger canoes are built with two skins, one sealed against the water, and the other smoothed for the wind, accommodating the different fluid dynamics in the sky and the sea.

Paper is made.

In China, a method of manufacturing a nicer and more portable medium for writing and artwork is invented.

The Sasanians and Byzantines are rival superpowers.

The Sasanian Empire of Persia is in its golden age. The two superpowers exhaust themselves by warring, leaving a gap through which a new empire can emerge.

Muhammad founds the religion of Islam.

Islam is a monotheistic religion that recognizes a succession of prophets of God; including Abraham, Moses, Jesus, and Muhammad.

Muhammad unites the warring tribes of the Arabian Peninsula. Most Arabs had been practicing polytheism, but some were already practicing monotheism. There were also minority populations of Jews and Christians living in the region. Muhammad stresses individual faith and consistent devotion for his followers and preaches that all Muslims are equal before God and that tolerance should be shown toward unbelievers.

Muhammad does not leave an heir and the dispute over who should succeed him begins soon after his death in 632.

What comes to be known as the Sunni position is that the caliph should be chosen on the basis of merit, while the Shiite position is that the successor to Muhammad should descend from a blood relative.

Islam will have a succession of four major caliphates; the Rashidun, Umayyad, Abbissid, and finally the Ottoman, which will last until the dissolution of the institution, in 1924, Additionally there are three times when rival or shadow caliphates compete.

In a dream, Muhammad flies to Jerusalem on a winged steed.

The mythical winged steed is called a Buraq and it flies. Muhammad's dream is called the 'Night Journey.' The site in Jerusalem will later be commemorated by the building of the mosque known as 'The Dome of the Rock.' This is the same site where Solomon's Temple is said to have been built.

Expansion under Muhammad, 622ᴄᴇ - 632ᴄᴇ
Expansion under the Rashidun Caliphate, 632ᴄᴇ - 661ᴄᴇ

China experiences a golden age during the Tang Dynasty.

The Tang Dynasty is established in 619 and presides until 907. The capital city, Chang An, is the largest city in the world. Chinese culture flourishes and further matures during this cosmopolitan period. The Silk Road is reopened (although it is not yet the thoroughfare it will become under Mongol rule) and trading resumes between China and Europe, although conflict with Tibet causes it to close from time to time. Buddhism becomes a major influence in Chinese culture. Gun powder is invented, wood block printing is refined, and national building standards are codified.

The Tang continue the system of organizing officials and bureaucrats under a civil service system that relies on recommendations and standardized tests. According to their census, they preside over a population of 50 million. Women enjoy greater rights than they will in later centuries; for example, foot binding is not yet practiced.

The population of China is estimated to increase to about 80 million people by the end of the Tang Dynasty.

Gunpowder is developed.

Gunpowder contains charcoal, salt peter (potassium nitrate), and sulphur. It might have been an accidental by-product made by alchemists searching for an elixir that would bring eternal life.

Fireworks are developed.

One of the Four Great Inventions of ancient China, gunpowder is reformulated to create fireworks.
Used in conjunction with other festival features, the original fireworks are hung from tall posts along with banners and other ornamentation. The explosive and sputtering fireworks displays are said to disperse evil spirits and bring good luck. Porcelain is also developed by the Tang.

Construction of the Great Wall of China continues.

In mountainous areas, local stones were used, while in the plains, earth was piled up and compacted by ramming.

The Grand Canal is completed

The Grand Canal stretches from Hangzhou in the south to Beijing in the north and is the largest man-made waterway in the world.

Chinese paper making technology spreads to the Islamic world, helping it achieve its golden age.

At the Battle of Talas, in 751, Islamic and Chinese forces fight in their first and only war. Talas marks the western extent of the Chinese empire and the most northeastern extent of the Islamic. Both sides employ mercenary troops. Tibetans, already fighting to maintain their independence from China, fight on the Muslim side. The Islamic forces prevail and take control of this region, which is especially valuable because it contains some of the routes of the Silk Road.

Afterward, Chinese paper-making skills and technology spread into the Middle East and later to Europe.

Widespread adoption of the horse and other improvements to agricultural methods allows Europe to move out of The Dark Ages.

In Northern Europe, population growth has been slow and the standard of living low because of the short growing season and the heavy, hard to plow soil. Agricultural technology that had been developed by the Romans is not applicable in most of Europe.

Islam spreads quickly across North Africa and into the Iberian Peninsula (Spain).

The Islamic Caliphate has grown far beyond the Arabian Peninsula and includes many non- Arabic speaking peoples. The second Abbissid caliph, al-Mansur, moves the capital to a more central location along the winding banks of the Tigris.

The capital is probably built atop older ruins, as a city of Baghdad is known in the Old Testament. Designs are drawn up in the Persian style of a circular layout with avenues radiating outward from the center.

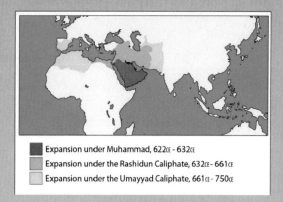

■ Expansion under Muhammad, 622ᴄᴇ - 632ᴄᴇ
■ Expansion under the Rashidun Caliphate, 632ᴄᴇ - 661ᴄᴇ
☐ Expansion under the Umayyad Caliphate, 661ᴄᴇ - 750ᴄᴇ

Abbas ibn Firnas is reputed to have flown.

The polymath Abbas ibn Firnas (810–887 CE) of Andalusia (Spain) is a physician, engineer, inventor, musician, and poet. Among his many inventions are a water clock called al-Maqata, a production process for making corrective eye lenses, a simulator of planetary motion, and a method for cutting minerals.

Legend says that he attempts to fly by jumping from a high eminence with a set of feathered wings strapped to his body. His alleged flight is marginally successful, with the contraption allowings him to glide and slowing his fall enough that he sustains only moderate injuries. The only contemporary source that seems to corroborate his flight is by Mu'min ibn Said, a poet in the court of Muhammad I. A translation of his account is "He flew faster than the phoenix in his flight when he dressed his body in the feathers of a vulture." This poet was usually critical of Abbas ibn Firnas when writing about his other achievements, which lends some credence to his account.

A more detailed account of his flight is by the Morrocan historian Ahmed Muhammad al-Maqqari in 1632, which is based on sources that no longer exist. The crater Ibn Firnas on the Moon is named after him as is the Ibn Firnas Airport in Baghdad.

850
CE

Triangular, or Lateen, sails are airfoils and give mariners more control over a boats' direction.

As sailing techniques are refined, the tools and vessels are also refined. In ages past, when only vessels with square sails were used, the wind had to be blowing in roughly the same direction that the sail was pointed. Directional changes of the boat were made by changing the angle of the rudder or by using oars.

When capturing the wind with more developed sails, wind power can be harnessed even when the wind is blowing at angles that seem to be in almost direct contrast to the overall direction of the boat's travel.

By employing a lateen sail, the sail can be aligned almost parallel to the wind direction. In this configuration, the sail acts as an airfoil, creating a pressure difference between the air on either side of the sail. Lift pulls the sail crosswise from its course. The keel of the boat provides enough resistance against this lift (the boat wants to move through the water along its keel) that the boat will move forward at an angle part way between the keel line and the direction of the wind.

The origin of the lateen sail is hotly debated and two models are proposed. The first places the credit with the Arabs or Persians, who brought it to the Mediterranean on trading ships. The second theory turns the former around and states that Mediterranean mariners were using the lateen sail around 2nd century CE. Introduction to the Muslim world would only happen later, with the lateen sail being introduced first to India and then beyond by Alexandrian/ Roman merchant vessels.

Islamic Empires expand rapidly in the centuries after the reign of Muhammad. Universities in Islamic cities are among the greatest centers of learning in the world.

Scholars write poems and literature and add words like algebra and algorithm to the vocabulary of math and science. They also translate many books and documents from Ancient Greece and preserve these texts.

Islamic lands are divided among rival caliphates.

In Andulasia (now Spain), another rebel, a descendent of the earlier Umayyad caliphs, sets up an independent kingdom but does not declare himself caliph. Universities, libraries and scholarship flourish and are visited by Europeans.

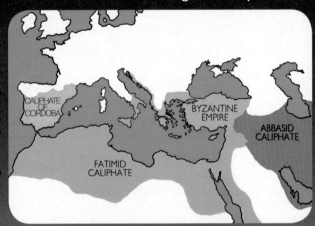

CALIPHATE OF CORDOBA

BYZANTINE EMPIRE

ABBASID CALIPHATE

FATIMID CALIPHATE

Cairo is founded by the Fatimids in 969.

A Shiite caliphate based in North Africa, the Fatimid, becomes a rival to the Sunni Abbasid Caliphate based in Baghdad. When the Fatimids have gained enough power, they move eastwards and take over the fertile lands of Egypt.

With control of the Egyptian breadbasket, Fatimid power increases. They take control of both shores of the Red Sea and the holy cities of Mecca and Medina, which adds to their prestige and 'soft power'.

The Crusades begin in 1095 under the instruction of Pope Urban II.

European soldiers are recruited from all echelons of society; some monarchs pledge their servants to accompany embarking nobles and prisons are emptied of convicts who are promised that their sins will be forgiven if they participate in this holy war. Some simply seek adventure, the chance to escape their defined role in feudal society, economic or political gain, while others sincerely believe that they can show the utmost devotion to God as a soldier of Christ.

The stated goal of the First Crusade is to restore Christian access to holy sites in and near Jerusalem. Jerusalem had been conquered by Islamic forces in 637. The crusaders take back the city in 1099 and the streets of Jerusalem run with blood with the wholesale massacre of the Muslim and Jewish inhabitants by the Christian soldiers.

The Crusades reopened trade routes to the Mediterranean and the cities of Genoa and Venice flourished. Although armies often pillaged, they would also trade for provisions along their route and Byzantine officials would sometimes organize markets for crusaders passing through their territories. Crusading consolidated the identities of European Christians and gave rise to medieval literature and philosophies but also strengthened ties between feudalism, militarism, and Christianity, and did not fulfill the stated aim of promoting peace.

Flight beckons the bright and the brave.

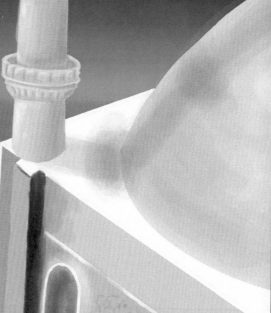

A bright super nova is visible.

In 1006, people from all around the world watch and wonder. The Egyptian astronomer Ali Ibn Ridwan writes a detailed account.

1006

A Turkish scholar jumps.

Likely inspired by the purported flight of 875, Abu Nasr Isma'il ibn Hammad al-Jawhari, a Turkish lexicographer, outfits himself with wings made of wood and attempts to fly by leaping from a mosque at Nishapur, a city in Northeastern Iran. He dies immediately upon hitting the ground and is remembered for his compilation of an Arabic dictionary, the al-Sihah fi al-Lugha, rather than for his failed flight,

Eilmer the monk jumps and glides.

Inspired by the Greek tale of Daedalus, Eilmer, a learned astrologer and monk, attaches wings to his hands and feet and launches himself from a tower at Malmesbury Abbey in Wiltshire, England in 1010. Accounts by medieval historian William of Malmesbury indicate that, by catching the wind upon launch, he flew for more than a furlong (about 200 meters) before landing and breaking both legs. Eilmer is said to have attributed the crash to lack of a tail for steering. The feasibility of the flight will be confirmed in 2010 by calculations indicating that a launch into the southwest wind could have enabled him to ride the air currents off the hillside and land where legend suggests.

Gunpowder is described.

The recipe for gunpowder is described in the 1044 text *Complete Essentials for the Military Classics* or *Wujing Zongyao*. Weapons that use the explosive powder, including incendiary projectiles, fire arrows, bombs, grenades, and smoke bombs are explained.

Damascus steel production takes off.

Syria, with its many water and wind powered mills for refining iron and forging steel, leads the world in production of these metals by 1100. Damascus becomes well known for the quality of swords produced there.

The compass is used for navigation.

Although there is much debate about exactly when and which culture invents the navigational compass, several sources note its use by the military of China's Song Dynasty. The first recorded mention of the compass being used for navigation at sea also occurs during the Song Dynasty.

The island of Hawai'i, which had been settled by Polynesians 500 years earlier, is invaded by a new wave of Polynesians from Tahiti.

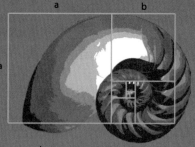

$$\frac{a+b}{a} = \frac{a}{b} = \varphi \approx 1.61803$$

Fibonacci brings Arabic numerals and the modern decimal number system to Europe.

Leonardo Fibonacci also popularizes the sequence of numbers that now bears his name.

0, 1, 1, 2, 3, 5, 8, 13, 21, 34 ...

Windmills are used in Europe.

Although the windmill has long been in use in Persia, Europe's earliest recorded windmill overlooks an estuary in Yorkshire, in 1185.

1200

In northwestern Europe, variable winds drive builders to create windmills that can swivel to face into the wind.

It is likely that these towering windmills were first built in the 12th century, perhaps in England. To prevent them from being blown over, these early windmills (called post mills) are built with their pivot post supports buried deep in the ground. Almost the entire building, from the specialized support beams (known as trestles) up, pivots with the wind. Eventually, post mills will be improved upon, often with modifications made to the trestles. Post mills use wind sails made of lattice work and very little solid surface. These windmills are used as power to grind grain almost as often as for drainage or irrigation pumps.

In Europe, cathedral building is in its heyday.

Europeans explore many building techniques. God is sometimes even depicted as an engineer.

Gunpowder is improved.

The Chinese invention of **gunpowder** moves out on the silk road. The Arabs improve the technology, which eventually reaches Europe.

Islamic empires flourish.

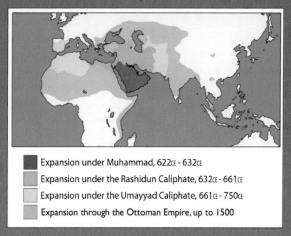

■ Expansion under Muhammad, 622CE - 632CE
■ Expansion under the Rashidun Caliphate, 632CE - 661CE
□ Expansion under the Umayyad Caliphate, 661CE - 750CE
■ Expansion through the Ottoman Empire, up to 1500

The Mongol fleet attacks Japan in 1274 and again in 1281. The Japanese are saved both times by the Kamikaze, or "Divine Wind."

The Mongols sack Baghdad in 1258, destroying the House of Wisdom, the world's largest library.

Traders and goods move safely and swiftly upon the Silk Road. Officially sanctioned travelers are identified by medallions that function like passports. They are provisioned and accommodated at stations located every forty kilometers or so along the many thousand mile long route. The Mongols do not tolerate banditry - they alone have a monopoly on violence. Tribute is paid to the Mongols by every village and town in the realm and petty wars between any of these entities are not tolerated.

Despite the annihilation of almost the entire population of Baghdad (the most important city in the Muslim world) and the destruction of the House of Wisdom, the Mamluks refuse to preemptively surrender when the Mongols threaten to destroy Cairo.

Some intrepid European travelers also journey along the Silk Road and visit India and China. Accounts by such authors as Marco Polo become best sellers in Europe and motivate future European explorations. Marco Polo writes of the riches of China and of the many barges that ply the yellow river with their loads of lumber, rice, paper, porcelain, and other resources. The economic output of China is much greater than that of Europe at this time.

In 1298, the Ottoman Empire coalesces.

In the 1340's, the Black Plague sweeps through the entire Eurasian continent.

The tower mill improves upon the windmill's design and efficiency.

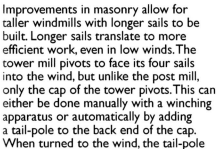

Improvements in masonry allow for taller windmills with longer sails to be built. Longer sails translate to more efficient work, even in low winds. The tower mill pivots to face its four sails into the wind, but unlike the post mill, only the cap of the tower pivots. This can either be done manually with a winching apparatus or automatically by adding a tail-pole to the back end of the cap. When turned to the wind, the tail-pole will act as an airfoil and be pushed back parallel to the wind, thus facing the windmill directly into the wind.

Mansa Musa, the king of Mali, makes the Hajj with 30,000 of his subjects in 1324.

When Mansa Musa makes the Hajj (the pilgrimage to Mecca), he carries with him a bounty of wealth to pay for the journey and as an offering to Mecca. So much of his gold is given out in Egypt that he accidentally devalues its worth there with his generosity. His visit does much to improve the image of Africa in the eyes of the Middle East, where Africans are mostly thought of as slaves.

Stories of Mansa Musa's pilgrimage and wave of gold endure, and inspire future generations of explorers to search for a giant vein of gold in Mali. His legend is a lure for Spanish and Portuguese mariners sailing down the coast. Future expeditions set out from Timbuktu in search of Musa's golden empire, only to find a wasteland.

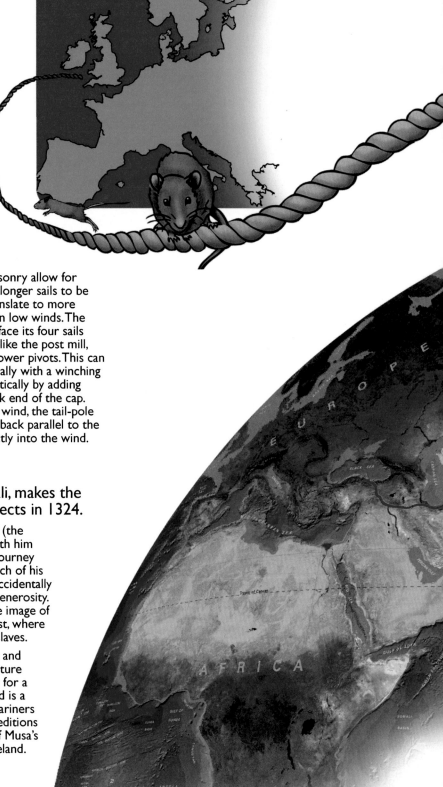

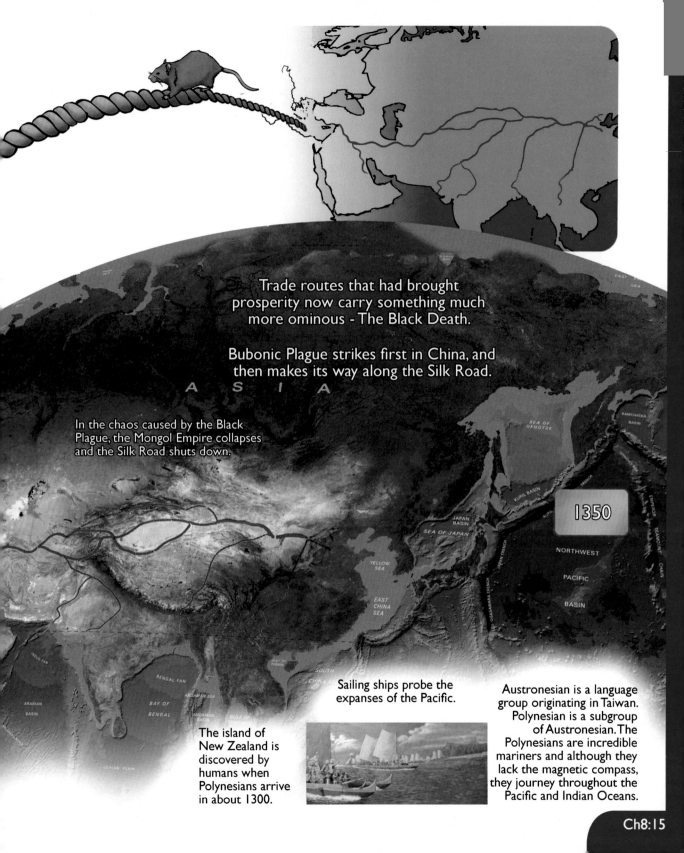

Trade routes that had brought prosperity now carry something much more ominous - The Black Death.

Bubonic Plague strikes first in China, and then makes its way along the Silk Road.

A S I A

In the chaos caused by the Black Plague, the Mongol Empire collapses and the Silk Road shuts down.

1350

Sailing ships probe the expanses of the Pacific.

The island of New Zealand is discovered by humans when Polynesians arrive in about 1300.

Austronesian is a language group originating in Taiwan. Polynesian is a subgroup of Austronesian. The Polynesians are incredible mariners and although they lack the magnetic compass, they journey throughout the Pacific and Indian Oceans.

0.36 Billion

World Population
stands at 360 million.

1400

China is freed from paying tribute to the Mongols and is independent once again. Population levels rebound from plague stricken lows. China's new emperor authorizes the building of a fleet of sailing ships to explore the adjacent coastlines and the world beyond.

The great expeditions begin in 1405 and Chinese sailors reach India, the middle East, and North Africa. The expeditions come to an abrupt end in 1433. Subsequent voyages are forbidden and China turns inward.

Most of the ships and their logbooks are destroyed. A new law is passed, making it a capital offense to build a ship with more than two masts.

Admiral Zeng He, working under the Yongle Emperor, administers the building of the fleet. These large sailing ships, some over 400 feet long, remain the largest wooden ships ever to be built.

Why did the Chinese curtail their explorations? Could some have feared that plague would again follow trade routes? Or did the emperor think that foreign influences would corrupt society or that China already had everything it needed and was better off remaining isolated?

The Huolongjing or Fire Dragon Manual is published.

Authored by the military strategists Jiao Yu and Liu Bowen of the Ming Dynasty, the text is an improvement on an earlier text that no longer exists. The earliest edition is published before 1395 and the oldest material included dates to 1280. Recipes for many different gunpowder formulas are described, as are weapons that use gunpowder, such as land mines, bombs, cannons, and primitive guns.

One remarkable innovation described in the manual is the **Fire Arrow**. Built around the modified shaft of an arrow, this is the first recorded rocket. Fueled by a solid-state gunpowder fuel cell, these weapons are launched from stands made from bamboo (the hollow shaft of the bamboo plant makes a good firing barrel). As this weapon becomes more refined, the tips of the arrow will be covered in flammable materials and devices will be built to launch as many as 1,000 Fire Arrows at the same time.

1420 - Giovanni da Fontana, an engineer and magician of the Italian renaissance, creates a "torpedo," which is said to have powered a model "dove," or small flying object, for flights up to 100 ft.

The Moa, the only wingless bird on the planet, is hunted to extinction.

The Moa, whose only predator prior to human contact was a massive eagle, radiated into New Zealand's niches and evolved nine distinct species. The two largest of these species reached a height of 12 ft when fully extended and weighed perhaps more than 500 pounds. Though scientists once thought the Moa was related to the largest members of the Ratite family, genetic testing has shown that their closest relatives are the Tinamous, a small South American bird capable of flight. Despite this relationship, every member of the Moa Order lacked the bones of a front limb, without even a vestigial wing. Moas will be hunted to extinction by the Maori people, subsequently leading to the extinction of their only natural predator, Haast's Eagle.

Wind speed is measured.

Leon Battista Alberti of Genoa creates an anemometer to measure wind speeds in 1450. With experience as an author, priest, architect, cryptographer, poet, and philosopher, Alberti is perhaps the definition of the 'Renaissance Man.' His first mechanical anemometer consists of a disk suspended perpendicular to the wind. Wind speed is calculated by the angle and speed of the disk's rotation.

Europeans lose access to overland trade routes with Asia and develop interest in finding a maritime route.

With the loss of Constantinople, European trade routes to India and China are severed. This will lead European navigators to seek maritime routes around Africa.

Constantinople falls to the Ottoman Empire in 1453.

1453

Portugal commissions an expedition to reach India by sailing all the way around Africa.

Bartolemeu Dias is commissioned by the king of Portugal to head the expedition in 1588. Nearing the southernmost tip of Africa, his two ships encounter a terrible storm. Dias orders them to head in a more southerly direction, which takes them farther from the rocky and dangerous shoreline, but also farther out to sea. It is likely that he was aware that the planet's winds usually blow from the southeast at extreme southern latitudes and that these winds would push him east, past the tip of Africa and into the Indian Ocean.

After some time, the expedition re-encounters the African coastline, this time on the eastern side. Now in warmer waters they proceed, but eventually the crew, worried about dwindling food supplies, threatens to mutiny and the expedition returns home. On the way back, they are able to see the tip of Africa, which Dias names 'Cape of Storms.' The king is dismayed that Dias did not reach India and has the cape renamed The Cape of Good Hope, in order to inspire future expeditions.

Dias searches for Prester John, a mythical priest fabled to lead an exotic band of Christians. Early legends place Prester John in India, Central Asia, or a Crusader State, but later accounts place him in Ethiopia. Rumors of gold in Africa may have fueled interest in searching for Prester John and his followers on that continent.

Cast of two pieces of solid bronze, a great cannon bombards the walls of Constantinople.

This cannon will remain in service for over 340 years. In 1807, when the British Royal Navy attempts to take possession of the Dardenelles (one of the two straits which mark the continental boundary between Europe and Asia), this cannon will be employed, earning it the moniker *The Dardanelles Gun*.

The Ottoman Empire has been expanding steadily westward through Turkey and arrives at the gates of Constantinople, the capital of the Byzantine Empire. The city is defeated by the Islamic armies of Mehmed the Conqueror.

Leonardo da Vinci illustrates flying machines.

Although da Vinci will never successfully achieve flight, his notebooks are filled with illustrations of flying machines.

Using the technologies of the day, along with his extensive research into body plans and the execution of flight in the animal kingdom, Da Vinci designs many devices. Some include mechanisms that flap to create lift, but others employ screw propellers to push air down (as a primitive helicopter rotor).

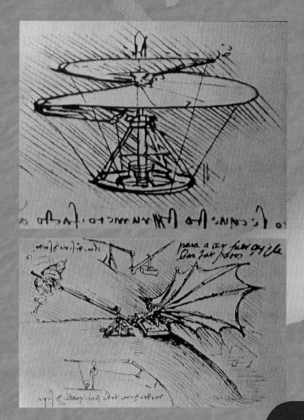

Da Vinci also makes the theory of fluid dynamics more rigorous.

1492

Columbus sets out across the Atlantic to reach India by sailing all the way around the globe.

The Americas are exposed to diseases that evolved in Eurasia.

Horses return.

The Spanish bring back horses, which originated in North America but became extinct there thousands of years ago. Meanwhile, back in Europe, Leonardo Da Vinci draws accurate depictions of both living horses and extinct organisms from the fossil record.

After the war to drive the Muslims from Spain is concluded, Christopher Columbus is finally able to convince Ferdinand and Isabella to sponsor his expedition. He sails westward to reach Asia by sea.

Columbus reaches the Caribbean and, assuming that he has reached India, calls the people he meets Indians. Little does he know, he has reached the shores of The Americas.

The Birdman of Stirling Castle launches from the ramparts.

John Damian de Falcuis, an Italian alchemist, charms his way into the court of King James IV with promises to turn base metals into gold. In an attempt to restore his reputation, which suffers from repeated alchemical failures, he attempts to fly by jumping off the highest tower of Stirling Castle with wings made of feathers and wood. Although the contraption, possibly based on the drawings of Leonardo DaVinci, whom he claims to know, may have allowed him to glide for a short time, he soon plunges to the ground, landing in a dung heap and breaking one of his legs. His flight is deemed a failure, especially by his competitor at the court, poet William Dunbar, who ridicules him mercilessly. However in the mid 1990's, Prof Charles McKean of the University of Dundee, hypothesized that he might actually have successfully glided a distance of half a mile based on the fact that the nearest dung heap is a half mile away from the tower, and deFalcuis survives what would otherwise have been a fatal fall with only a broken leg.

Leonardo da Vinci studies the flight of birds and writes a *Codex*.

Codex on the Flight of Birds, published in 1506, documents the flight behavior of several species of birds, describes how gravity affects different materials (i.e., feathers), how the center of gravity of a flying creature differs from their center of pressure, and many other phenomena.

Copernicus puts the sun at the center.

Earth orbits the sun!

It is the sun and not the Earth that is the center of our system.

Copernicus waits until he is on his deathbed to publish *On the Revolutions of the Celestial Spheres*. The heliocentric view of the solar system allows the orbits of Earth and the other planets to be described and predicted in a simple straightforward manner, much more easily than the Earth centered model of Ptolemy with its many epi-cycles.

Although it may not seem that way, everything around us including ourselves is in motion. The earth rotates on its axis, and orbits the sun. Our solar system rotates around the center of the Milky Way galaxy, and the galaxies are moving away from each other. To us, this motion is imperceptible (without the aid of scientific instruments). With everything moving—in an absolute sense—we do not sense any motion because we are moving at the same speed and in the same direction as everything around us.

A storm blows a Portuguese ship off course and to the isle of Japan. This ushers in a period of trade and the spread of Christianity in Japan.

Silver is mined, refined, and shipped to China.

Mines are opened after the artistic treasures of the Aztecs and the Incas have already been shipped to Seville. Larger ships are built to haul the silver from Mexico and Peru across the world's largest ocean, the Pacific, to China. China's economy is booming and expanding.

Spain produces about 85% of the world's silver from mines in Mexico, Bolivia, and Peru. China is poor in precious metals, which led them to develop paper money long ago, but paper money became obsolete when they overprinted it, resulting in inflation and a loss of trust. China trades silk, porcelain, and tea for Europe's silver. China needs currency to facilitate its thriving economy and remove the burden of the barter system. China's restructured tax system requires that taxes be paid in currency rather than in goods, which encourages people to participate in the wage economy as well as in markets to sell their agricultural products.

Since the first voyage of Columbus, species of plants and animals that had evolved in different ecosystems on separate continents have been interchanged.

This interchange of species, known as the Columbian Exchange, is still going on today. It is a wholesale mixing of ecosystems that extends far beyond deliberately intended imports; other species, diseases and pests tag along. Exchanged crops greatly expand the inventory of crops on all continents. For example, the potato is farmed in areas that were too cool or damp for any domestic European crop to grow. Domesticated animals are also exchanged, which has a greater effect in the Americas, as almost all domesticated animals are of Eurasian origin. Horses, the most cherished of the domestic animals, which originally evolved in the Americas but had become extinct there about 10,000 years ago, were brought back, influencing Native American culture.

Spanish and Portuguese colonies in The Caribbean, Brazil, Mexico, and elsewhere cultivate sugarcane, coffee, and other crops. Disease devastates Native populations, so African slaves are imported to labor under European immigrant masters. Malaria accompanies the Africans, who have partial immunity to it, which will prevent the potential use of European indentured labor and encourage Europeans to try to govern their colonies *in absentia* as much as possible.

De Re Metallica ("On the Nature of Metals") explains the mining, refining, and smelting of metals.

Germanic mining techniques are state of the art. Georg Bauer, a forceful intellect who first studies literature, linguistics, medicine, physics, and chemistry, works as a physician in a mining town. He gathers information, codifies it, and creates the brilliant text, *De Re Metallica,* which is published in 1556. It is written in Latin, which can be read by any educated European. It replaces Pliny the Elder's work *Historia Naturalis* as the most practical source of information on mining and metals and will remain so for almost 2 centuries.

Smock-style windmills can be built on marginal sites.

Smock mills build off the tower style of windmill, where only the cap of the building rotates to present the sails to the wind. Smock mills, however, are built of a sloping frame of wood that is usually octagonal. The frame is then thatched or covered with clapboard, making them far lighter than previous masonry-based designs, which makes it possible for them to be built in places with unstable subsoil.

The Transatlantic slave trade begins.

Sugar plantations make the most use of slave labor, but coffee, cotton, and other crops are grown in the colonies of the New World as well, and are worked by African slaves.

The cannon and other firearms are developed by Muslim engineers. The Moghul, Ottoman, and Safavid Empires come to be known as Gunpowder Empires.

Drift whaling, harvesting dead whales that wash ashore, is practiced by Europeans and many other peoples.

1588

The English navy, with its new cannons, defeats the Spanish Armada.

With the blessing of the Pope, Spain sends out its mighty fleet, the largest in the world, to force England back into the Catholic fold. The English Navy, meanwhile, has learned to optimize ship cannons rather than using their ships primarily for transport of troops or to board enemy ships to engage in hand to hand combat. In a dramatic upset, the English Navy defeats the Spanish Armada in battle, in 1588. Only half of Spain's ships are able to limp home. Having already spent all the tons of gold looted in the initial conquest of the Americas on wars against Protestants and to maintain its European empire, Spain will never recover its superpower status.

Dutch industry, especially shipbuilding, thrives. The lowlands of the Netherlands have an abundant and unusual fuel supply, peat.

Peat is ancient, non-decomposed swamp material. It is harvested by scooping it up in nets, and when dried out, it can be burned as a fuel. Canals in the swampy landscape act as highways for transport. Winds blowing across the flat terrain power windmills.

Waterwheels are scarce in Holland because most areas don't have enough difference in elevation to drive them. Wind power is used instead, especially for pumping water out of the lowest areas.

A problem of subsidence occurs when the land is dried out or peat is removed. Peat shrinks much further in volume when it is dried out; fields that are dried out function well for years but then start to subside and then become flooded. Any fields that subside below sea level must be protected by earthen dikes in order to maintain agricultural productivity. The organization and maintenance of the vast and intricate water works that evolve leads to cooperation and political unification of the people.

Lippershey tries to patent the first telescope.

A Dutchman named Lippershey applies for a patent for a refracting spyglass in 1608. He is denied and informed that other spectacle-makers have simultaneously made similar devices, but the government rewards him anyway and pays him for his designs.

Whale blubber is used as fuel.

American colonists have been hunting whales since 1644. When a whale is spotted off shore, boats are launched and the whale is harpooned and towed in. On the beach, the whale is butchered and its blubber boiled into oil.

Galileo observes the moon.

Astronomer Galileo Galilei makes some improvements to Lippershey's device, which is intended for viewing faraway ships, and then turns it upward in 1609. He observes the topography of the moon, which shows that the moon is an actual place, not some ethereal orb or perfect sphere. Galileo also sees that Venus goes through phases, waxing and waning like the moon. These phases must mean that Venus orbits the sun.

Galileo observes the small.

Though the early history of the microscope is fogged with claims of primacy, in 1625 Galileo publishes extremely detailed illustrations of insects observed under a microscope - the first such documentation of a compound microscope. Galileo had previously referred to this instrument as his *occhiolino* ("little eye"), and it was later named the 'microscope' by botanist Giovanni Faber.

Kepler publishes three laws of planetary motion.

By analyzing the observational work of Tycho Brahe concerning the motion of Mars, astronomer Johannes Kepler publishes *Astronomia Nova* in 1609, outlining his first two laws of planetary motion.

One: Planets move in elliptical orbits with the sun at one focus point.

Two: The speed of a planet changes at each moment, so that the time between two positions is proportional to the area 'swept out' between these two positions and the sun.

Johannes Kepler further proves his theory of the elliptical nature of planetary orbits in 1619 in his book, *Epitome Astronomiae Copernicanae*.

Three: The square of a planet's orbital period is in proportion to the cube of the semi-major axis of its orbit.

Both the English East India and Dutch East India Companies are founded.

The English East India Company is founded in 1600, shortly before the Dutch East India Company. Spain had failed to unite Europe under a Spanish empire and its mighty treasure had been spent, leaving a legacy of decentralized groups, well-heeled opposition groups (Protestants), competing groups, and a decentralized authority of economic decision-making; in short, it left an atmosphere in which the scientific and industrial revolutions would thrive.

Evangelista Torricelli, solving a dispute about water pumps, invents the barometer.

Due to its density, water can only be raised to a height of 10 meters with a suction pump, as previously described by Galileo. In 1643, in order to find a way to pump water higher, Torricelli filled a meter-long tube (sealed on top) with mercury and placed it

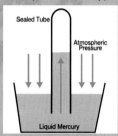

Sealed Tube

Atmospheric Pressure

Liquid Mercury

upright in bowl of mercury. The mercury, with a density almost fourteen times that of water, settled down from the top of the tube, creating a *Torricellian Vacuum* above it. This vacuum is extremely sensitive and responsive to atmospheric pressure and signals the invention of the **barometer**.

The first coffee house opens in Europe in Venice in 1645. Soon thereafter, coffee houses gain popularity in Europe.

The **Magdeburg hemispheres** demonstrate the principles of atmospheric pressure.

Scientist and mayor of the town of Magdeburg, Germany, Otto von Guericke is inspired by Torricelli's work on vacuum pumps. Guericke builds a pair of copper hemispheres that fit together to form a sphere. Using a vacuum pump of his own invention, he sucks the air out of the sphere. The resulting air pressure gradient keeps the two hemispheres tightly mated together.

To demonstrate the principles of air pressure discovered along the way, Guericke attaches a team of eight horses to either side of the sphere and challenges the team's handlers to pull the hemispheres apart. Because of the hemisphere's effectiveness, the horses are unable to pull them apart until the valve is opened and the vacuum seal broken.

A Dutch travel writer observes Chinese windmills.

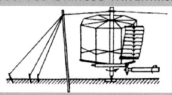

A travel writer by trade, Jan Nieuhof was hired by the East India Trading company to accompany the Dutch Ambassador to Peking. He recorded a detailed account of everything he saw. As he walked along a canal in Chiangsu, he saw many large octagonal drums spinning in the wind. These devices have eight wind-catching surfaces made from the same materials as junk sails, each attached to a vertical shaft on which they swung freely. As the wind catches them, they act as airfoils and the whole device turns. These windmills are 15 ft in diameter and are used to power desalination and irrigation pumps.

The Earth itself is a magnet.

A treatise is published on the "Magnet and Magnetic Bodies," and on "That Great Magnet the Earth." Author William Gilbert is meticulous in his descriptions of his experiments with magnetism, static electricity, and compasses, making *De Magnete* a highly influential text. The navigational compass has been in use and has been refined over the centuries, but explorers have found that there are discrepancies between magnetic north and true north. Gilbert explains this by positing that the Earth itself is a magnet.

To prove this, he creates a *terrella,* a small sphere created out of a lodestone that acts as a working model of the planet. He proves the "magnetic inclination," or the difference

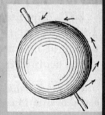

between the true north heading and that of magnetic north by using both horizontal compasses and dip needle compasses on the *terrella.* The mechanisms that influence compasses have previously been explained as mythical or supernatural. *De Magnete* finally puts these ideas to rest.

Saturn's largest moon, Titan, is discovered by Christiaan Huygens in 1655.

Giovanni Cassini observes polar ice caps on Mars and determines the rotation periods of Mars and Jupiter.

An airship is designed.

In 1663, Francesco Lana de Terzi, an Italian polymath, designs a theoretical flying ship that would use hollow copper spheres from which the air had been pumped out.

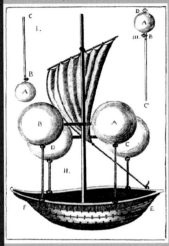

After witnessing a demonstration of the Magdeburg Hemispheres, de Terzi draws up plans for a flying boat, which are published in a volume called *Prodomo*, in 1670. The ship is to be suspended in the atmosphere by the vaccuum provided by the evacuated copper spheres.

Manufacturing the copper spheres to be thin is a physical impossibility of the time, so the design will remain untested, but de Terzi is perhaps relieved. His first philosophical thoughts on the lighter-than-air ship are its possible catastrophic military ramifications.

Plant reproduction and anatomy are explained and described in detail.

The "Father of Plant Anatomy," Nehemiah Grew, a physiologist and anatomist, turns his attention from human physiology toward the world of plant life. Over his long and storied career, he publishes numerous treatises on plant anatomy and, in 1682, publishes the compendium *The Anatomy of Plants*.

Divided into four sections, the compendium examines vegetables, roots, tree trunks and leaves, flowers, seeds, and fruit in great detail. The last of these treatises contains the world's first microscopic examination and description of pollen. Grew correctly hypothesizes on the reproductive mechanisms of flowers, all of which set the stage for further understanding of plant life.

A New Theory of the Earth is published.

William Whiston, in 1696, describes the Earth as a divine creation, built from the atmosphere of a comet. He also attributes all major catastrophes and changes in Earth's history, including a global flood, to comets.

The Archimedian screw is developed and patented as a ship propeller.

Although little is known of the innovators Toogood and Hays, the two describe a method of boat propulsion in 1661, far ahead of its time. While they inadvertently add to the creation of the modern propeller, the two are, in fact, describing a process of creating waterjet-based propulsion.

English physicist Robert Hooke proposes the use of a "windmill-like device" to propel boats.

In 1676, Van Leeuwenhoek reports the discovery of micro-organisms, which he calls *animalcules*.

A stock market forms. $

A stock market opens at Jonathan's coffee house in London in the 1690's, using capital generated by sugar, tobacco, and the slave trade.

Borelli conceptualizes a self-contained underwater breathing apparatus and submarine.

Giovanni Alfonso Borelli, Italian physiologist and physicist, is the first person to propose that body mechanics are governed by muscle contraction, that forward motion by humans is a matter of shifting our center of gravity, and that swinging of arms helps to maintain balance. Additionally, Borelli designed (but never built or tested) a self-contained underwater breathing apparatus. Consisting of a brass helmet and an exhalation cooling tube, the helmet was conceived of as a companion to his primitive submarine designs.

Isaac Newton strives to explain gravity.

 Through careful observation and calculation, Newton is able to describe gravity in equations. While his equations work as rules of thumb and can accurately predict almost all known motion, he comes to no solid explanation for how gravity works. His rules, known as Newtonian Physics, are unable to describe the orbit of Mercury, always resulting in predictions that are off by a small factor.

Newton explains how objects like the Moon stay in orbit.

The moon is moving away from the Earth at the same speed that it is falling toward it. When an object is moving tangentially away from another body at the same speed that it is falling toward that body, these factors cancel each other and the object stays in orbit.

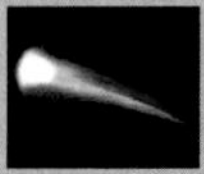

Phantoms of flight, comets periodically appear and Edmund Halley surmises that some of them make repeat visits.

Halley analyzes the historical records of comet sightings and postulates that three of the sightings describe the same comet and that this comet orbits the sun with a periodicity of 75 years. He predicts that it will come again in 1758.

This is a scientific prediction that, if it later proves true, will be a good test of the theory that comets orbit the sun. The comet that now bears his name had most recently appeared in 1531, 1607, and 1682.

1698 Thomas Savery patents a pump that uses hand-operated valves to create suction from condensing steam, thus raising water from mines.

1712 Thomas Newcomen develops a steam engine that uses a piston to separate the condensing steam from the water.

Shipping continues to connect far flung peoples and goods into one world wide web.

Ships cannot travel on any route but must sail with prevailing winds and ocean currents.

1700

Mariners have been describing these winds and currents for centuries. A systematic study is presented by Edmund Halley in 1686 and he identifies solar heating as the engine that drives these atmospheric motions.

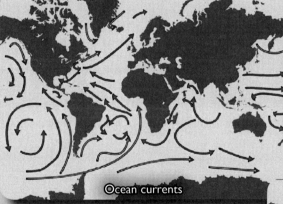

Ocean currents

Earth's winds and currents flow in directions determined from a few simple rules: the sun's heat is greater near the equator, and winds and waters flow from warm areas to cooler ones. The spinning of Earth on its axis adds complication.

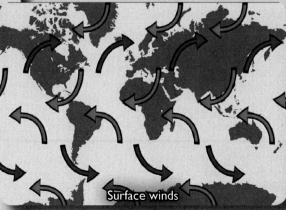

Surface winds

Wind and ocean currents are mapped

On a rotating planet, air and water masses are deflected at a slight angle as they move along and the atmosphere has three vertical convective cells in each hemisphere. These moving currents are deflected in a way that is similar to attempts to draw a straight line on a spinning turntable, and they end up being curved. This is due to the **Coriolis Force**; in the northern hemisphere, the moving current is deflected to the right and in the southern hemisphere it's deflected to the left.

Heat flows from hot to cold areas and not the other way around (in accordance with the second law of thermodynamics). The hot areas occur where the sun beats in near the equator, and the cooler areas are the polar regions and up high in the atmosphere (warm Earth radiates heat into cold space). Also, air masses on the day side of Earth warm in the sun and migrate toward the night side.

In 1738 Bernoulli publishes his book on fluid dynamics.

Henri Pitot creates a tube system to measure fluid velocity.

Young Henri doesn't have much interest in education until he discovers a geometry text at the age of 19. Soon he is studying astronomy and physics as well, and he wins election to the Academy of Sciences in 1724.

He turns his attention to problems with the flow of water in the River Seine and the canals of Paris. He realizes that some of the old ideas about fluid velocity, like the notion that fluid speed increases with depth, are wrong. He sets out to find a way to directly measure the speed of flowing water and, in 1732, he creates a tube system to measure fluid velocity.

Pitot points one end of his tube upstream where flowing molecules of water push on water molecules already inside. The water molecules in the tube are allowed to move into a vertical part of the tube system, where the height of the water column can be measured.

A greater height is achieved by a stronger current. By measuring the height of the contained fluid column, Pitot can use Bernoulli's Principle to calculate the velocity of the fluid flow.

The fluid rises to a height in the column that is proportional to the square of the velocity of the current. For example, if the velocity of the current increases by a factor of 4, the height of the water column in the tube increases by a factor of 2.

A triangular trading pattern develops.

Ships sail between ports on the Atlantic coasts in a clockwise pattern in order to follow winds and currents. Even today, ships powered by modern engines try to go with rather than against ocean currents for greater speed and economy.

The Triangle Trade transports slaves from Africa to The Americas, carries cargo from North America to Europe, and then moves manufactured goods from Europe to Africa to trade for more slaves.

Firewood grows scarce in England.

The growing population clears forests to plant crops and needs wood for fuel and lumber. Wood is also turned into charcoal - a cleaner, higher quality fuel - and used in iron smelting. Coal is available as an energy substitute but it burns with a smoky haze and can't be used in iron making because it contains so many impurities that get into the iron and make it brittle.

Wood from the great forests of North America is processed into charcoal and shipped across the Atlantic. The tallest trees in the forests are scouted out and reserved for building masts for the ships of the British Navy. In 1709, a new way to process coal into a cleaner derivative product called coke, is invented by Darby in Shropshire, England.

The Saud-Wahhab pact creates the Kingdom of Saudi Arabia.

In the middle of the Arabian Peninsula, in the small oasis town of Diriyah, the ambitious prince Muhammad ibn Saud offers refuge to the controversial fundamentalist leader Muhammad al-Wahhab. The two cement their alliance through a marriage between their children. Wahhab will dictate his intolerant, fundamentalist brand of religion and Saud and his heirs will rule over the state and enforce the religious dictates.

Of the four different schools of Islamic law (Sharia), al-Wahhab belongs to the Hanbali school, which is the smallest and most conservative. The Saud-Wahhab forces soon attack neighboring oasis towns. Each bloody victory augments their power and the ranks of their army swell with conscripts and zealots. Towns that resist are dealt with harshly. Across the interior of the Arabian Peninsula, tombs are destroyed, people forced to abide by the Wahhab religious decrees, and many Shia Muslims are killed.

The Ottoman Empire controls most of the Islamic world, including the perimeter of the Arabian Peninsula, but does not pay much attention to the interior.

Prevailing winds blow from different directions at different latitudes.

Warm, moisture-laden air rises at the equator. As it rises, it cools and the moisture condenses out as rain. When this air later descends again, at about 30 degrees north or south of the equator, most of the moisture has already been wrung out of it. Furthermore, descending air warms up as it descends and whatever moisture is still in it stays suspended even more easily. Sometimes clouds are visible in the desert but disappear without raining as they approach the ground. Most of Earth's deserts are located at about 30 degrees of either side of the equator.

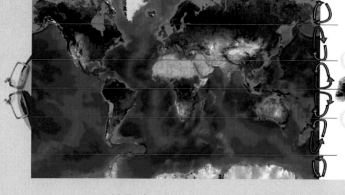

There might be other galaxies.

Astronomers have found many wispy clusters of stars and patches of bright dust and are unsure what these objects are. The idea that Andromeda, which appears as a smeared-out star to the unaided eye, might be a separate galaxy like our own, is introduced in 1755 by Immanuel Kant, who referred to it as an 'Island Universe.'

James Watt improves the steam engine.

1765 James Watt improves Newcomen's engine by adding a separate condenser in order to avoid heating and cooling the cylinder with each stroke. Watt develops another engine that uses a rotating shaft rather than the up-and-down motion of a pump.

Halley's comet shows up in 1758 as predicted. It is a big victory for science, popularizing the notion that scientific theories make testable predictions.

Windmills turn into the wind.

An English blacksmith creates and patents an apparatus for automatically turning windmills into the wind. Edmund Lee patents the fantail in 1745. The fantail is a beam that extends backward from the tower cap with its own small windmill mounted at 90 degrees to the main sails. When the wind strikes the sails of the fantail windmill at any angle other than parallel, a complex system of gears turn to pivot the main windmill sails into the wind.

Benjamin Franklin advocates for the use of the lightning rod, which reduces the chance of a building being struck by lightning, and minimizes the damage if it does get struck.

Lightning is finally explained when Benjamin Franklin describes it as a static-electric phenomenon. It had previously been described in a variety of ways, often as the action of an angry god. Contemporary church leaders attribute it to God's anger at people for their sinfulness.

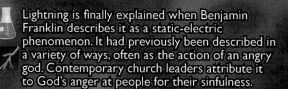

Church opposition to the lightning rod continues for another few decades, during which time many bell ringers are killed by lightning.

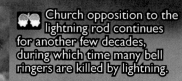

Lightning rods were used long before Franklin's time by Sinhalese kings in Sri Lanka thousands of years ago, but they are a novel invention in Boston.

In 1755, an earthquake rocks Boston and the East Coast of North America.

Opposition to the lightning rod increases after the earthquake and it takes courage for people to choose science over superstition.

The first automobile drives forth.

Nicolas-Joseph Cugnot harnesses the energetic motion of a steam piston to turn one of three wheels of his "fardier à vapeur" or "steam dray." The vehicle performs poorly due mostly to the distribution of weight, but Cugnot receives a hefty pension from the King for his efforts.

A 'spiral oar' screw-propeller is sketched out.

In 1770, while working on a canal, James Watt writes to a friend about the feasibility of two 'wheels' or a 'spiral oar' for boat propulsion. He supplies a sketch of a four-turned screw propeller very similar to those which will be used years later.

American colonists demand freedom from the British and a democratic government that cherishes liberty.

France brings its fleet to aid the Americans.

After the first year of the war, the situation worsens for the rebellious Americans. Lafayette, the young French aristocrat who joined the cause for freedom at the onset, is persuaded to return to France. He convinces his king to send the fleet and the tides are turned.

A duck, a sheep and a rooster go for the first hot air balloon ride in 1783.

The flight hints at the potential for a whole new mode of transport and the reality of air as a substance.

The balloon is designed by the Montgolfier brothers, whose family is in the business of manufacturing paper. After noticing that pockets of hot air caught by pieces of laundry drying above a fire cause the fabric to billow upward, Joseph experiments with a large, open-bottomed box built of thin pieces of wood and lightweight taffeta cloth. He mounts the box on a stand and lights a fire underneath it. Soon the box rises upward, ascending rapidly until it collides with the ceiling, where it remains for a while.

The brothers then build a larger, round balloon, out of fabric-lined paper. This device has so much more lift than they expect that they can't hold on to it and it sails off for a few minutes of free flight over the Vidalon paper mills on the river Deûme in Davézieux Parish near Annonay, France. No one of any note sees it. Anxious for an officially recognized flight, and to show off their invention, they build a new balloon and fly it at Annonay in front of a group of dignitaries from the États particuliers.

Humans fly just months after the hot air balloon test flight with animals

Ben Franklin, the U.S. ambassador to France, is in attendance.

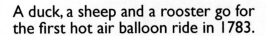

Word of their flight reaches Paris, and the brothers collaborate with wallpaper manufacturer Jean-Baptiste Réveillon to build *Aérostat Réveillon*, a beautifully decorated sky-blue balloon that is big enough to carry passengers. Though the king suggests that the first passengers should be convicted criminals, to assess the effects of flight on humans, the balloon instead carries farm animals.

A duck, a creature accustomed to flight, is included to assess if some ill effects are created by the balloon rather than the altitude. A sheep is chosen to approximate the effect on human health. A ground dwelling bird, the rooster, is added as a further control.

The demonstration is held at the Palace of Versailles before Louis XVI and Queen Marie Antoinette. The balloon soars to an altitude of at least 450 meters and travels 3 kilometers during the 8 minute flight before landing safely.

Hydrogen, a lighter-than-air gas, is used to make a balloon buoyant.

Less than two weeks after the Mongolfier flight, French physicist Jacques Charles uses hydrogen to fill the *Charlière* balloon. The balloon is made of silk coated with rubber, using a new technique developed by Nicolas Robert. Unlike hot air balloons, which rely on burners to heat the air to make it less dense and therefore buoyant, the *Charlière* balloon is filled with hydrogen, which is lighter than air and provides lift without heating. Charles flies it in the Tuileries Gardens before an audience of 400,000. The flight exceeds that of the Montgolfiers in both time in the air and distance traveled and the balloon's design becomes the blueprint for hydrogen balloons for the next 200 years.

In 1785, Jean-Pierre Blanchard crosses the English Channel in a balloon. He use three sail-like appendages - two for flapping like a bird's wings and one for steering like a bird's tail - with which he intends to produce propulsion.

In the 1780's Lieutenant Jean Baptiste Marie Meusnier experiments with dirigible designs.

Dirigible comes from the Latin *dirigere*, meaning "to steer."

Liberty, Equality, and Fraternity.

The established order of France is overturned by the French Revolution.

French chemist Lavoisier isolates, describes and names the elements oxygen in 1778 and hydrogen in 1783.

American whaling ships sail into the Pacific.

In 1790, the whaling ship *Amelia* rounds the Cape of Good Hope and ventures into the Pacific, establishing new fishing grounds for whalers.

The industrial technology of England is copied in the U.S.

Samuel Slater has been working in cotton mills in England since the age of ten, and upon the death of his father he becomes indentured as an apprentice millwright. Learning that Americans hope to build similar mills, he memorizes the plans and embarks for America as soon as he is released from his apprenticeship. He partners with American businessmen to build the Slater Mill in Pawtucket, Rhode Island, opening in 1793.

Technological innovations can have paradoxical consequences.

The cotton gin is invented in 1793. This labor-saving device will make cotton farming so profitable that, ironically, it creates a huge demand for labor to farm the cotton fields that will become the mainstay of the American south.

Henry Cort of Funtly Iron Mills in England uses grooved rolls for rolling iron bars, producing 15 times more iron per day than was possible with a hammer.

The four forces of flight are **lift** and **weight**, **thrust** and **drag**.

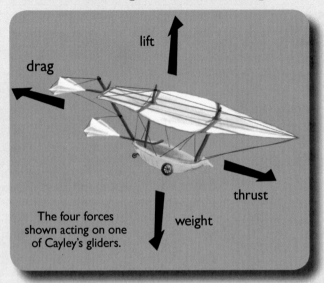

lift

drag

thrust

weight

The four forces shown acting on one of Cayley's gliders.

George Cayley separates dynamic lift from propulsion.

In 1799, the engineer/inventor George Cayley identifies the four forces: lift and weight, and thrust and drag. Each pair must balance for a machine to achieve equilibrium in the air. Before Cayley, inventors designed their heavier-than-air machines to mimic birds, whose wings combine lift and propulsion. Cayley realizes that these two forces need to be separate and imagines an aircraft that does not flap.

The flap of a bird wing combines lift and propulsion. Humans were able to achieve flight once they no longer attempted to replicate the movement of a bird wing and instead separated lift and propulsion into two different parts of a flight machine.

After observing that seagulls soar for long distance without flapping, Cayley imagines an aircraft that develops lift as air moves past it rather than trying to replicate bird flapping.

A steamboat plods slowly upstream.

A practical steamboat plods slowly upstream against a headwind, towing two heavy barges almost 20 miles. Despite a history of disappearing funders and design flaws, inventor William Symington persists in his endeavors to build the world's first viable steam-powered paddle boats. Named the *Charlotte Dundas*, after the daughter of his current sponsor, Lord Dundas, the boat's second sailing was along the Forth and Clyde Canal toward Glasgow, Scotland in 1803, against a headwind and towing two barges weighing seventy-tons each.

Oil is scooped up out of shallow, hand-dug wells in the Baku Khanate of Azerbaijan beginning in the early 1800's. It is shipped off, primarily to Persia, for lighting fuel and for use in ointments.

In 1803, Richard Trevithick builds the first steam locomotive, which makes a successful run on a horsecar route in Wales in 1804.

In 1807, the steamboat comes to the US -In 1807, Robert Fulton uses a steam engine on a passenger boat.

Heat can be caused by **friction**.

Heat can be caused by friction. In 1797, Rumford notices that boring out cannon barrels to create a smooth interior causes them to heat up. He asserts that there is some equivalence between heat and work. He challenges the existing theory that heat is a substance. This will lead to the modern theory of thermodynamics.

In 1798, John Malthus says that if fed, a population will increase exponentially. Therefore, increases in agricultural yield, which are usually incremental, won't be able to keep up with the exponential growth and cycles of famine will recur.

In 1799, Napoleon conquers Egypt and orders a feasibility analysis for building a canal from the Red Sea to the Mediterranean (where the Suez canal will eventually be built). His engineers wrongly report that the two bodies of water are not at the same elevation, which will necessitate the building of locks and pumping systems. Because of the extra expense predicted, Napoleon does not start the project.

England achieves naval supremacy.

England's navy destroys the fleets of both France and Spain at the Battle of Trafalgar in 1805.

New tactics are employed by Admiral Lord Nelson. His 27 British warships defeat the combined forces of 33 French and Spanish ships of the line. Rather than arranging themselves in the customary single line for battle, which allows for easy signaling, maximum firing speed for cannon, and rapid disengagement, Nelson splits his forces into 2 groups and engages the enemy's single battle line from a perpendicular direction.

Nelson is shot by a French musketeer and dies shortly after the decisive victory. During this period of the Napoleonic Wars (1803-1815), France is allied with Spain.

Carrier pigeons transport the news of Waterloo to London.

Legend claims that carrier pigeons transport the news of Napoleon's defeat at Waterloo to the banker, Nathan Rothschild, in London, allowing him to profit by buying up British government bonds before others learn the outcome of the war.

In fact, the five sons of the Rothschild family, who are distributed among different European cities, communicate efficiently through a system of horseback messengers, and will only use carrier pigeons later in the century. Their messenger *does* reach London two days before the government's messenger arrives, and the news is made public. The Rothschilds had helped to finance the war through bonds sold to the British government and they profit because the government is able to repay.

Although they likely make some profit off the early news, the later claims that the profits were immense and that carrier pigeons were used are probably a fabrication by those seeking to discredit the family.

Aluminum is identified

In 1808, Humphry Davy, a chemist from Cornwall, isolates the metallic element in aluminum salts, calling it "alumium." The salt had been called "alumine" by French chemist Louise-Bernard Guyton de Morveau, in 1782.

The coal reserves of England fuel the industrial revolution.

The coal was formed back in the Carboniferous times, when ferns evolved the molecule lignin, which allowed them to grow as tall as trees. Microbes that could digest this tough molecule were slow to evolve and the vegetative matter lay without decomposing. Coal represents the solar energy that those ferns converted into hydrocarbons almost 300 mya.

The first geologic map is made.

While working as a surveyor on the new canal systems, William 'Strata' Smith notices that the distinctive, layered patterns of rock strata in places where rock is exposed are similar throughout the region. The same layers always seem to occur in the same relative positions. He observes that many layers contain distinctive fossils that can be used as identification. Smith sets out to make a composite map of the whole country by analyzing the layers where they are exposed, determined to see if the patterns that he sees in his local region are consistent over a larger area. He publishes his map in 1815.

As the Industrial Revolution intensifies, the transportation industry must grow in kind.

Systems of interconnecting canals have been in use since the 16th century, but the English Industrial Revolution necessitates a vast expansion of these waterways. Notably, a heavy transport system is needed to bring coal from mines in the north and southwest to fuel the factories in urban centers such as Liverpool, Manchester, and London.

A Baron of Germany, Karl von Drais, invents the *Laufmaschine*, the "running machine."

Also known as the *velocipede*, *dandy horse*, or *draisine*, these two-wheeled vehicles rely on the rider's legs to provide propulsion and are widely regarded as an archetype for the bicycle. After the first reported ride, in 1817, these contraptions will be briefly popular throughout Europe, with many manufacturers producing their own versions.

The Monroe Doctrine is established.

The United States develops the policy in 1823 to discourage European powers from forming colonies or meddling anywhere in the Americas, with the exception of Spain's continued control over Cuba.

Factories become larger and more numerous in Britain, while smaller makeshift workplaces exist alongside them.

The fast pace of England's industrialization has high social costs.

In England, even as breakthroughs in science continue to be made, industrial production reaches high levels and working people suffer. In the 1820's, the young Charles Dickens is among the many children forced to labor in factories.

Young Charles Darwin sails out.

The mission of the *HMS Beagle* includes charting the water depth along the coast of South America and conducting other surveys aimed at enhancing Britain's control of the seas. The 22 year old Darwin receives an unexpected invitation to join the expedition in 1831.

Darwin's job is to act as naturalist; observing the different landscapes, environments, and their flora and fauna. With only weeks to prepare for the two year voyage, Darwin scurries to procure his supplies, packing scientific instruments, guns, his bible, and the latest scientific texts.

Darwin has an eye for observation and notices similarities and differences and patterns between places and the organisms in them. He notices that all land animals, except insects, have four limbs and a similar pattern of bones comprising their limbs.

The selective breeding of dogs had been popular in England; new breeds with exotic and hereditary characteristics are on display. Darwin extrapolates the idea of selective breeding to selective evolution in the wild.

It will be 5 years before Darwin returns to England. He will meet Renous and many other people and his discoveries will transform him as well as science.

Two inventors separately file patents in Britain for screw propeller designs.

Francis Pettit Smith, having filed his patent on the last day of May in 1835, builds a 6hp, 30 ft long boat called the *Francis Smith*. Fitted with a wooden propeller of his design, the boat was demonstrated and experimented on for over a year in a canal off of the Thames River. A serendipitous accident broke his screw propeller, reducing it to only one turn of the screw, which doubled the boat's speed. He immediately re-filed his patent to keep this happy mistake in the design. Based on this new single-turn screw propeller, Smith will oversee the construction of the world's first screw-propelled warship, the British Royal Navy's *SS Archimedes*.

Steam locomotives become economically viable.

The use of steam engines on railways becomes a commercial success, in 1829, with the Rocket, a locomotive designed by engineer George Stephenson.

John Ericsson, a Swedish engineer living and working in London, filed a similar design six weeks after Smith's initial patent. Concurrent with Smith's work, Ericsson built a screw-propeller steamboat, forty-five ft in length. The boat was poorly received despite its impressive speeds, due to the thought that screw propellers would be unseaworthy, but Ericsson was undaunted. In 1839, he built a much larger screw propeller steamboat with secondary sails, the *Robert F. Stockton*. Sailing to the US, Ericsson will soon design their Navy's first warship with a screw propeller, the *USS Princeton*.

Caterpillars become fliers.

German-born amateur entomologist, Juan Renous, having lived in Chile since 1825, studies the local insects closely. He declares that beautiful butterflies metamorphose from crawling caterpillars and this statement lands him in prison. He is eventually released when experiments prove him to be right.

The telegraph is invented.

The bone arrangement of whale limbs has been modified for aquatic propulsion.

Whales have the same arrangement of bones as land animals but they have been modified for aquatic propulsion. The bones of their front flippers clearly exhibit the pattern, as do the bones of their hind legs, which are still present in most species although drastically reduced in size. Darwin concludes that whales are tetrapods that have returned to the sea.

Whales share some similarities to fish because both animals adapt to the same aquatic environment. This type of relationship is called convergent evolution. Likewise, the wings of insects share some similarities with the wings of birds because both adapt to flying in air by developing lightweight wings. Unravelling the relationships takes a bit of detective work.

The Morse Telegraph is invented in 1837 by Samuel Morse, allowing messages to be transmitted quickly over wire.

The Gold Rush creates demand for fast transport.

BEST ROUTE TO CALIFORNIA.

Inventor and founder of *Scientific American* magazine, Rufus Porter dreams and comprehensively plans an "Aerial Locomotive" to fly prospectors west. An advertisement titled, *Aerial Navigation: The Practicality of Traveling Pleasantly and Safely from New York to California in Three Days*, is published in 1849. Models are made of the planned 800 foot long steam powered airship but it is never produced.

Models depict powered airships.

In 1850, Pierre Jullien of Villejuif demonstrates a cigar-shaped model airship at the Paris Hippodrome. The model airship is equipped with a rudder, elevator, and gondola stationed in the prow, while a small clockwork motor drives two airscrews mounted on each side of the center line. This model never actually flies..

The physics of work and heat are discovered.

James Joule publishes "The Mechanical Equivalent of Heat." In his experiment, in 1845, Joule repeatedly drops a weight that turns a paddle wheel that is immersed in water. The temperature of the water increases every time the weight is dropped. The temperature increases more if the weight is dropped from a greater height.

This will lead to the First Law of Thermodynamics, which states that energy can be converted from one form to another but that it cannot be created or destroyed. In physics, work is defined as "weight lifted through a height."

Traveling lecturers spread information.

The largely self-taught, eighteen-year-old Thaddeus Lowe attends a lecture event on chemistry in 1850. The lecturer, recognizing Thad's intelligence and enthusiasm, offers him a job as his assistant. The lecture circuit business is lucrative, and after 2 years of making displays, traveling around, and putting on shows, Thad buys the business. He develops advanced theories in meteorology and aeronautics and dreams of making a trans-Atlantic balloon flight. He will later use his aeronautical talents in the Civil War.

The Leviathan telescope is completed.

This new telescope, built in Ireland, sees its first light in 1845 and will be the largest ever built until 1917. WAstronomers William and Mary Parsons will discover many more of the wispy patches of stars that are referred to as 'nebula' and hypothesized to possibly be separate galaxies. They are able to resolve some of the nebula into disc shaped collections of stars and make drawings of them. The spiral arrangements of the nebula hint at some kind of organization based on 'dynamical laws'.

Carrier pigeon networks improve.

The future founder of Reuters news agency, Paul Reuter, uses a fleet of around 50 homing pigeons the send messages between European cities.

The Pitot tube is improved.

Engineer Henry Darcy modifies the Pitot tube into the modern device.

Robinson improves the anemometer by replacing discs with hemispherical cups, in 1846.

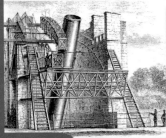

A powered and steerable lighter-than-air craft steams its way along for almost 20 miles!

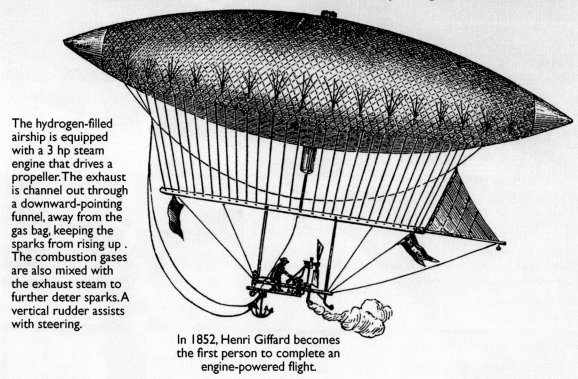

The hydrogen-filled airship is equipped with a 3 hp steam engine that drives a propeller. The exhaust is channel out through a downward-pointing funnel, away from the gas bag, keeping the sparks from rising up . The combustion gases are also mixed with the exhaust steam to further deter sparks. A vertical rudder assists with steering.

In 1852, Henri Giffard becomes the first person to complete an engine-powered flight.

A Crystal Palace is built for the Great Exhibition.

New technologies are brought into public view in 1851. The Crystal Palace itself is a wonder, showing off the new technology of cast plate glass. It is the first of the Worlds Fair Exhibitions. In about 10 years, it will host an aeronautical exhibition.

The Crimean War breaks out.

Russia and an alliance of European powers compete for influence and control of territories of the declining Ottoman Empire. The Crimean War, 1853-1856, is the first war to be extensively documented by photographers and war correspondents.

The Russian Black Sea fleet destroys a Turkish Squadron in 1853.

To compete with already industrialized nations, Russia begins to emancipate its serfs.

Russia's defeat in the Crimean War motivates the Tsar to modernize his country and to deal with the problem of serfdom. The serfs did not fight with the dedication or handle industrial technologies with the prowess shown by British soldiers of all social classes.

There are some 50 million serfs in Russia out of a total population of about 60 million.

Americans demand trade with Japan.

Commodore Perry orders his ships to run on steam power as he makes his entrance into Edo Bay in 1853. He fires blank shot from his 73 cannons and demands an audience. One of the American objectives is to establish a coaling station, so that steam ships can be refueled.

Aerial photographs are made.

The earliest aerial photographs, taken by balloonist Gaspard-Félix Tournachon also known as 'Nadar', while flying over Paris in 1858, no longer exist, although his feat is depicted in a contemporary cartoon.

'Boston, as the Eagle and the Wild Goose See It' is made 2 years later by James Wallace Black and the balloonist Samuel Archer King.

A solar flare causes a huge solar storm on Earth.

A giant sunspot produces a solar flare that releases a packet of charged particles that reach Earth. The charged particles are mostly deflected by Earth's magnetic field but some slip in between the field lines, near the poles where the field lines come together. Telegraph communication fails and brilliant auroras are seen as far from the poles as the Caribbean and Australia.

The Pennsylvania Oil Boom begins.

In 1859, a drill strikes oil 69 feet down. Soon, others will dig wells nearby, and in just the first year an estimated 2,000-4,500 barrels are produced.

Darwin publishes *The Origin of Species* .

Darwin hesitates to publish his ideas, fearing anger from the church and the public but scientific achievement brings prestige. It is only when another biologist, Wallace, is about to publish his similar theory of evolution that Darwin finally finds the fortitude, in 1859. The pursuit of Science is driven not only by curiosity.

A generator produces an electrical current by using some fuel source to rotate a magnet around a coil of wire or to spin a coil of wire around a magnet.

Maxwell shows that electricity and magnetism are two expressions of the same force.

Electricity and magnetism had been considered to be completely different forces but in 1865, James Clerk Maxwell shows that they are different expressions of the same thing.

Maxwell shows how the motion of a magnet can induce an electric current in a wire and conversely how an electric current passing through a wire can make an electromagnet.

Maxwell's equations are simple, symmetrical, and elegant. Their beauty resonates in the minds of mathematicians.

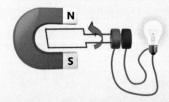

The U.S. Civil War breaks out between the industrialized North and the agricultural South.

Railroads transport raw materials and manufactured goods to and from factories and bring supplies and troops to battlefields. The North has many more miles of track as well as telegraph lines than does the South. President Lincoln recognizes the importance of information flow in coordinating the war and expands the network of rails and lines early in the war.

In the U.S., one out of every seven persons is enslaved.

Freedom and equality sprout naturally from the human heart. Injustice and inequality can only be maintained by the use of force and the creation of an ideology to rationalize it. Outright slavery requires an extreme ideology; African-American slaves are purported to be stupid, dirty, and sub-human. This makes it seem more reasonable to treat them harshly, in a self-perpetuating cycle.

Pedals are added to the bicycle.

Pedals are added to the front axle of the velocipede In 1863, in the Paris workshop of Pierre Michaux, pedals are added to the front axle of the velocipede, providing a new, more efficient method of propulsion. It is unclear whether the addition was made by Michaux himself or by his employee, Pierre Lallement.

Joined by the Olivier brothers, Michaux and Lallement become the first in the world to mass produce bicycles. Their two-wheeled, pedal-propelled *Boneshaker* is made entirely of wood. Michaux and Lallement contiue to argue over ownership of the design.

A coal barge is converted to the first aircraft carrier.

The *George Washington Parke Custis* is a coal barge requisitioned and modified for the war effort. The deck is cleared and set up for launching balloons. Overseen by Thaddeus Lowe, the Union's Chief Aeronaut, this carrier-tethered balloon is used as a mobile observation platform. Other barges will be likewise converted to provide troops with battlefield intel on rivers across the eastern states.

Stationary tethered balloons are used as observation platforms

Submarines are built.

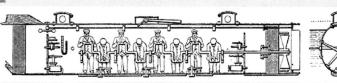

Jules Verne publishes *From the Earth to the Moon* in 1865.

The Confederacy builds the *H. L. Hunley* which sinks a Union warship. It is itself sunk three times and resurrected twice.

The bloody civil war ends in 1865 and slavery is finally abolished in America.

The world becomes dramatically more inter-connected.

The world's web of transportation corridors ramps up and the time required to move people or goods drops markedly in the single year of 1869.

1869

The American Transcontinental Railroad is completed.

At Promontory Point in Utah, the Golden Spike unites America's transcontinental railroad in 1869.

Helium is detected

Two astronomers, Jules Janssen and Norman Lockyer, observe the 1868 solar eclipse through spectroscopes. Watching from British India and England respectively, they both notice a bright yellow line within the spectra of the impressive solar prominences. This is the first known detection of helium, so named for the Greek Sun god, Helios.

Aeronautical Societies are founded.

The Aeronautical Society of Great Britain is founded in 1866 and another is founded in France in 1869. These societies serve as forums for early aviation enthusiasts to meet and discuss theory, materials, and designs, and to share new ideas with like minds.

The bicycle becomes popular in the U.S.

Following his dispute with Michaux over ownership of the design of the two-wheeled, pedal-powered bicycle, Lallement moves to New Haven CT and is granted a patent for "improvements in velocipedes" in 1866. The Hanlon brothers of New York improve the design even further and Americans begin to take notice. By 1869, a number of carriage builders have begun to build bicycles and the sport has become popular on college campuses. Some cities forbid the use of the bicycles, which are heavy and require a lot of strength and coordination to operate, on pedestrian sidewalks and the craze dies down.

A simple pattern is discovered among the multitude of elements.

Chemists have long been trying to discover all of the fundamental units of matter, which they call atoms. They have found dozens. Substances once believed to be fundamental - like water, for instance - were found to be composed of smaller parts; water is composed of hydrogen and oxygen atoms.

Chemists seek to organize the different kinds of atoms into groups with similar properties and endeavor to find an explanation for or relationship between all the different types of atoms. Dmitri Mendeleev has the intuition to organize them by weight and publishes his **Periodic Table of the Elements** in 1869. The smallest atoms are listed in the first row, larger elements in the next row, and so on.

Mendeleev doesn't know why the rows should be of these particular lengths, but after trying many combinations, he comes across this arrangement, in which patterns emerge in the columns. For example, the precious metals copper, silver, and gold line up in a middle column and all of the inert gasses are in the last column. He surmises that there must be intrinsic properties in the nature of the atoms that are somehow showcased by this arrangement. He predicts that elements will, in time, be discovered to fill the empty spaces in the table.

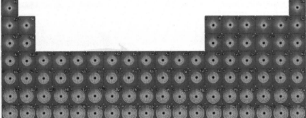

Germany becomes a nation state.

As a minister of the Prussian king, Otto von Bismarck, pursues his dream of creating a German state. Through shrewd military tactics and a conniving political strategy, he engineers a short series of foreign wars to unite germanic speaking city states and territories into an alliance with Prussia and forms the German Empire in 1871. He uses his diplomatic skills to avoid unwanted wars and balances foreign powers against each other which helps to keep peace in Europe. He cleverly shifts his domestic allegiances to stay in power; balancing the interests of the Junker elite, of whom he is a member, and the growing forces of liberalism that gain more support during the economic downturn which begins in 1873. It is the first large downturn for the German region since the surge of its industrial capacity in the 1850s. Known as the Long Depression, the downturn affects both Europe and America.

The new genre, Invasion Literature, is established by Chesney's 1871 novella, *The Battle of Dorking*. It imagines the invasion of Britain by Prussia after the introduction of a wonder-weapon that destroys the British navy.

The Suez Canal opens.

The canal opens in 1869, linking the Mediterranean Sea to the Indian Ocean by ship. It is no longer necessary to sail around Africa to get from Europe to the Indian Ocean.

Construction was organized by the French diplomat turned developer Ferdinand de Lesseps, He used some of the connections he made as a diplomat, to secure a 99 year lease/concession from Egypt. Construction began using forced labor and took 10 years.

A wind tunnel improves aerodynamic testing.

Francis Wenham builds the first wind tunnel in 1871. In a wind tunnel, moving air is blown past a stationary object. It is an improvement over the whirling arm.

Japan decides to industrialize.

Japanese leaders realize that the industrialized nations are colonizing the non-industrialized nations and decide to industrialize Japan.

The Meiji Restoration begins in 1867, after the Shogun is persuaded to retire and the Emperor, who had been but a figure head, is made the official ruler along with a body of advisors in a quasi-parliamentary system. French advisers are hired to modernize the army and the navy is reorganized according to the British model.

Additional schools are built and all children are taught to read and write. Foreign teachers are recruited to teach science, medicine, math, engineering, and languages. Steam ships are purchased and plans are made to build a railroad between Nagasaki and Edo, a telegraph line, and a steel mill.

Industrialization is a suite of social systems as well as technology.

Russia expands eastward and founds Vladivostok.

The trans-Siberian Railroad will soon be built.

Haenlein designs an airship with an internal combustion engine.

The engine uses gas from the envelope, rather than carrying a separate fuel supply. While it doesn't make a successful flight, it paves the way for a type of dirigible design.

Oil is used as a fuel for motors.

By 1873, the oil rush in Pennsylvania is producing 10 million barrels a year. Petroleum oil is not only replacing whale oil as the fuel for lamps and as a lubricant but is also being used to power engines.

Mars has moons.

Phobos and Deimos, the moons of Mars, are discovered in 1877.

Thomas Baldwin brings hot air balloons to the circus.

After working as a brakeman on the Illinois railroad, Baldwin joins a circus and works as an acrobat. He uses a hot air balloon in his trapeze act, in 1875.

The circus is a popular venue

Balloons are a popular attraction at circuses

The large wheel of the High-Roller bicycle leverages pedal power.

The earliest Penny-Farthings had spokes that radiated out straight from the hub. Tangentially radiating spokes soon replace that simple pattern, spreading the load over a greater portion of the rim and helping the wheel resist deformation. These early bicycles quickly become popular for entertainment and transportation, although great balance is required to ride a High-Roller.

Small scale industrial production fosters innovation.

Bicycle production is an industrial process that requires pressing and stamping metal, welding, working with rubber tires, spokes, and understanding drive trains. It is also a simple business that does not require a monumental investment in tools or factory space.

Kites are used for photography.

In the 1880s, kite photography becomes popular. The resulting aerial photograph prints are generally sold as novelties, postcards, destination advertisements, and posters.

Ball bearings are created.

Ball bearings are created to reduce friction between a bicycle wheel and axle in 1877.

Columbia bicycles are manufactured

In 1878, under the trade name "Columbia," Albert A Pope becomes the first American bicycle manufacturer.

The British have built a network of railways across India.

British troops can be deployed anywhere in the country along a web of rail lines, allowing a relatively small force to occupy such a large country. Finished goods, manufactured in England, are brought to markets in India, and raw materials are transported out.

Octave Chanute is an engineer with a passion for aviation.

Chanute made his living designing bridges, such as the Hannibal Bridge which opened in 1869. It was later damaged in a storm and repaired and is shown here.

Chanute had watched a balloon take off in Peoria, Illinois in 1856 and become interested in aviation.

He will later be instrumental in collecting information about flight and disseminating it to inventors.

The Nobel brothers improve oil tankers.

The brothers begin to improve the design of oil tankers, and build them, in 1877. Further design improvements take place in 1883 when they divide the hold - which until now consisted of one or two large tanks - into many smaller holds that run the length of the ship. This makes the ships less susceptible to rolling over when the oil sloshes back and forth.

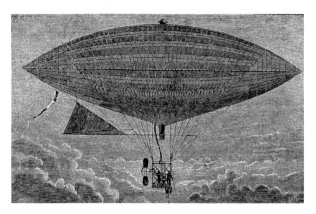

An airship flies with electric propulsion.

1883 sees the first electric-powered lighter-than-air flight. Gaston Tissandier connects a Siemens 1.5 horsepower electric motor to an airship.

A double-bladed fan propeller powers a boat.

A fisherman by trade, John Patch of Nova Scotia builds a hand-cranked double-bladed fan propeller. In 1883, he attaches the propeller to a coastal schooner of 25 tons called the Royal George. On a calm day, when all other boats in the Bay of Fundy are stalled out, the propeller allows him to maneuver the boat in the bay. He attempts to patent the design, but is refused by both Canada and the U.S. for lack of funds, and lack of citizenship, respectively. Patch will continue to improve his propeller and, in 1949, when the U.S. government amends its policy on patents, Patch will finally receive recognition.

Thomas Baldwin parachutes from a balloon.

Thomas Baldwin jumps from a balloon and parachutes safely to the ground in 1885. Working as an entertainer, he makes several more jumps. He earns $3000 jumping from 3000 feet over Golden Gate Park, in 1887. On a jump over the water at Rockaway Beach, he has parachute problems but survives.

Construction begins on the Eiffel Tower.

Construction on the Tower begins in January of 1887, with the excavation of its footprint and the construction of the extensive pylons it sits on. Constructed out of precisely designed segments of wrought iron that arrive by horse-drawn wagon, the tower draws protest from many, notably Parisian artists. It is largely considered to be an eyesore and an egotistical attempt to dominate the city's skyline with a work of engineering rather than a thing of beauty.

The tower will serve as the gate to the Paris World's Fair, timed to celebrate the French Revolution's centennial anniversary.

Standard Oil establishes a monopoly.

Through efficiency, connivance, and economy of scale, the Standard Oil Trust establishes a monopoly. By 1882, Rockefeller's Standard Oil Company has purchased or driven out of business most of its competitors. In a move that would later be challenged in court, Rockefeller establishes the Standard Oil Trust, a monopoly that controls the vast majority of supply, production, refinement, and distribution of oil in the U.S.

The Safety Bicycle Replaces the high roller.

Immediately popular for its safe handling, affordability, and simplicity, millions of bikes will be sold in just over 10 years.

In 1882, Captain Jack Fisher advocates that British war ships be converted to run on oil.

Coal had ignited the Industrial Revolution and Britain still has plenty of it. The mighty ships of the British navy run on coal. Although oil-powered ships would most likely be faster, more maneuverable, have longer ranges, and refuel quickly, the idea of switching fuels is met with fierce resistance because Britain does not have any oil reserves. Some doubt whether there is enough oil in the whole world to fuel the British fleet. Oil is found the following year in Sumatra by the Dutch.

Samuel Cody, the eventual kite builder, is foremost a showman.

Born in Iowa (as Franklin Samuel Cowdery), Samuel Cody shrouds his past in tall-tales and self-made legends. His version of events starts in Texas, where he was orphaned young and went to work on the famous Chisholm cattle trail. Having learned to break horses and live as a cowboy, Cody is employed with several different traveling shows, including the Philideliphia-based circus, the *Great Forepaugh Show* and Annie Oakley's show.

Often billing himself as the son of Buffalo Bill, Cody faces frequent legal action for infringement. Perhaps as a result, he and his family move to the stages of London as a troupe of wild west performers.

Langley experiments with aerodynamics.

In 1887, at the Western University of Pennsylvania, Langley runs a secret research program called "experiments in pneumatics." There he constructs a steam-powered "whirling table" device that measures the lift and drift (drag) of flat surfaces set at various angles to air blowing at velocities up to 70 mph. Around this time, the study of wind currents and updrafts began to utilize anemometers to anemometers and small lifting surfaces that were raised to the top of tall poles.

The Wright Brothers begin working with bicycles.

The brothers already had a successful printing business. In addition to repairing existing bikes, they create innovative new improvements and will eventually manufacture their own brand.

The safety belt is patented.

Edward Claghorn patents a safety belt in 1885. Though originally intended as a harness to secure people into devices for raising and lowering, such as firefighters or painters working alongside a tall building, the device furthers the evolution of the automobile seat belt.

A contemporary example of Natural Selection is found.

The color of moths in England has changed. Dark colored forms of the Peppered Moth had been extremely rare before the Industrial Revolution, but when soot from smokestacks coats the bark of trees, the black variety becomes more common and the light one less. The entomologist J.W.Tutt hypothesizes that when the tree bark was lighter, the light colored moths were safely camouflaged and the dark colored ones were easily preyed on by birds. But now, Natural Selection favors darker moths, which are camouflaged against the soot.

Octave Chanute collects aviation data and expertise from all available sources.

He retires from the railroad in 1883 and devotes his time to furthering the science of aviation. He collects all available data gathered by aviators to date and, applying his knowledge as a civil engineer, prepares a series of articles.

Langley's interest is sparked.

Langley's enthusiasm for heavier-than-air flight is sparked by the work of Israel Lancaster, an amateur aeronatical experimenter. Lancaster had presented his work at a meeting of the American Association for the Advancement of Science in 1886, and was met with roars of laughter from those in attendance, who, given the theoretical errors in Lancaster's work, disbelieved the theory that his wooden models could soar without power for up to 15 minutes. Octave Chanute, who had planned the program, was disappointed, but Langley was intrigued.

Kaiser Wilhelm II ascends to the German throne.

Wilhelm is the eldest grandchild of Britain's Queen Victoria, and is related to many of the monarchs and princes of Europe, including Emperor Nicholas II of Russia.

Wilhelm has been enthralled with all things military since his childhood days, playing war games against his English cousins at their grandmother's summer residence. He loves to dress up in elaborate uniforms. Shortly after he is crowned Emperor of Germany, in 1888, he dismisses Otto von Bismarck, the statesman who had been carefully maintaining a balance of power in Europe.

England has long had the world's finest navy, but Germany has been steadily catching up. Under Wilhelm II, industrial production of ships, munitions, and other military supplies will dramatically expand.

The National Geographic Society is founded, in 1888.

Paleozoic plant life, including spores that drifted, is studied and catalogued by Kidston, in 1883.

Otto Lilienthal studies birds in flight.

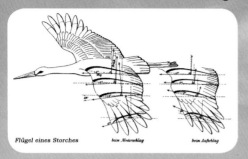

Flügel eines Storches   beim Niederschlag   beim Aufschlag

He authors some of the most comprehensive texts on the mechanics of bird flight. Using polar diagrams to describe wing movements and map the shapes of birds' wings (particularly those of storks), Lilienthal shows how shape affects lift and other principles of flight.

Using the findings from his study of birds, Lilienthal designs heavier-than-air aircraft, creates a dozen monoplanes, two biplanes, and an aircraft with flapping wings. He applies the knowledge he gains systematically; one of his glider designs is re-engineered in eight separate iterations.

Clouds can be shaped by winds.

When winds aloft blow at a different speed and direction than winds below, rolling clouds that look like ocean waves can form at the boundary layer. A large difference in the density of the air masses will enhance the effect. Known as Kelvin Helmholtz clouds, they indicate wind shear and turbulence. It is possible that they provided the inspiration for Vincent van Gogh to paint his now famous masterpiece, ' Starry Night.'

The Michelin brothers create a removable pneumatic tire.

In 1889, Édouard and André Michelin were the owners of a rubber factory in central France. A cyclist happened by one day, asking for assistance with a flat tire. Though the tire was a very modern pneumatic design, the adhesive used to append the tire to the wheel rim was excessively difficult to remove and reapply, and the repaired tire went flat shortly thereafter. The two brothers set about to create a removable pneumatic tire, and several months later incorporate the Michelin company. The removable pneumatic tire will revolutionize not only the bicycle industry, but the automobile as well.

Paris hosts a World's Fair.

The gateway to The Exposition Universelle of 1889 is through the Eiffel Tower, the tallest man-made structure in the world. It is attended by inventors such as Tesla and Edison and many dignitaries. Buffalo Bill's Wild West is the most popular attraction.

Alfred Mahan publishes a definitive book on the importance of naval power.

Sea power has been the most important factor in geo-politics since 1660. Mahan considers different elements that contribute to international supremacy; possession of the biggest, most powerful fleet of ships is foremost. His book, *The Influence of Sea Power upon History,* is published in 1890.

Clement Ader flies his heavier-than-air craft.

In 1890, Clement Ader's *Éole* achieves flight at the Chateau d'Armainvilliers in Brie, France. The success of the *Éole* is due largely to the power of the lightweight, alcohol-burning steam engine invented by Ader. Some consider the *Éole* the first true airplane, given that it left the ground under its own power and carried a person through the air. Others protest that the *Éole* lacks an adequate steering mechanism.

1890

Octave Chanute becomes a node in a network; collecting and distributing aviation knowledge.

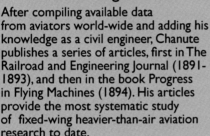

After compiling available data from aviators world-wide and adding his knowledge as a civil engineer, Chanute publishes a series of articles, first in The Railroad and Engineering Journal (1891-1893), and then in the book Progress in Flying Machines (1894). His articles provide the most systematic study of fixed-wing heavier-than-air aviation research to date.

Langley believes powered heavier-than air flight is possible with better engines.

He writes the paper 'Experiments in Aerodynamics' in 1891. Perhaps his most significant conclusion is that 'mechanical flight was possible with engines we could then build.'

Otto Lilienthal flies a succession of gliders of increasing sophistication.

Starting in the summer of 1891, Otto Lilienthal builds and flies eighteen different gliders over the course of five years.

The *Murex* is the first tanker to pass through the Suez Canal, in 1892.

Rudolf Diesel patents his engine in 1892

Pennsylvanian oil peaks.
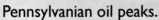

The Pennsylvania oil rush reaches its peak in 1891 with 31 million barrels of oil. Oil production in Ohio will surpass Pennsylvanian oil in 13 years.

Alexander Graham Bell places the first New York to Chicago telephone call in 1892.

Langley's Aërodrome No. 5 in Flight, May 6, 1896
From instantaneous photograph by Alexander Graham Bell

Samuel Langley's model aircraft flies.

Smithsonian Secretary Samuel Langley uses a spring-loaded catapult to launch his models, which he calls Aerodromes, in 1896 from the roof of his houseboat on the Potomac River in Virginia. Number 5, the model shown here, weighs 11 kg. It makes 2 flights, flying 700 and then 1000 meters.

Marconi's radio reaches out.

After studying the work of German phsyicist Heinrich Hertz, Marconi builds his own wave generating machine capable of transmitting signals up to a mile.

Young Glenn Curtiss wins bicycle races.

Eventually he will equip bicycles with engines and later adapt engines for aircraft.

Japan flexes its new-found industrial muscle.

The First Sino-Japanese War, August 1894 – April 1895, is fought between Qing Dynasty China and Meiji Japan, primarily over control of Korea.

1895

The Lowell Observatory is established.

This observatory, built in 1894 in Flagstaff Arizona, is the first to be sited at a place selected for its optical properties. It is at a high elevation without much water vapor and far from city lights. Lowell becomes obsessed with finding canals on Mars. Pluto will be discovered from this observatory in 1930 and it will be used in the 1960s to locate suitable landing sites for the Apollo moon missions.

Lilienthal's gliders impress.

Otto Lilienthal patents his "bar" design, in which the pilot hangs on a bar structure in the center of the craft, shifting the center of gravity by moving his legs and lower body, in 1894. Many pictures of his flights exist, including the one on this page from 1895. During a test flight, in August of 1896, a shift in wind direction causes his glider to stall and he drops more than 50 ft, breaking his neck. He dies the next day.

Chanute's glider flies.

Originally designed as a triplane, Chanute's glider is modified to become a biplane, reducing the amount of lift at the front. The rigid, lightweight structure serves as a model for future aircraft.

A piloted catapult-assisted aircraft is launched.

After the successful flights of the model aerodrome, a full sized aircraft is constructed. Piloted by Langley's assistant and protege, Charles Manly, the craft is again launched from the roof of the houseboat. Neither is successful and Manly plunges into the Potomac.

Women ride toward suffrage on the bicycle.

Personal mechanized transport is as freeing as horseback riding had been centuries earlier. It fosters independence and the optimism that

mobility brings. The rising popularity of the bicycle as a method of transportation happens to coincide with the first wave of the women's rights movement in the 1890's. The bicycle, which requires that women give up their corsets and skirts for more versatile and utilitarian bloomers and pants, allows women, who had until then relied on men for transportation, more control over where they go, and when. The bicycle quickly becomes associated with the ideal of the "New Woman" of the Progressive era - young, educated, upwardly mobile, athletic, and determined to gain equality.

Langley finds funding.

In 1898, based on the success of his models, Langley receives a War Department grant of $50,000 and a Smithsonian grant of $20,000 to develop a piloted airplane, which he called an *"Aerodrome"* (coined from Greek words roughly translated as "air runner").

Passenger pigeon airmail connects New Zealand to Australia in 1897.

Special stamps are used to pay for this new service.

Marconi's radio signals reach across the English Channel

After successfully transmitting a signal across the English Channel, Marconi travels to the U.S. to provide wireless coverage of the America's Cup yacht race.

The French Military cuts Ader's funding.

Although Ader constructed the flying machines *Avion II* and *Avion III* with funding from the French Ministry of War following the flight of the *Eole*, it's not certain that either ever flew. The French military will cut his funding in 1902, acknowledging the military potential of his machines, but choosing not to fund them and swearing him to secrecy.

The alphabet is modified for radio.

Even as radio equipment development makes frequency tuning and noise reduction easier for users, in high-stakes situations, clear communication and enunciation is critical. Letters and sounds that are easily confused in the English language are given new monikers. In 1898 and again in 1904, the War Office of Britain releases guides to Signalling Regulations. These regulations spell the letters of the alphabet, but use different pronunciations for those letters most often confused: "Ack Beer/ Bar C D E F G H I J K L eMma N O Pip Q R eSses Toc U Vic W X Y Z"

Glenn Curtiss becomes a self taught engineer.

Although his formal education ended in the 8th grade, Glenn Curtiss exhibits an uncanny ability for engineering. He gets a job at the Eastman Dry Plate and Film Company in Rochester, NY and invents a stencil machine that is adopted at the plant. Later he builds a camera to study photography

Glenn Curtiss gets married and begins his career as a Western Union bicycle messenger, a bicycle racer, and a bicycle shop owner.

A rigid airship with an aluminum envelope is built in 1897.

Hungarian-Croatian engineer David Schwarz builds a rigid airship with an aluminum envelope in 1897. He dies before it flies from Berlin. Some sources say that Count Ferdinand von Zeppelin pays a small fortune to his widow for the patent to the airship design.

Count Ferdinand Graf von Zeppelin's first craft, the *LZ1*, flies.

Patent law in the U.S. changes dramatically when the new category of 'Pioneer Patent' is created in 1898.

This ruling will often be referred to just as 'Westinghouse' but the pioneer patent comes from 'Westinghouse v. Boyden Power Brake Co.,' in which Westinghouse claimed that Boyden had violated their patent for a quick-action triple-valve airbrake.

The ruling, which states that a patent may be granted only for "... a function never before performed, a wholly novel device, or one of such novelty and importance as to mark a distinct step in the progress of the art, as distinguished from a mere improvement or perfection of what has gone before, " *(U.S. Supreme Court, Westinghouse v. Boyden Power Brake Co., 170 U.S. 537 (1898)),* set the precedent for the aviation patent wars soon to come.

Propellers create thrust

The spinning motion of an aircraft engine must be converted into a rearward motion of air by the propeller. Some of this movement of air will be used by the wings to create the lift that holds the weight of the plane up against gravity and some will be the propulsion that thrusts the plane forward. Propeller blades, which are airfoils shaped much like airplane wings, create high and low pressure pockets as they spin, actually generating lift themselves, but this lift only moves the air backward, it does not lift the plane. The propellers are mounted on the nose (or tail) of an airplane so the air is moved backwards in line with the fuselage and opposite the direction of travel. Incoming air particles are thrown out behind the propeller, moving the aircraft forward. The amount of air thrown backward per unit of time must be at least equal to the weight of the aircraft times its forward speed.

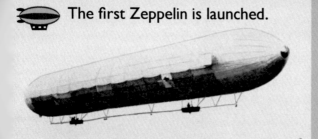

The first Zeppelin is launched.

1.6 billion

Count von Zeppelin launches the first of his fleet, the Zeppelin LZ1 in 1900, the flagship of what will become the most successful airships in history. Zeppelins use a lighter-than-air gas inside balloons housed in a ribbed structured hull.

Baldwin uses pedal-power

After creating his first pedal-powered airship in 1900, Thomas Baldwin, financed by the American Aerial Navigation Company of San Francisco, goes on to construct the *California Eagle,* an airship that uses both pedal power and an automotive engine

Giant kites fly.

Though not much is known of the source of his original interest or education in the science of kite-building, Samuel Cody becomes enamored with kites around 1899. He builds kites that can reach heights of over 10,000 ft and which provide excellent platforms for meteorological research. In fact, Cody is made an Honorary Fellow of the Royal Meteorological Society for his contributions. 'Cody Kites' consist of strings of double-cell box kites, capable of ascending thousands of feet into the air, or carrying humans in a gondola.

1900

Santos-Dumont rounds the Eiffel Tower.

In April 1900, a prize of 100,000 francs is offered by industrialist Henri Deutsch de la Meurthe to be awarded to the first aviator to complete a proscribed circuit of 11 km around the Eiffel Tower within 30 minutes.

Santos-Dumont builds a new airship, larger than the ones he had been flying since 1898. During one of his early attempts in this new ship, called *No. 5* and shown here rounding the Eiffel Tower, he begins to lose hydrogen and descends, crashing into the Trocadero Hotel. After hanging from the side of the building, he is rescued by the Paris fire brigade but the ship is a loss.

With ship *No. 6,* he makes it to the tower in only 9 minutes but then his engine fails. He has to climb over the gondola rail, without a safety harness, to restart the engine but still crosses the finish line in 29 minutes and 30 seconds. However, the mooring line was not secured immediately and the adjudicating committee refused to approve the flight even though de la Meurthe is present and declares the flight satisfactory. Public opinion is outraged and a compromise is reached; Santos-Dumont is awarded the prize but he gives half to his crew and half to the poor of Paris.

Santos-Dumont becomes an international celebrity and is often seen flying at roof top level along the boulevards of Paris, sometimes landing at an outdoor cafe for lunch.

Industrial power is a complex package.

Great Britain was the first nation to industrialize on a large scale, with North America and other European nations quickly following suit. Russia and Japan become aware of the power of industrialization, and deliberately reorganize their societies through governmental policies to adopt an industrial package. This package contains the hardware of iron, steel, and mass production, as well as the social software of a wage-earning class and increased access to education.

The Eight-Nation Alliance of imperial powers consists of 20,000 well armed troops from Austria-Hungary, France, Germany, Italy, Japan, Russia, the United Kingdom, and the U.S.

The Northern Lights are explained.

Kristian Birkeland leads several Norwegian Polar Expeditions in 1899 and 1900 to study the Earth's magnetic field. He experiments in the lab using x-rays, recently discovered, and with cathodes and magnets in vacuum environments. He creates a model of the aurora borealis by sending a stream of particles, representing the solar wind, around a magnetized sphere. Birkeland not only explains the existence of the aurora, but also maps the pattern of electric currents passing around and through Earth.

Gustav Whitehead purportedly flies a heavier-than-air craft in 1901.

Whitehead contributes to the quest of aviation, whether or not he ever flew a controlled powered flight. He had been apprenticed as a boy as a machinist-mechanic and later works with a variety of mechanics and engineers in the US. In an 1897 interview he showed a reporter for the *New York Herald* two flying machines. One was a copy of the latest technology being developed by Octave Chanute and Augustus Moore Herring. The other craft had bat-like wings.

The first gusher in Texas pours forth oil in 1901.

Coal continues to be mined by men but sorted by 'Breaker Boys'.

China is subjugated.

A rebellion in China is easily crushed by the Eight-Nation Alliance of industrialized powers, who then divide the spoils among themselves.

The Wright Brothers build a glider and then a wind tunnel.

The brothers build a wind tunnel superior to that built by Wenham a few decades earlier. They spend two months extensively testing miniatures of their wing designs in it.

Louis Renault introduces the first standard drum brakes for automobiles.

A newspaper article, written by a supposed eyewitness, describes Whitehead's August 14, 1901 flight in Connecticut. The unsigned article (purported by later research to be written by a man named Richard Howell) appears in the Bridgeport Herald, accompanied by an illustration of the aircraft, called *Number 21*, in flight. If this is indeed the first successful controlled powered flight of an airplane, it precedes the Wright Brothers by more than two years and travels farther (852 ft) than their best flight. Whitehead will act as a designer and advisor to other early aviators. His name will later fall into obscurity but evidence of his possible flight has recently become the object of new scholarship and debate.

Bicycle power changes gear.

Gearing allows the rider to pedal uphill easily and to go fast downhill. The mechanism must be strong but light. The derailleur gear change system is invented in 1899 and the Sturmey-Archer three-speed hub becomes available in 1902.

The oil industry illegally crushes competitors.

Ida Tarbell writes a piece of investigative journalism about John Rockefeller's oil monopoly for McClure's Magazine in 1903. Ida's father was a Pennsylvania oil man whose enterprise was ruined as Rockefeller monopolized the business by legal and illegal means.

A Russian school teacher publishes about exploring space via rockets.

Konstantin Tsiolkovsky publishes *The Exploration of Cosmic Space by Means of Rocket Devices.* Theorizing about many aspects of space exploration, travel, habitation, and means of escaping planetary gravity wells, the self-taught Russian scientist Tsiolkovsky draws up plans for multistage rockets, all-metal dirigibles, and, in 1903, the first instance of a space elevator.

August Gareth flies a dirigible over San Francisco.

In 1903, after 6 years of experimentation and construction, Dr. August Gareth completes the California Eagle, an 80-ft hydrogen-filled dirigible with two propellers, driven by a 500-lb, 12hp automobile engine. After testing the craft in a tethered, unmanned flight over Market St. in San Francisco, Gareth flies his craft to a height of 2000 ft. until the sun heats the gas bag to such a degree that he is forced to vent hydrogen in order to maintain altitude. At the same time, the engine dies and Gareth descends into San Francisco Bay.

Aviators test Chanute's gliders

Chanute is a bit too old to fly his own glider designs, so he hires younger aviators to collaborate on new designs and test fly them.

America, promising freedom, democracy, and the potential to profit by one's own hard work, beckons immigrants.

Immigrants are now coming from Eastern and Southern Europe, whereas previous waves of immigrants had been from Northern and Western Europe. French Canadians also immigrate by migrating south to work in the industrialized textile industry in the New England states.

Einstein publishes the Theory of Special Relativity.

Published in 1905, has many implications, including that the speed of light in a vacuum is the same for all observers regardless of the motion of the light source, that time is not absolute but dependent on position and reference frame, and that mass and energy are interchangeable.

$$E = mc^2$$

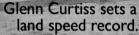

Glenn Curtiss sets a land speed record.

Glenn Curtiss an avid bicyclist and engine enthusiast, manufactures his own single cylinder engine, the first of which uses a tomato can for a carburetor. He sets a land speed record of 64 mph on a motorcycle. sets a land speed record of 64 mph on a motorcycle.

An aluminum alloy is developed.

Duralumin, an aluminum-copper-magnesium-manganese heat-treatable alloy, is developed by German chemists. Chemists in the United States develop their own version of Duralumin, called Alloy 17S-T. Both countries use this alloy in the production of airships with rigid frameworks during the Great War. Duralumin is also ideal for making tools because of its strength-to-weight ratio.

The Wright Brothers successfully achieve controlled, powered flight with a heavier-than-air craft, but keep their experiment secret.

Marconi's radio transmits across the Atlantic Ocean

In January of 1903, Marconi sends a message from Cape Cod to the U.K. It is the first successful radio transmission to reach across the Atlantic from the United States.

On December 17, 1903, in a secret experiment, Orville and Wilbur Wright make the first piloted, powered, controlled, and sustained heavier-than-air flight. Wilbur, as pilot of the Wright Flyer I, travels 120 ft in just under 15 seconds, using hand controls and a hip harness as he lies prone on the lower set of two wings. Brother Orville runs alongside, ready to stabilize the craft if needed. The craft reaches an altitude of several feet above the ground. They keep the flight secret and other aviators continue to develop their own designs.

The Wright Brothers fly in secret at Kitty Hawk.

1903

Chanute's glider is shown at the St. Louis World's Fair

Constructed with mahogany and spruce, the glider uses durable dacron rather than silk as a wing covering,

In January of 1904, the Wrights hire the experienced patent attorney Harry A. Toulmin. He advises them that seeking a patent for a 'flying machine' rather than a soaring machine would be complex and expensive, so they decide to try to patent a glider and control system. Toulmin assures them that such a patent would not preclude the later addition of a motor.

Toulmin files at the U.S. Patent Office in March of 1904. He doesn't file to patent a specific device for adjusting the wings, but the very idea of adjusting the wings in opposite directions to achieve lateral control. With such an overarching patent, the hope to force any subsequent inventor, even if using a completely different method to adjust the wings, to require a license from them in order to operate.

Toulmin is also asked to file for patents in England, Germany, France, Russia, Austria, and Belgium.

Japan's power grows.

Japan shows the world that the power of industrialization can be adopted and used by non-Western countries.

Russia completes its Trans-Siberian Railroad, and reaches the Pacific, in 1904.

The Russo-Japanese War will be fought not in either country but in northern China and Korea. It begins with a surprise attack on Port Arthur by the Japanese. The cutting-edge technologies used in this war do not include airplanes.

The Vuia 1 hops.

Santos Dumont Flies.

Traian Vuia, a Romanian engineer, designs and flies a fixed-wing, self-propelled aircraft in France. The *Vuia I* sports wings shaped much like those of Lilienthal's gliders and manages to make hops of 12 and 24 m on separate flights in 1906, but is unable to sustain flight.

In September of 1906, Alberto Santos-Dumont makes the first public flight of his 14-bis. This flight, in a public park in Paris, is the first confirmed heavier-than-air flight in the world and Dumont is hailed as the inventor of the airplane. Later, the Wrights assert they had flown first, in a secretive experiment at Kitty Hawk in 1903.

1906

The Mount Wilson Observatory is built.

The Hale Telescope sees 'First Light' and becomes operational in 1908. George Ellery Hale received the 1.5 m glass blank for the mirror in 1896. The disk is 19 cm thick and weighs 860 kg. Grinding the disk into its precise shape takes 2 years and begins in 1905, after reception of a grant from the Carnegie Institution. Some parts of the mounting structure were built in San Francisco but survived the 1906 earthquake and were eventually transported to the observatory at the top of Mt. Wilson in the hills outside Los Angeles.

Astronomers get a Standard Candle.

It is difficult for astronomers to determine if dim stars are small and close by or if they are large and far away, but Henrietta Leavitt discovers a way to determine the absolute brightness of a particular type of star. This kind of star, called a Cepheid Variable, pulsates, its brightness varying over time.

Leavitt realizes that the rate at which the pulsating stars pulse is related to their brightness; the brighter ones have longer periods.

All of the Cepheid Variable stars she observes follow the same rule so it will be possible to use them to deduce distances; the absolute brightness of the star can be compared to its relative brightness and its distance away can be determined.

Cody's kites find military use.

After many demonstrations of his kites' viability around London, the War Office hires Samuel Cody to build kites to serve as military observation platforms. Previously, stationary balloons had been used for such lookout posts, but these could only fly in light winds, whereas Cody's Kites can be used in winds in excess of 60 mph.

Cody's relationship with the British Air Battalion (the arm of the Army which will become the Air Force) flourishes when he is appointed Chief Kiting Instructor at the Balloon School. Together with military engineers, Cody designs and facilitates Britain's first airship, *Nulli Secundus*.

Cody will also go on to develop piloted glider-kites designed to be launched from a removable tether, allowing the pilot maneuverability beyond the launch location.

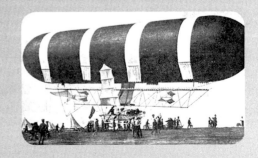

Radial engines are improved.

The Seguin brothers, Louis, Laurent, and Augustin, are French mechanical engineers who produce stationary engines for powering industrial production. The three turn their attention to creating radial engines around 1907, with the particular application to aviation in mind.

Using the highest quality machining technology and the most modern alloys, the Seguin brothers create the 7-cylinder, air-cooled, radial Gnome Omega engine. By milling all of the components from solid nickel steel, they make an engine capable of delivering an astonishing power-to-weight ratio of 1hp x 1kg.

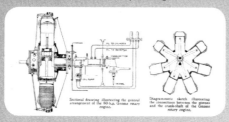

Sectional drawing illustrating the general arrangement of the 50 h.p. Gnome rotary engine.

Diagrammatic sketch illustrating the connection between the pistons and the crank-shaft of the Gnome rotary engine.

Henry Farman enters and wins the 1908 *Grand Prix d'Aviation* in Paris, flying a Voisin biplane. Farman's flight sets distance and speed records and garners popularity for the Gnome Omega engine, which enabled such a feat.

An arms race is underway.

England was the first industrial power and still enjoys a preeminent position. The industrial and economic power of Germany, first surged in the 1850's and grew quickly following unification in 1871. Kaiser Wilhelm 11 increased the industrial production of military goods such as ships and munitions dramatically after assuming the throne in 1888. Stockpiles of these goods are growing larger and Germany's industrial might can no longer be dismissed and ignored. The other industrialized nations also enter the arms race and military spending increases by 50% in the five years before the 'Great War' breaks out.

The Model-T rolls out.

Henry Ford strives to create an automobile "for the great multitude," affordable, of good quality, and with interchangeable parts such that "no man making a good salary will be unable to own one…" The mass-produced Model-T rolls off of Ford's moving assembly line, in 1908.

Alfred Wegener is a young German who attains a degree in Astronomy but soon switches to the new academic discipline of meteorology. He wins the kite flying record and then sets off to Antarctica. His multi-disciplinary and enterprising approach to life will aid him in envisioning **Continental Drift**, which will soon shake the foundations of earth science.

Airports are just large, level fields. Planes can take off and approach in any direction that the wind favors. Most airfields are grassy, which can create drag on takeoff, but is preferable to dirt, which can only be used in dry weather.

In an attempt to encourage aviation innovations in the U.S., *Scientific American* and the Aero Club of America partner to create the Scientific American Aeronautical Trophy. The trophy is to be awarded yearly as acknowledgement of significant achievements in the field, with the first recognition going to the first aviator to fly a straight line a kilometer in length.

Telephones ring in individual homes, connected by an operator who connects the call through a switchboard.

Glenn Curtiss is the "Fastest Man on Earth."

Glenn Curtiss clocks 136.6 mph on his V8 powered motorcycle, earning him  the moniker "Fastest Man on Earth." He writes to the Wright brothers, offering them a free engine for their flying machine. They refuse. He joins the Aerial Experiment Association, or AEA, a group founded by Alexander Graham Bell.

Oil is discovered in Persia.

Oil is found in Iran in 1908. After 5 years of searching, a geologist finally finds oil for the Anglo Persian Oil Company.

H.G. Wells writes *The War in the Air*.

Wells doesn't use the term 'science fiction' but calls the genre Fantasias of possibility. He writes the book in four months and it is published in 1908.

Airplanes mean that not just the front but everywhere, behind the lines etc. Indecisiveness as airpower takes out other war machines but cannot occupy the country.

The world's first commercial airline is established, using airships.

Count Ferdinand von Zeppelin founds the Deutsche Luftschiffarhrts-Aktiengesellschaft (DELAG) or "German Airship Travel Corporation" in 1909. The airline begins as a pleasure cruise company in the hopes of proving their viability to the German military. In 1911, The *LZ 10 Schwaben* is launched. This ship flies more than 200 flights, carrying more than 1,500 fare-paying passengers. This marks the beginning of a true passenger-based airline.

Aviation meets gain popularity.

The first Gordon Bennett Aviation Competition takes place at the *Grande Semaine d'Aviation de la Champagne* in 1909 near Reims, France. The aviation meet increases the popularity of heavier-than-air aviation. Gordon Bennett, heir to the New York Herald fortune, international playboy, and financial backer to Henry Morton Stanley, sponsors a timed airplane race. Glenn Curtiss wins the 12 mile race with a time of just under 16 minutes in his *No. 2 flyer.* By the rules of the race, this dictates that the next Bennett competition will be held in the US.

1909

Claiming patent infringement, the Wrights file suit.

They seek to ban Curtiss from all sales and exhibitions of his aircraft.

Glenn Curtiss sets heavier-than-air distance records.

Glenn Curtiss flies his *Golden Flyer* a distance of 24.7 miles, establishing a world record for distance and claiming the second leg of the Scientific American Trophy. The next year, 1910, he flies his *Hudson Flyer* from Albany to NYC in 2 hours 51 minutes, the longest airplane flight to date, winning him the third leg of the Scientific American trophy and a $10,000 prize. The Wrights offer him a licensing agreement, but he refuses, insisting that his aileron control system of steering is inherently different from their wing-warping system

Knowledge is sometimes shared.

In 1910, The Aero Club of Illinois is founded, with Chanute as its first president - a position he maintains until his death, 9 months later. Chanute corresponded at length with the Wright brothers, freely sharing his knowledge and theories about aviation. He believed that, though inventions should be patented by their inventors, information should be shared with anyone who is interested. The Wright brothers disagreed; although they utilized all of the codified knowledge available they did not share what they had discovered. The three remained friends in spite of this difference of opinion, and Wilbur Wright wrote a eulogy for Chanute, reading it at a meeting of the Aero Club shortly after his death.

Over 11 days, the Los Angeles International Air Meet attracts more than 200,000 spectators and is the first major U.S. air show. Aviators travel to compete for prestige and cash prizes with airplanes, balloons, and dirigibles. Many famous aviators are in attendance, including Glenn Curtiss (who was also involved in organizing the meet), Roy Knabenshue, Lincoln Beachey, and Louis Paulhan.

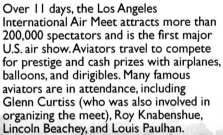

Theodore Roosevelt takes the first presidential flight.

At a racetrack in Long Island, New York, many famous and up-and-coming pilots gather for the Belmont International Aviation Tournament. In the weeks before the tournament, aviation teams gather to test equipment that had been shipped long distances and to practice. Theodore Roosevelt, having left the office of President and on the campaign trail to support the subsequent Taft administration when he passes through Long Island, in 1910. Pilot Arch Hoxsey offers the former president a ride in the famous *Wright Flyer*.

Curtiss gets a Navy contract.

In 1911, after demonstrating airplanes' military potential for the Navy, Curtiss receives the first Navy contract to build planes and train pilots, earning him the informal title *"Father of Naval Aviation."*

Charles T Weymann reaches speeds of over 120 kph and wins the 1911 Bennett Aviation Trophy on a *Nieuport II* powered by a 100hp Gnome double Omega engine.

The airplane is used in war.

In 1911, during the Turkish-Italian War, the first airplane used in war flies over Libya.

Wilbur Wright is contracted to train two pilots from the United States Army Signal Corps to fly a Wright Type-A biplane, the government's first. An airport is built to serve this purpose. College Park Airport of Maryland is one of the oldest airports still in operation.

Publisher William Randolph Hearst offers a $50,000 prize to the first person to fly across the U.S. within 30 days. Rodgers is the first to make the flight across, in 1911, but he misses the deadline and can not collect the prize.

A catapult driven by compressed air assists the takeoff of a piloted aircraft.

Theodore Ellyson, a Commander in the U.S. Navy, is sent to San Diego to learn aviation under Glenn Curtiss in 1910. In January of the following year, Ellyson makes his first solo flight in a Curtiss "grass cutter," narrowly avoiding injury following a wing-first landing. That same month, after helping Curtiss design pontoons to create floatplanes, Ellyson became the first passenger to go aloft in a floatplane. While on the Naval Base in Annapolis, Maryland, Ellyson became the first pilot to successfully use the then-experimental compressed-air catapult system.

The first seaplane fliies.

Henri Fabre pilots a powered seaplane, traveling about a third of a mile, in 1910. Fabre builds the craft, which he calls a **Hydravion**, with a former mechanic of the French army, Marius Burdin, and naval architect, Leon Sebille. The craft, known as *The Fabre* and nicknamed *Le Canard, The Duck,* is pushed by a single propeller, powered by a 50 horsepower Gnome Omega piston engine. Although Fabre's overall design is soon superseded by new ones, his basic design of the floats that keep the craft buoyant continues to be used.

The British attempt to build an airship.

Constructed by Vickers, Sons, and Maxim, *His Majesty's Airship Number 1* (which was referred to by the crew as *The Mayfly*) was to be the British answer to Germany's Zeppelins. *The Mayfly* is attached to *HMS Hermoine*, a battle cruiser with a mooring shed built onboard, and is Britain's first attempt to build a rigid airship. It is wrecked by high winds on the 24th of September, 1911, before its first test flight.

The German military buys zeppelins.

The German military buys its first zeppelin in 1912. Within a year it will commission two airship bases and a fleet of ten airships.

Over the course of several years, Francois Denhaut builds the world's first flying boat. A flight instructor by trade, Denhaut imagined the flying boat a year before and modified a plane he had been building to be able to land on the water.

The model includes a fuselage that acts as the main float for the aircraft, landing gear that can be replaced with water floats, and an angled plate below the rectangular nose, to aid in hydrodynamic lift.

Technology aids weary pilots.

As the range of airplanes is extended, the continuous hours of attention necessary on the part of the pilot is extended. To address this issue, and the fatigue that it can create, the Sperry Corporation creates the first aircraft autopilot in 1912. Combining hydraulic elevators and rudder with gyroscopic heading and attitude indicators, this device allows the plane to be flown straight along a level compass course without a pilot's attention.

The feasibility of the autopilot device is then displayed at a 1914 safety contest in Paris. Lawrence Sperry demonstrates the device by flying his plane low enough for the crowd to see that his hands are away from the controls.

A French tailor attempts to fly with a wing suit.

An attempt to fly with a wing suit from the Eiffel Tower is made in 1912. Franz Reichelt tests his invention, unfortunately with fatal results. The 33 year old tailor, claiming that he was going to use a dummy to test the suit misleads the guards to get access to the tower. After much hesitation he finally jumps but impacts the ground head first.

A French ship is converted into a Seaplane Carrier.

The *Foudre* was originally constructed to carry and launch and service torpedo boats at sea. After the ship's conversion, four torpedo-carrying seaplanes can be stored on board. The *Foudre* already possessed the needed crane and gantry setup to pull seaplanes back aboard after a water landing. A ten-meter deck is installed on the ship's bow, allowing for 'land' takeoffs.

The first seaplane used aboard the *Foudre* is a Canard Voisin.

Continental Drift is postulated.

German scientist Alfred Wegener notices just how well South America and Africa fit together and that in the past the same kinds of plants had grown on both. He finds much evidence to support his theory that those continents, now separated by an ocean, had once been adjacent.

Other evidence includes the fact that southern South America, Southern Africa, India, Australia, and Antarctica were all covered by glaciers in the past (implying that they may all have been together at the south pole), and that mountain ranges on the edges of continents are the same age, circumstantially indicating that the mountains were created when the continents had joined.

Wilbur Wright dies.

Wilbur Wright dies of Typhoid fever on May 30th, 1912. He contracted the fever a month earlier and died in his bed at the family home in Dayton, Ohio surrounded by his brother Orville, his father, his sister, and his other brothers. He had been an inventor and an aviator but had spent the last years of his life involved in litigation and the pursuit of wealth and fame, and the stress had taken its toll.

Over a thousand telegrams deliver condolences to the family within 24 hours of his death. President Taft proclaims Wilbur to have been the "father of the great new science of aeronautics."

A flight recorder is built.

George Miller Dyott builds the flight recording device into his planes, as standard equipment, in 1913. The device records warp, elevation, and rudder movement individually by drawing on paper pulled along by rotating drums.

Though his first successful test-flight won't occur until 1926, Robert Goddard, a professor in Massachusetts, patents multi-stage rockets and liquid-fueled rockets, in 1914.

War erupts in 1914.

Jubilant, newly registered, soldiers travel to the front. The war is widely expected to be a short one. People on both sides are impressed with their new technologies and stockpiles of ammunition. Almost everyone expects to be home before Christmas.

Trenches are dug and the Great War soon becomes a terrible stalemate.

Zeppelins drop bombs on London.

Zeppelins are first used in reconnaissance but soon drop bombs over London. The leviathans spread fear and panic among the civilian population, who call them "baby killers." Early attempts to shoot them down are ineffective but engineers soon create incendiary bullets, which explode upon impact.

IT IS FAR BETTER TO FACE THE BULLETS THAN TO BE KILLED AT HOME BY A BOMB

JOIN THE ARMY AT ONCE & HELP TO STOP AN AIR RAID

GOD SAVE THE KING

They create holes in the airships large enough to allow outside air, which contains oxygen, to mix with the hydrogen and catch fire. By the end of 1914, the German fleet is reduced to just four ships.

The British navy converts its ships to oil.

Some engineers and policy makers – notably Winston Churchill – push to build oil-powered ships. When these ships, including the *HMS Queen Elizabeth*, launch in 1913, all reservations are dispelled. The new class of battleships, the super-dreadnaughts, will prove reliable in the upcoming wars.

The airplane finds utility in reconnaissance.

Reconnaissance planes keep either side from surprising the other. The information they provide also helps artillery teams to aim their guns more effectively.

Map sketchers are recruited to accompany pilots and take notes on enemy troop movements. Photographs are more detailed, accurate, and reliable than sketches. Beginning in 1913, Germany routinely uses cameras on reconnaissance missions. France enters the war with several dozen Blériot planes equipped for reconnaissance, including cameras. Systems are created to develop photos quickly in the field, getting information to leaders at unprecedented speeds.

Experiments with stereoscopic photography start around 1914, allowing for more accurate cartographic information and greater insight into the heights of hills and buildings.

Trenches stretch on for hundreds of kilometers and aerial reconnaissance maps them out. Both sides have intimate knowledge of the others' movements; savage battles are fought for little more than kilometers of territory, only to be ceded to the other side in the next skirmish.

1914

Einstein expands his theory of relativity to include gravity.

Einstein expands his Theory of Special Relativity to include gravity and publishes his General Theory of Relativity in 1915.

Gravity is no longer the unexplained, almost magical force that it was in Newtonian physics, where objects with mass just pull together across vast distances as if with an invisible rubber band. In the new theory, objects move toward other objects because they are sliding down unseen inclines in the topography of space/time. The inclines are due to depressions caused by the presence of objects of matter.

Objects of matter, Einstein postulates, distort the fabric of space/time much as a bowling bowl distorts the fabric of a trampoline, causing topographic anomalies through which other objects must move.

Gravity is redefined by the new physics, not as a force but as the consequence of objects moving naturally and freely through the contours of the topography of space In our solar system, the most massive object is the sun and it creates a deep gravitational well around itself.

Each of the planets also creates its own small well. The planets would roll down the gravitational hill into the sun but each one is perched on the lip of its own small well, like a boulder on a mountainside, that doesn't roll downhill because it is slightly dug in. Thus the planets orbit the sun.

A ship is purpose-built as a seaplane carrier.

The *HMS Ark Royal* was purchased in 1914 by the Royal British Navy when the ship was still only a framed hull, allowing naval engineers to build to purpose. When completed, the Ark Royal can carry, launch, and service 8 floatplanes, and sees first service in 1915.

Safety devices are not welcomed.

Everard Calthrop, a British railroad engineer for most of his life, turns his attention to aviation safety in his later years. A close friend of Rolls-Royce's Charles Rolls, who dies in 1910 after losing control of his biplane, Calthrop begins building life-saving emergency parachute systems. In 1916, he patents one that uses compressed air to eject the pilot from the plane. Afraid that the use of parachutes might negatively affect the "fighting spirit" of pilots, the RAF will not use parachutes or ejection seats in World War I.

The UK and Germany fight over oil in Iran.

Planning and construction for the joint German-Ottoman railroad projects continues.

Japan seeks to expand its own influence and joins the war, siding against Germany.

The Japanese navy secures sea lanes against the Germans in the South Pacific and Indian oceans.

The war exacerbates the discord already threatening imperial rule in Russia.

The Tzar had hoped a foreign war would bring him prestige and unite the ethnic groups within his empire. Although he had taken some steps to modernize, including the building of railroads and reforming serfdom, the Russian army is no match for fully industrialized Germany. By the end of 1916, five million Russian soldiers are killed, wounded, taken prisoner, or missing in action.

Engineers experiment with ways to fire a gun forward without hitting their own propellers.

An attempt is made to install a forward-firing gun on this French Morane-Saulnier L.

The Migratory Bird Treaty of 1916 attempts to protect some birds moving between the U.S. and Canada.

The Lafayette Escadrille is formed

In the early days of WWI, before the U.S. officially joined the Allied Forces, Americans eager to offer their services were able to enlist in the French Foreign Legion as ambulance drivers, foot soldiers, and aviators. In 1916, the French government forms the Escadrille Americaine, a squadron of American pilots led by French commander Captain Georges Thenault. The squadron quickly becomes known for its heroic exploits, and Germany files an official complaint with the U.S., a supposedly neutral nation, about the use of the name "Americaine." France changes the name to Escadrille Lafayette in honor of the Marquis de Lafayette, hero of the French and American revolutions. A total of 38 Americans will fly with the squadron, while many more fly with the "Aéronautique militaire," France's air service. Collectively, these pilots become known as The Lafayette Flying Corps.

Ace pilots emerge.

Aerial photography becomes so important that skirmishes take place as pilots seek to drive away enemy pilots taking pictures over their own trenches.
The French Marquis de Montferato, Jean Casale, requests a transfer to aviation duty, where he advances quickly through the ranks and scores 13 aerial victories. He will be one of the few aces to survive the entire course of the war.

Britain's King George V and officials inspect a munitions factory in 1917

The long ailing and debt ridden Ottoman Empire collapses.

The Ottomans lose battles on many fronts. British forces defeat the Ottoman army and capture Bagdad in 1917.

Aluminum is recycled for the war effort.

Aluminum recycling factories open in Chicago and Cleveland.

 The 100-Inch Hooker Telescope at Mount Wilson is completed in 1917.

The U.S. aircraft industry finally gets going.

At the start of WWI, the US is not producing any aircraft of its own design due to patent wars instigated by the Wright Brothers. At the request of the government, the various manufacturers form the Manufacturers Aircraft Association, which provides licensing agreements that allow for cross-company use of patented technology, bringing to an end the legal monopoly established by the Wrights.

Naval Aircraft Factory (NAF) is established in the Philadelphia Shipyards to design and produce wartime aircraft. By 1918, the U.S. aircraft industry will employ 200,000 people. Still, due to delays in innovation and production caused by the patent wars, most U.S. pilots in Europe fly French-made planes.

The Aviation Act of 1917 budgets over $50 million for U.S. Army aviation. Some 13 million of it is earmarked for aviation infrastructure facilities. Before the war, the military possessed three airfields, by the end of the war, they will have almost forty.

Baldwin makes Captain

Thomas Baldwain, who had been building airships for the U.S. Navy as a member of the Connecticut Aircraft Co., since 1914, becomes a Captain in the Army Signal Corps. in 1917. He supervises inspection of all airships and balloons built in the U.S.

The Curtiss Aeroplane and Motor company is formed, providing training and aircraft for the US military

Curtiss envisions a flying car.

The Curtiss Autoplane is a triplane incorporating the wings from a Curtiss Model L, a 100 hp Curtiss OXX engine, canard nose wings, a pusher propeller, and four automobile wheels with front-wheel drive. The three-seat cabin resembles a Ford Model T, with room for one driver up front and two passengers in back. The Autoplane is able to 'hop,' but never achieves true flight.

The Red Baron is the most famous ace.

Manfred von Richthofen, the Red Baron, is perhaps the best-known ace pilot of all time. Born in Prussia, Richthofen joined the Polish Uhlan cavalry (serving the German military) at age 19. As World War I became thoroughly a trench-based war, most cavalry units were used as dispatch messengers, which bothered him greatly. A transfer request was accepted and Richthofen joined the Imperial German Army Air Service in 1915.

Starting his career first as a reconnaissance observer, Richthofen switched to pilot's training when he met German ace pilot Oswald Boelcke. The moniker of the Red Baron comes from his familial status and the bright red planes he flew; most famously the Fokker Dr.I triplane, but originally the Albatross D.III. Though his official tally of 80 downed enemy aircraft will be surpassed, the Red Baron's name and story will outlive those of many other ace fighter pilots.

The Lafayette Flying Corps disbands.

The Lafayette Flying Corps disbands after the U.S. officially enters the war in 1917, with many American pilots transferring into the U.S. Army Air Service as the 103d Aero Squadron and many French pilots forming the Escadrille SPA.124 Jeanne d'Arc. The 2006 film Flyboys will be based loosely on the experiences of the Lafayette Flying Corps

World War I finally ends on November 11, 1918.

The war leaves much of Europe in ruins.

1918

The Junkers D.I is all metal.

The Junkers D.I is a single seat monoplane and the first all-metal fighter plane to enter service. The D.I is found to not be maneuverable enough to merit flying as a front-line fighter, so instead flies for the Imperial German Navy. Junkers uses corrugated duralumin to skin the fuselage and wings, forever changing the way that planes are constructed.

The cost of the war proves high.

More than 35 million casualties result from WWI, including 9 million soldiers killed. Russia suffers the highest numbers with more than 9 million casualties including 1.7 million soldiers killed. Germany also sees approximately 1.7 million soldiers killed. The U.S. enters the war late and suffers 320,700 casualties.

A new strain of flu is deadly.

More than 50 million people will die from the influenza pandemic of 1918.

The Flu usually kills only weak, sick, elderly, or very young individuals. The pandemic of 1918, strangely, kills mostly young adults in their prime. It is still uncertain why this virus, the first outbreak of the N1H1, reacted the way it did. Did the conditions during the war mold a more virulent strain or did the high levels of human stress cause an unusual reaction? Returning soldiers carry the disease to every corner of the world.

The U.S. mail gets airborne.

President Wilson and huge crowd gather to watch as George Boyle pilots the inaugural flight of the Washington, DC to Philadelphia to New York route. Boyle, well connected but lacking experience, is given a crude map and told to follow train tracks north to Union Station. It's an inauspicious start; Boyle gets lost and heads south.

The Treaty of Versailles is signed.

Germany is forbidden to have an airforce.

Germany is saddled with a heavy burden of debt, more than it could probably ever repay. The utter devastation of the war is blamed on Germany and a vengeful attitude prevails among the victors. Ironically, the very measures taken to ensure Germany stays too weak to enter another war will actually set the stage for the next one.

Vietnam hopes for independence.

Vietnam had been under the dominion of the French and, before them, the Chinese. Ho Chi Mihn journeys to Paris but is not invited to the negotiations of the Paris Peace Conference and must make his case from outside.

Amid much talk of a lasting peace and the rights of nations to be unmolested by aggressors, France, having suffered greatly in the war, insists on retaining its colonies.

The lands of the defeated Ottoman Empire are partitioned up amongst the prevailing European powers.

The British had taken Palestine, including Jerusalem, from the Ottomans shortly after the Ottomans entered the war. Iraq becomes a League of Nations mandate under British control. Egypt remains a British protectorate; it had been an autonomous vassal state in the Ottoman Empire until taken by Britain in 1914 after Britain became apprehensive of Egyptian support of the Young Turks, who had advocated for an alliance with Germany.

France presides over Syria and Lebanon as mandates and retains its North African colonies of Algeria, Tunisia, and Morocco that it had taken from the ailing Ottoman Empire some decades before. Italy retains control of Libya. Iran was not part of the Ottoman Empire and had already been partitioned in 1907 between Britain and Russia.

The first trans-Atlantic airplane flight takes 19 days.

In May 1919, six crew members pilot a Curtiss flying boat, the NC-4, in the first transatlantic flight. Beginning in New York State, the trip takes 19 days, stopping in Massachusetts, Nova Scotia, Newfoundland, and the Azores Islands before landing in Lisbon, Portugal.

Relativity is put to the test.

A more effective test of Einstein's Theory of Relativity is devised; the new test will establish if light rays really do bend when passing by a strong gravitational source like a star. Because the change of a light beam's path will be difficult to measure, it will be measured with our own nearby star, during an eclipse, in 1919.

Amelia Earhart yearns to fly.

In December of 1920, Amelia Earhart takes a brief flight with Frank Hawks and then immediately sets out to work a myriad odd jobs to save up for flying lessons. She becomes a student of Anita Snook and learns in a Curtiss JN-4. Just six months later, Earhart will purchase a Kinner Airster ("The Canary").

Bessie Coleman perseveres in her dream to fly. The African American, is not accepted to any American flight school, so she learns French and goes to France to fly, in 1920.

The first nonstop trans-Atlantic airplane flight takes 16 hours.

Two weeks later, the first nonstop transatlantic flight is completed by two British Air Force pilots in just under 16 hours, eclipsing the previous achievement. John Alcock and Arthur Whitten Brown modified a Vickers Vimy bomber from WWI and flew it almost 2000 miles from Newfoundland to Ireland, winning a long-standing contest posed by the Daily Mail, a London Newspaper, with a 10,000 pound prize.

Many pilots, trained to fly in World War I, turn to barnstorming.

Spectators demand risky, ever more thrilling performances as the Roaring Twenties roll out.

1921

The first helium airship flies.

Airship C-7 lifts off on the first of December, 1921; the first successful flight of an airship filled with helium instead of hydrogen.

The C-class of airships, patrol ships developed by Goodyear and Goodrich for the U.S. Navy, are an improvement upon the previous B-type. Originally, 30 ships are ordered to be sent to Europe, but production was delayed enough that the 10 ships produced arrive too late to participate in World War I. Spread out amongst naval bases for training and experimentation purposes, the C-class will only be used until 1922.

Test pilot Lieutenant Harold R. Harris pilots the world's first high-altitude flight with a cabin pressurization system, in a modified (and Americanized) Airco DH.9A from McCook Field in Dayton, Ohio in 1921.

Queen Bess takes to the sky

Bessie Coleman becomes the first woman of African American descent, as well as the first Native American, to receive a pilots license, which she earns in France. After returning from France, she receives a surprising amount of press. She also realizes that she will have to work as a barn stormer to make a living. Unable to find an instructor in aerobatics who will take her, she heads back to Europe.

Helium is rare on Earth.

While the element helium is one of the most abundant atoms in the Universe (second only to hydrogen), it is rare on Earth. Helium was blown away and out of the inner solar system by the solar wind shortly after the formation of the sun.

The helium nucleus is emitted as an alpha particle when large, radioactive elements in the Earth's crust break down. After being released, the helium nucleus attracts two electrons and rises upward in the crust. It will escape into the atmosphere and eventually be lost to space unless it is trapped, usually along with natural gas.

Floatplanes are modified to more easily escape water surface suction.

John Cyril Porte, a retired British Navy Lieutenant, acquires many flying boat models from the American aviator and inventor Glenn Curtiss for the British Navy at the outset of World War I. Early models of Curtiss' aircraft were plagued by trouble breaking the water suction that occurs at takeoff and poor maneuverability. Porte acquires permission to modify and experiment on the Curtiss models, leading to innovations like the "Felixstowe notch," a hull modification that overcomes the water suction issue. Following the innovation of this notch, Porte's seaplanes and flying boats were labeled the Felixstowe line. Over one hundred Felixstowe F.2's were built and employed over the course of World War I, primarily for patrol and light bombing runs, with F.3, F.4, and F.5 models running different types of missions through 1925.

An airplane is said to stall when the wing is unable to continue generating lift.

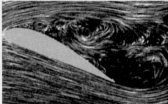

This occurs at low speeds or too high an angle of attack. Instead of the air flowing smoothly over the surface of the wing, it breaks away and forms turbulent burbles.

When one wing is stalled but the other continues to generate lift, a plane can fall into a dangerous spin.

Gallaudet Aircraft Company liquidates its inventory the same year that GM closes the Dayton-Wright Company. Reuben H. Fleet buys up most of the remaining inventory of both companies. Fleet founds Consolidated Aircraft in 1923, concentrating on its line of flying boats.

The oil tanker *J.A. Moffet* (owned by Standard Oil) is the first ship to use an autopilot device to aid its crew.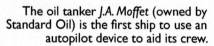

Airports begin employing rotating lights, like upward-facing lighthouses, to signal to night-flying pilots.

Physicists define four forces that govern the Universe.

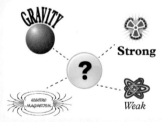

The International Astronomical Union is formed in 1922. It acts as the authority for naming celestial bodies and categorizing them as comets, asteroids, planets, etc.

In 1923, Amelia Earhart is issued pilot's license #6017, becoming the 16th woman to hold one.

Oil continues to gush out of the ground in Texas.

The all-metal Ford Tri-Motor is a popular airliner.

Dubbed *"The Tin Goose"* and built almost entirely of corrugated aluminum, the Trimotor's design is straightforward.

Although it is simple and sturdy, its unrefined exterior creates a lot of drag.

The design is built upon the work of German aeronautical engineer Hugo Junkers. Original designer William Bushnell Stout's plans only include one engine, but when Ford buys out his company in 1925, the *Tin Goose* is redesigned with three radial Curtiss-Wright air-cooled engines. Ford claims that the all-aluminum nature of the plane and its multiple engines makes it "the safest airliner around."

Astronomers engage in the *Great Debate* about whether or not there are any other galaxies besides our own.

Some astronomers believe that nebula, the tiny bright wispy patches, are actually separate galaxies. Most, however, insist that these nebula are within our own Milky Way galaxy, and that it is the only galaxy in the universe.

To determine if the nebula are far-away separate galaxies, astronomers need a new technique to measure vast distances.

The Soviet physicist Alexander Friedmann follows Einstein's equations and postulates, in 1924, that the Universe could be expanding.

Igor Sikorsky establishes the Sikorsky Aircraft Corporation in 1925. Initially, development and production is concentrated on multi-engine landplanes, but soon amphibious aircraft will be added.

Sikorsky Aircraft is incorporated.

1925

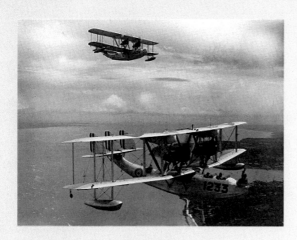

Based on the plans for the 10-seater passenger flying boat the *Supermarine Swan*, the *Supermarine Southampton* is built in 1925. It soon replaces previous flying boat models from World War I, running missions ranging from morale-boosting shows to air mail deliveries to military excursions (there are three machine gun positions and a bomb bay).

'Airmindedness,' or straightforward thinking and the willingness to embrace modern ideas about the role of flight, emerges.

In 1926, the Air Commerce Act establishes parameters for pilots' licensing, certifying and inspecting aircraft, and traffic rules (among many other areas), under the oversight of the Secretary of Commerce.

Bessie Coleman dies.

Bessie Coleman flies in many exhibitions and occasionally makes parachute jumps. She only appears at desegregated venues in which all spectators use the same entrance gates. Her dream is to start a flight school. Having just made the final payment on an old Jenny JN-4 with an OX-5 engine, she and a mechanic make a test flight in 1926. When the plane malfunctions, Bessie Coleman falls from the open cockpit several hundred feet to the ground. More than 15,000 people attend her funeral services.

Tesla predicts drones, smartphones, and gender equality.

In an interview with Collier's magazine in 1926, engineer/inventor Nikola Tesla predicts that new inventions and new ways of thinking will dramatically change society in the near future. While most of his predictions will come to pass, the application of wireless energy for the propulsion of flying machines that carry no fuel is still but a dream.

"When wireless is perfectly applied the whole earth will be converted into a huge brain, which in fact it is, all things being particles of a real and rhythmic whole. We shall be able to communicate with one another instantly, irrespective of distance. Not only this, but through television and telephony we shall see and hear one another as perfectly as though we were face to face, despite intervening distances of thousands of miles; and the instruments through which we shall be able to do his will be amazingly simple compared with our present telephone. A man will be able to carry one in his vest pocket."

Pilgrim flies safely with helium.

An executive at Goodyear Tire and Rubber, Paul Litchfield, envisions airships as an inland analogue for yachts. *Pilgrim* is the first of their blimps to be converted to fly with helium. The pilot and two passengers travel in luxury; the gondola is covered in velour and mahogany.

World population is rising at an exponential rate, seeming without bound, and ticks off the second billion mark.

2 billion

Though unpublished, Peruvian scientist Pedro Paulet experiments with liquid-fueled rockets in 1927.

Elmer Ambrose Sperry, Sr. creates a gyroscopic instrument that indicates the orientation of the aircraft relative to the earth, the **artificial horizon**.

Freon facilitates refrigeration.

Frigidaire synthesizes Freon, making a safer home refrigerator.

The German airline company Lufthansa opens in 1927.

The Treaty of Versailles had forbidden Germany to ever have an airforce but the passenger airline provides generic pilot training.

Pan American World Airlines opens for service in 1927.

Pan Am establishes many routes in the Americas, beginning with scheduled air mail service between Key West, Florida and Havana, Cuba.

The Cleveland National Air Races begin.

The National Air Races, which had originally been sponsored by the publisher Ralph Pulitzer, in 1920, move to Cleveland, in 1929. Running for as long as ten days, this collection of races features both pylon course flying and cross country races. It will showcase great pilots such as James Doolittle and Roscoe Turner.

Astronomers work to determine if other galaxies might exist.

Edwin Hubble, using the 100 inch Telescope at Mount Wilson, examines the wispy nebulas to determine if they are just strange stars or if they are other galaxies. He looks for Cepheid Variable Stars which have a known brightness and can thus be used as 'standard candles.' He shows that the Cepheids in Andromeda and the other nebulas are dimmer and therefore much farther away.

Just as the headlights of an automobile appear bright if the car is near and dim if the car is far away, a star with a particular brightness should appear bright if it is in our own galaxy and dimmer if it is farther away. Some stars, however, are bigger and brighter than others. The recent discovery that a particular kind of star, called a Cepheid variable, always has the same brightness will allow astronomers to measure absolute distances.

Evidence of the expansion of the Universe is both theoretical and observational.

In 1927, Georges Lemaître publishes a paper titled "Un Univers homogène de masse constante et de rayon croissant rendant compte de la vitesse radiale des nébuleuses extragalactiques" (A homogeneous Universe of constant mass and growing radius accounting for the radial velocity of extragalactic nebulae").

In his paper, he presents his measurements of Doppler shift of Galaxies and shows that the spectra of far off galaxies are redshifted more than nearby ones. He presents the idea that the Universe is expanding and makes a rough calculation of the pace of expansion.

Unfortunately, the journal in which he publishes is not widely read. Two years later, Edwin Hubble will derive the same result and popularize the idea.

The Ford Flivver.

On the heels of Ford's success with both the Trimotor and the Model T, Henry Ford pitches the idea of an aircraft in every family's garage. With Otto Koppen as head designer, Ford claimed that the one-seater Flivver would "fit in his office." Test pilot Harry J. Brooks regularly flew the prototype from his garage at home to work, and Charles Lindbergh was the only other pilot to fly one. After a few botched test flights, Brooks dies and the project is put to rest.

Instruments allow for 'blind flight'.

James "Jimmy" H. Doolittle and Benjamin S. Kelsey make a historic 'blind flight.' The two U.S. Air Force lieutenants take off from Mitchel Field in Long Island, NY in September of 1929, in a NY-2 biplane. In the front cockpit, Kelsey sits with his arms outstretched and hands off the controls, while Doolittle pilots from the rear cockpit with a canvas tarpaulin masking his view. The two are able to take off, fly, and land, relying only on their instruments.

In 1929, the Curtiss Wright Corp is formed, bringing the patent wars to an end once and for all.

The Empire State Building is designed with a mooring mast for airships.

The high winds at the top are too great to land, and there wouldn't be enough room for a ground crew, but the Art-Deco spire serves as a beautiful ornament.

A more compact and dependable version of Sperry Corporation's autopilot device is created and keeps an Army Air Corps Ford Tri-Motor on course for three hours without straying from its heading or altitude.

The "Catapult-able cockpit" is invented.

Anastase Dragomir tests and patents an ejection seat at Paris-Orly Airport in August of 1929. The "catapult-able cockpit" design opens a hatch in the floor of the plane and ejects the pilot with a highly maneuverable cell-parachute attached to his back.

The late 1920's and 1930's see regular air transport between North America and Europe, due largely to rising confidence in the reliability of flying boats. During this time, airborne refueling is perfected, allowing flying boats to load on more fuel than they could take off with. This makes long distance travel far more accessible to both the military and passenger services.

1929

Aircraft carrier catapults are tested.

Many early aircraft carriers cater only to seaplanes which land in the water beside the ship and are then winched up on board. Before taking off again, the planes are prepped and refueled and lower back into the water. In 1930 *HMS Ark Royal* is recommissioned from her active seaplane carrier status to a training ship for seaplane pilots and as a proving ground for aircraft catapults. Although a variety of catapults have previously been tested and successful launches have been made, a practical system has not yet been perfected.

Parachutists employ wingsuits to glide.

The 19 year old parachutist, Rex Finney, of Los Angeles, uses a wing suit in 1930 in an attempt to add a horizontal component to his jumps; in other words, to glide. Silk, whalebone, wood, canvas, and metals were all used in the creation of early suits. Other notable "birdmen" are Clem Sohn and Leo Valentin, who are said to have glided for miles.

Aviator, inventor, and innovator Glenn Curtiss dies in 1930

Pluto is discovered.

Pluto is discovered in 1930 by Clyde Tombaugh at the Lowell Observatory. Originally called 'Planet X,' Pluto will hold the title of the solar system's ninth planet until the IAU reclassifies its definition of 'planet.'

Airports begin to install runway lighting. These early forms attempt to indicate the correct angle of approach and descent, however the colors and strobe rates are not yet standardized.

Balloonists explore the stratosphere.

Balloonist Auguste Piccard invents a pressurized gondola, enabling the exploration and research of the earth's upper atmosphere. Piccard and Paul Kipner set an altitude record of 15,781 meters in 1931 while gathering data on the stratosphere and cosmic rays. The following autumn, Piccard will break his own record and ascend to 16,201m.

Howard Hughes hits Hollywood.

A young Howard Hughes inherits his family tool company, a multi-million dollar fortune built on oil drilling machinery. After his parents' deaths, Hughes drops out of Rice University at 19 years old and at 20 follows his uncle Rupert to Hollywood.

Founding his own production company and releasing several acclaimed movies in short order, Hughes begins to prove himself as a film maker.

His credibility begins to wane, however, as he begins filming his WWI opus, Hell's Angels. Hughes will push his staff and crew, budget, and public opinion to produce the film he wants. During the extremely protracted production, Hughes watches a "talkie" movie, *The Jazz Singer*, and sees silent films as a thing of the past. Production screeches to a halt and he orders the whole film reshot in sound, with many script and actor changes. With a price tag of $3.95 million, it is the highest budgeted film in the world, but box office sales bring in over $8 million. Hughes himself is hospitalized after attempting an impossibly steep dive for the final scene and several pilots lose their lives during filming.

During the filming of *Hell's Angels*, Hughes employs Glenn Odekirk to oversee the maintenance of his fleet of aircraft. Hughes and Odekirk's friendship and professional relationship is cemented during the film's production and the two will work on innovative aircraft designs in the years to come.

Einstein journeys to Mt. Wilson.

Einstein journeys to Mt. Wilson in 1931 to look at the evidence that the Universe is expanding. After his visit, he stops arguing against the hypothesis.

Einstein's dislike for the idea, which actually stems from implications of his own equations, is further intensified by the fact that it is a priest, Lemaître, who proposes the new hypothesis of an expanding Universe.

If the Universe is expanding, then it must be expanding from some source, a point of origin. Every religion includes a proposed origin for the world, a creation story. Since the time of Newton, scientists have been content to assume that the Universe is eternal and unchanging in its fundamental aspects. In earlier centuries, the Church had tortured many people for considering that the earth might be round and orbit the sun.

When Isaac Newton had proposed the paradigm that the Universe is infinite and eternal, conditions which don't require or preclude a creator, the Church did not engage in a debate about it. This allowed a kind of truce between science and the Church.

Lemaître, who is a dedicated physicist but also a priest, calls his idea 'the Primeval Atom' hypothesis, further agitating scientists who fear that the church is attempting to reassert itself into the affairs of science.

The German engineer, Werner von Braun, former colleague and student of Hermann Oberth, begins working on liquid-fuel rockets on an Ordinance Department grant. He will continue working with the Nazi military to develop what will become the V-2 rocket.

At the end of 1931, the Goodyear Pilgrim is retired. After six years this airship's flight record is impressive, with over 5,000 passengers carried on 4,765 flights.

 ## TransAtlantic flights by airship follow regular schedules.

Pan American World Airlines flies many routes in the Americas.

At large scales, every patch of the universe seems to be similar to every other.

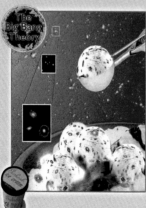

Any model of the Universe that we make depends upon the premise that our sector of the Universe, the part of it that we can see, is representative of the whole.

We don't find any trends with direction; for example, galaxies are not bigger in one area or farther apart in another. This means that the Universe is isotropic. Some substances, like vanilla ice cream, are homogenous and isotropic. Others, like Rocky Road ice cream, are heterogeneous but still isotropic.

When sampled with a small spoon, every spoonful of vanilla is the same as every other but spoonfuls of the Rocky Road are quite different from one another; one spoonful can contain a walnut while another has a piece of chocolate. However, if you use a large enough scoop to dish it out, every scoop will contain roughly the same proportion of nuts and candy as every other.

Astronomers have found that every volume of space that we have been able to sample is statistically similar to every other as long as we use a 'scoop size' of about 300,000 light years.

The German Junkers Ju 49 is built to test cabin pressurization.

With an initial goal of operating at 20,000 ft., the Ju 49 is already making flights at 30,000 ft. by 1933.

Jean Piccard designs a balloon for the World's Fair.

With help from his twin brother Auguste, Jean Felix Piccard designs the world's biggest balloon for the 1933 World's Fair, held in Chicago. The *Century of Progress* balloon takes over 700 cylinders of hydrogen to fill and is over 100 feet at its widest point. Contemporary aeronautic regulations require balloonists to hold a U.S. pilot's license, and Swiss-born Jean Felix is not allowed to fly. In his stead, U.S. Navy pilots demonstrate the balloon.

Joseph Goebbels, who will become the Nazi Minister of Propaganda, makes effective use of technology; even his earliest speeches are broadcast on radio.

Superman is born.

Two high school students bring the most popular superhero to life. Joe Shuster and Jerry Siegel create the comic *"The Reign of the Superman"* in 1933. The protagonist uses his new-found psychic powers for malicious personal gain. This first version of the story is not popular.

The Stinson is reliant.

Following its debut in 1933, more than 1,327 Reliants of various models will be made. It will serve as a cargo plane and trainer in WWII.

In 1934, the Aeronautics Branch of the U.S. Department of Commerce is renamed the Bureau of Air Commerce and the first three Air Traffic Control centers are built.

The Shah of Iran shocks the world by contesting the country's oil concession with Anglo-Persian Oil Company.

The share of the profits that Iran receives from the British-controlled company come only from the money made off of the crude oil, excluding Iran from any of the proceeds from the highly profitable process and products of oil refinery. Less than a year after striking the original deal, the Shah renegotiates with APOC, asking for a higher percentage of the crude oil profits based on the market price of oil. The APOC refuses to budge on the main issue. The Shah's only small victory is that Persia's approximately 17% share will now be 21%, but it will be a share of a fixed price, regardless of the market value of the oil at the time of its production. The ghost of what is lost in this concession will follow him throughout his time as Shah.

Following the Shah's decision to officially refer to Persia as Iran, the British-based Anglo-Persian Oil Company renames itself to the 'Anglo-Iranian Oil Company.'

Radio and ranging is used in meteorology.

The first radar for radio and ranging detection of meteorological use is demonstrated in 1935. Robert Watson-Watt, a British meteorologist and engineer (as well as a descendent of James Watt), maps the radio signals given off by lightning to better map the positions of moving thunderstorms. With the looming threat of air and sea raids, many in the scientific community bring their attention to furthering the war effort. Watson-Watt proves the application of radar to the Air Ministry in what is known as the 'Daventry Experiment,' detecting a Handley Page Heyford bomber as it flies along a preset path.

The project is scaled up to increase the devices' power and range, and in June, a Supermarine Scapa is detected at 17 miles away. The British Treasury orders the building of Chain Home, a system of five radar stations, for £60,000.

A woman flies in the stratosphere.

Jeannette Piccard, accompanied by her husband Jean Felix and their pet turtle, pilots the Century of Progress balloon from Dearborn, Michigan to Cadiz, Ohio. The flight takes over eight hours, passing over Lake Eerie, and the two ascend 17,550 meters, crossing into the stratosphere. She will hold the record for first woman to reach the stratosphere for almost 30 years, until the first woman launches into space in 1963.

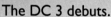

The DC 3 debuts.

The prototype DST (Douglas Sleeper Transport) flies on December 17, 1935, and is a success. Its cabin is outfitted with 21 seats instead of 14–16 sleeping berths and it is given the new designation DC-3. The first DC-3s roll off the production line and are delivered directly to American Airlines.

The Hughes H-1 Racer is fast.

The first aircraft produced by the Hughes Aircraft Company, the H-1 Racer, immediately breaks records. Although the design process began only the previous year with scale models, Hughes and Odekirk have labored over innovations included in the design of the H-1 since the filming of Hell's Angels. With countersunk screws, flat rivets, retractable landing gear, and Hughes flying, the H-1 Racer sets the world's landplane speed record at 352.39 mph. Hughes crashlands in a nearby beet field and is quoted as saying, "We can fix her; she'll go faster." Attempts to sell the plans to the Army Air Corps as a pursuit plane are unsuccessful.

1935

Airplane fuselages are pressurized.

The Soviet Union furthers cabin pressurization technologies; now, the entire fuselage can be pressurized, not just the cockpit. Built by the Bureau of Special Design (part of the Central Aerodynamics and Hydrodynamics Institute), the Chizhevski BOK-1 was based on the success of the German Junkers Ju 49 and a hermetically sealed balloon gondola that the Bureau had previously built. The BOK-1 began with a Tupolev RD airframe chassis, and a sealed cabin was built of aluminum alloys. Air exchange was controled by a dump valve and replaced with stored oxygen, and radiators kept the cabin warm. The BOK-1 is capable of cruising up to 46,000 feet while maintaining the standard cabin pressure of 26,000 altitude feet.

Japan invades China in 1931 and declares all-out war in 1937.

High altitude balloons are improved.

Jean and Jeannette Piccard invent the plastic balloon, that can fly higher due to its low weight. The balloon, made by Jean's students, consists of cellophane sections which are taped together. Instruments on board the unmanned craft send back pressure and temperature data, until the transmitter freezes at 50,000 ft. Jean Piccard also develops cluster balloons (in an attempt to save weight) and the frost-free window and the liquid oxygen converter.

Hitler unveils the Luftwaffe.

The Treaty of Versailles forbade Germany from developing an airforce, but Hitler built one secretly.

The age of Aluminum dawns.

Alloy 7075 is secretly developed by Sumitomo Metal Industries of Japan. It will be used in the production of the Mitsubishi A6M Zero airframe. This alloy makes the Zero fighter aircraft lighter, stronger, more resilient and easier to produce.

Lockheed builds a monocoque aircraft.

Monocoque refers to using the 'skin' or exterior surface of a vehicle to provide load support, rather than relying entirely on interior supports. The Lockheed XC-35 will become the basis of many subsequent pressurized aircraft.

With one unfortunate accident, the airship industry deflates.

When the Nazi party comes to power in Germany, Zeppelins become a tool for disseminating propaganda. By 1933, the swastika is prominently displayed on the tail fins and loud speakers attached to the gondola play speeches and march music to crowds across Germany.

Zeppelin behemoths like The Hindenburg were filled with Hydrogen gas. At the time, the United States controls the supply of helium, the slightly heavier but non-flammable, gas. The LZ 129 Hindenburg was used for transatlantic passenger service.

On the 6th of May, 1937, after a transatlantic trip, the Hindenburg caught fire. There were 97 people on board, including 36 passengers and 61 crew members. A total of 35 people are killed; 13 passengers, 22 crew, and one worker in the ground crew. Its arrival in Lakehurst, New Jersey is recorded by Herbert Morrison's blow-by-blow narration which is broadcast the following day.

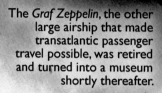

The *Graf Zeppelin*, the other large airship that made transatlantic passenger travel possible, was retired and turned into a museum shortly thereafter.

An American icon is born on a distant planet.

Following the poor sales of *Reign of the Superman*, Shuster and Siegel reinvent the character as a hero, rather than a villain. In 1938 **The Superman** is published as the cover feature for *Action Comics* No. 1.

Sent to Earth as the only surviving inhabitant of the destroyed planet Krypton, baby Kal-El is found in a rocket vessel by Kansas farmers. They raise him as Clark Kent and he attempts to blend with humans, even as his superpowers begin to manifest. With a strong sense of morality, Kent goes to work at a newspaper in the fictional city of Metropolis. To hide his true identity from the public, he dons his blue and red flying outfit with the iconic **S** emblazoned on his chest when fighting crime as Superman. Often on the scene as journalist Clark Kent, Superman frequently makes use of public telephone booths to change outfits.

In 1938, the Civil Aeronautics Act creates the Civil Aeronautics Authority; all civil aviation oversight is transferred from the Bureau of Air Commerce. Buick introduces the "Flash-Way Directional Signal," an innovation that will facilitate traffic flow and safety.

The British RAF Balloon Command is established.

As war looms over Europe, Britain turns to plans that date back to WWI: aerial mines strung on balloons. Known as barrage balloons, these lighter-than-air mines are tethered together with cables. When a plane flies between them, snagging the cables, they explode and deploy parachutes, grounding the plane to great effect. By deploying barrage balloons in aprons around a strategic location, the RAF is able to direct enemy planes to fly above them, making them prime targets for anti-aircraft guns.

In 1937, British military balloonists are based out of four stations spread around the south of the country. By 1938, the Balloon Command is established to take over the tasks of deploying, operating, and repairing the balloons and equipment. Within the year, almost 50 squadrons are formed.

The Nazis send several Zeppelins on a reconnaissance mission.

 In August of 1939, several Zeppelins head to the coast of Great Britain on a reconnaissance mission. Loaded with radio, magnetic, and photographic devices, the airships attempt to tap into Britain's aircraft radio frequencies. The range of frequencies searched is too high, however, and the mission is a failure. Soon afterward, Goering declares the Zeppelin line to be useless and decommissions all military Zeppelins in use.

Britain's radar outposts begin to network their findings in real time, allowing control centers to map out enemy plane movements.

British pilots fight to repel the German invasion of their homeland.

After their unsuccessful attempt to help the French resist the westward advance of the Germans on the mainland, the British were barely able to evacuate their troops home from Dunkirk and now they must brace for a German invasion. The Battle of Britain takes place in 1940 as German fighter planes embark from their bases in defeated France and fly across the channel to bomb airfields, infrastructure and London itself. With as little as 10 hours training, young pilots bravely dog fight the superior forces of the Luftwaffe. British pilots inflict significant losses but do not actually defeat the German campaign, rather Hitler resets his sights eastward and moves the bulk of his forces toward Russia.

1940

Cocky young U-boat captains sink venerable British ships.

This is a propaganda coup, making Germany seem agile and unstoppable and marring the facade of British supremacy.

The U-boat commander Friedrich Guggenberger, born in 1915, eventually sinks 17 ships before his capture in 1943. He sinks the British aircraft carrier HMS Ark Royal in 1941

More Stinson Reliants are produced.

Stinson Reliants are used as training planes and to haul cargo, fulfilling many civilian and military needs. They are constructed of steel tubing and fabric.

Airliners are pressurized.

The Boeing 307 Stratoliner, employed by TWA and Pan Am, carries more than 30 passengers and a crew of six. Innovations in fuselage design enable the Stratoliner to fly comfortably at 20,000 ft.

Supplies are dropped behind enemy lines.

The U.S. Air Force develops a specialized container, more accurate than a parachute for dropping supplies. The "*Sky Hook*" is a bulbous case made of hard plastic and capable of carrying about 65 pounds of supplies. Based on the shape and principles that make maple tree seeds effective, the "*Sky Hook*" possesses a single wooden-framed wing covered in airplane cloth.

America enters the war, after the attack on Pearl Harbor.

Almost the entire American Pacific Theatre Fleet is anchored in Hawai'i, in December of 1941, making an easy target for the Japanese. However, the three largest aircraft carriers are absent, out at sea. Most Americans had been unwilling to enter the war, but American industry responds to the attack by immediately ramping up and recruits sign up for service.

The Army Air Corps splits away from the Army and becomes the U.S. Air Force.

An all-black flying unit is formed.

Alfred "Chief" Anderson of the Tuskegee Institute becomes the first black pilot to fly a First Lady when he takes Eleanor Roosevelt up for a short flight in 1941. This garners much positive publicity for the program. Mrs. Roosevelt herself arranges to loan almost $200,000 to build a dedicated airfield.

Moton Field in Tuskegee, Alabama will serve as the home base and place of instruction for all African-American pilots during the segregated Jim Crow years. The term **Tuskegee Airmen** refers to both pilots and support crew.

The first all-black flying unit is formed— the 99th Pursuit Squadron.

In 1941, the RAF Balloon Command employs women as Fabric Operators. Soon, women in the Air Force are operating balloons. By 1942, 15,700 women have replaced some 10,000 men in the Balloon Command ranks. Squadrons of Barrage Balloons abroad, however, are still deployed by male operators.

Germany can't maintain synthetic oil production levels and moves to take Crimean oil fields.

The Germans make oil from their own coal reserves. The oil and gas fields and pipelines of Ukraine are also strategic resources.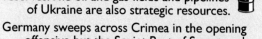

Germany sweeps across Crimea in the opening offensive but the Soviet Port of Sevastopol, home to the Russian Black Sea Fleet, holds out for months.

Industry expands not just by producing ships, planes, and guns, but also rations and cigarettes for the troops; the tobacco lobby persuades the war department to give cigarettes to all GIs.

It is the perfect war to unite Americans, industrialize America further, and allow the captains of industry to consolidate power at home and set the stage for later international expansion.

American production lines ramp up.

A Bat Bomb is envisioned.

A dentist, while on vacation at Carlsbad Caverns, watches the colony of bats and envisions a new weapon to use on the flammable structures found throughout Japan. If bats were to be released over Japan just before dawn with small, timed bombs strapped onto them, they would carry the bombs to hard-to-reach places as they search for roosts among the bamboo and rice paper structures. He imagines the extensive damage and suggests the idea to his friend, First Lady Eleanor Roosevelt.

The inventor of napalm will be brought in to head the project, which will progress despite accidents caused when the bats roost under fuel tanks at the testing grounds, until the nuclear bomb program is well under way.

Aircraft carriers change naval strategy.

The Battle of the Coral Sea takes place during four days in May of 1942, and is the first naval battle where ships from the opposing sides had no visual contact with one another, and aircraft were the sole determinants of the outcome.

While it may be recorded that the Japanese Naval forces are able to win a tactical victory over those four days in the Coral Sea, Allied forces are able to disable two fleet carriers and prevent them from engaging in the Battle of Midway the following month.

American industry and society change in response and reaction to the war.

America comes closer to realizing some of its original dreams of democracy in the war against the Nazis.

Women and African Americans are allowed access to a greater variety of jobs as men are mobilized to the war theater. Americans meet other Americans, breaking down regional and class barriers. Americans are treated as liberators – even by many in the Axis.

Japanese Americans are interred, however, and government propaganda foments hatred against "The Yellow Peril." Protests against the war effort are few. Many German-Americans change their surnames.

Many planes are shipped overseas, reassembled, and tested by brave test pilots.

Heinkel *Uhu* comes with ejection seats.

This night-fighter rolls off the production-line with twin ejection seats, advanced radar gear mounted on the nose, a pressurized cockpit, and remote control gun turrets.

American aluminum improves.

The U.S. and other countries begin producing their own 7075 aluminum. This alloy will soon replace most currently-used aluminum mixtures in airplane production. It works well under compression loading and has a 70,000 psi yield strength. Aluminum begins to replace wood or other metal alloys for structural members, and as plating and sheeting to replace fabric skins. Demand for aluminum in the U.S. for airplane manufacture prompts scrap metal drives.

The German V-2 rocket is deadly.

March 1942 sees the first test launches of the V-2, the "wonder weapon" Hitler had dreamed of, the world's first **ballistic missile**. Early models were controlled by onboard analogue computers, with later models using radio signals to direct flight.

The V-2 rocket successfully kills 12,000 people, while 20,000 more die working in the V-2 production slave labor camps.

Buoyant aircraft carriers built of ice are tested.

The idea of using ice or other unusual materials to build ships is not new. The U.S. and Canada had previously built a 1,000 ton ship at Patricia Lake in the Canadian Rockies. Although the ship took only a month to build and resisted melting away for more than a season, it was not viable because the plain ice it was made of was too fragile, even at thicknesses in excess of a foot.

Japanese pilots begin to fly Kamikaze missions.

Aluminum begins to be used to replace wood or other metal alloy structural members, and as plating and sheeting to replace fabric skins.

FDR flies in a requisitioned Pan Am Boeing 314 "Dixie Clipper" 5,500 miles to the Casablanca Conference to meet with the Allies to decide the course of the war.

Henry Ford, distraught by the death of test pilot Harry J Brooks, a personal friend who died in 1931 while testing the Ford Flivver, finally rebrands the project and resumes development under the name "SkyCar." With a rear-mounted pusher propeller and room for two people riding tandem, the SkyCar is designed to be a short-distance commuter.

Ford is quoted saying, "Mark my word: a combination airplane and motorcar is coming. You may smile, but it will come."

The V-2 rocket causes mass destruction when its payloads reach London.

Then the principal advocate for the ice ship project, Geoffry Pyke comes across a report written by Herman Mark, a polymer scientists displaced from his home of Vienna, Austria by the Nazis. The report describes using wood pulp or cotton fibers to strengthen plastics that are brittle when pure. Pyke directs those working on the ice ship project (codenamed *Project Habakkuk*) to experiment with wood pulp, creating what would come to be known as 'Pykrete'.

Women Airforce Service Pilots fly.

The WASPs are trained to fly U.S. military aircraft. With their male counterparts busy flying combat missions, the women transport cargo, ferry aircraft from factories to military bases, test newly repaired and overhauled planes, and tow aerial targets for simulated strafing missions with live ammunition. Between 1942 and 1944, they fly more than 60 million miles in a variety of aircraft, providing services essential to the war effort.

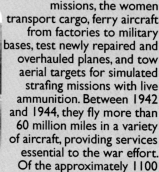

Of the approximately 1100 WASP pilots to serve, 11 will die in training and 27 will die in active duty. Those killed are considered civilians rather than official members of the military and their bodies are sent home at family expense, without military honors or notes of heroism or even a flag draped over their casket.

Barrage balloons defend coastlines.

After designing large kites for advertising purposes, Domina Jalbert files a patent for a balloon with a stiffened flexible wing and is hired to design and manufacture barrage balloons to protect the coastline of the Western U.S. In 1944, he files a patent for a combination kite-balloon with a stiffened flexible wing, forming what is now known as a "kytoon."

The U.S. is the only country to employ piloted airships during World War II. Airships are used by the Navy for everything from search and rescue, reconnaissance, and minesweeping to marine escort and submarine spotting. Balloons, however, were used by both Allied and Axis powers.

De-icing systems improve.

A rubberized electric heating coil is run along the leading edges of wings and propellers. This system, created by the U.S. Rubber Co. can prevent icing or eliminate ice that has already formed.

Japan uses the Jet Stream to create an intercontinental weapon, the Fire Balloon.

Between November 1944 and April 1945, over 9,000 hydrogen balloons are released from the island of Honshu, Japan under the direction of General Kusaba. Each carries a payload of explosive or incendiary devices, designed to be carried by the newly-discovered Jet Stream for several days and dropped onto U.S. and Canadian cities, farmland, and forests. Carrying over 1,000 lbs of equipment, each of these balloons is able to correct its own altitude by dropping ballast or venting hydrogen to better stay within the air current.

Only around 300 of these balloons will be found, with many more estimated to have landed in remote locations. While Fire Balloons will be found as far east as the outskirts of Detroit, the only casualties of this attack are a Sunday School teacher and five pupils in Oregon.

An autopilot device controls the takeoff, transatlantic flight, and landing of a U.S. Air Force C-54.

Bombing targets and techniques change.

Many pilots, especially American pilots, are reluctant to target population centers instead of military targets.

The city of Dresden, with its narrow streets and large buildings, is selected to attempt to create a **fire-storm**.

In the first round Blockbuster bombs rip into roofs and blow off doors. Then a huge number of incendiary bombs are dropped

As the buildings burn, a column of hot air rises. As air on the ground moves in to replace the rising air, winds in the narrow streets reach hurricane force. This bombing technique is so effective that people are killed even in basements two stories deep.

1945

German engineers develop jet fighters..

The single-engine Heinkel He 162A Spatz, the fastest of the first generation of jets, is built with a new type of ejection seat. Cartridges fire when activated, launching the seat up along a set of rails and out of the plane.

A crash proof flight recorder is built.

This device inscribes the various data being collected during flight onto copper foil spools. By the end of the war, these devices prove so useful that the British Ministry of Aircraft Production will pressure the inventors, Len Harrison and Vic Husband, to sign over their rights to it.

America drops the atomic bomb.

Americans win the race to develop the atomic bomb and unleash it on Japan to prove their power and hasten the war's end.

The Enola Gay, a B29, drops the bomb on Hiroshima

German rocket scientists are recruited

After the war ends, more than 1,600 German scientists, engineers, and technicians, among them Wernher von Braun and his V-2 rocket team, are recruited to work for the U.S. government under the program known as Operation Paperclip.

The Electric Boat Company buys Canadair from the Canadian government for $10 million in 1946. At the time of purchase, the company and production line are in shambles but this is soon reversed.

In 1946, the U.S. Congress approves federal financial aid to expand and promote civilian airport development, radar is applied to civilian air traffic control centers, and the Civil Aeronautics Administration (CAA) takes over the responsibility of takeoff and landing operations at airports.

Fulton attempts a flyable car.

In 1946, Robert Edison Fulton Jr. begins work on a roadable aircraft called the Airphibian. With four aircraft-sized independently suspended wheels, a detachable aluminum-body car, and fabric wings, the prototype is certified by the CAA in 1950. This design leaves the wings and tail of the craft at the airport, allowing the car section to be driven off. Without any formal training, Fulton will log more than 100,000 miles testing the Airphibian. Fulton's later financial problems will force him to sell the Continental Inc. company, and the project will be discontinued.

The first picture of Earth from space is taken.

Shortly after World War II, the U.S. reassembles captured Nazi V-2 rockets and uses them in a series of atmospheric tests. Rockets sent into the stratosphere sample atmospheric pressure and gas composition, and help pave the way for human space travel. In 1946 a V-2 rocket reaches 65 miles in altitude, and takes the first pictures of Earth from space.

The International Civil Aviation Organization (or ICAO) is formed. This organization establishes aviation standards for aeronautics to ensure safety. One immediate and lasting effect of the ICAO is the standardization of the types, patterns, colors, and strobe rates of runway approach lighting and beacons.

The *Spruce Goose* flies once.

Howard Hughes seeks to change the way that troops and supplies are transported around the world from the United States. The *H-4 Hercules* is the world's largest flying boat, intended to circumvent the constant threats to Allied ships presented by German U-boats. Wartime rationing, however, restricts the use of aluminum so the plane is built out of wood. With a wingspan of 320 feet, it is built to carry over 700 troops or 60 tons of supplies (including vehicles) across the Atlantic. The war ends before it is completed and it makes only one flight, with Hughes at the controls in 1947.

In 1946, the Bell Model 47B becomes the first certified civilian helicopter. Morphs of this chopper will serve in the Korean War, as crop dusters, training ships, aerial photography vessels, and power line patrollers.

Previously under the oversight of the Army, the U.S. Air Force becomes an independent entity within the military in 1947.

Truman signs the National Security Act of 1947 aboard the *Sacred Cow*, a C-54 Skymaster. Commissioned by FDR for official transportation, the *Sacred Cow* had a radio phone, sleep section, and a specially-designed wheelchair lift for FDR.

Test pilots break the sound barrier.

Flown by Air Force Captain Chuck Yeager, a bright orange "X-1" named *Glamorous Glennis*, flies faster than the speed of sound on October 17, 1947. Built by Bell Aircraft, the X-1 also carries the first Pitot-static tube to pass through the sound barrier.

Super Sonic flight is achieved in 1947.

Pilots must pay close attention to the danger of **wake turbulence**.

Wakes are patterns of turbulence. Boaters must deal with them too; the wake left by a passing ship can upset or at least affect small boats nearby. Wake turbulence from aircraft has two components, jet wash and wingtip vortices. Jet wash is caused by gasses expelled by the jet engines and, although this is extremely turbulent, it is of short duration. Wingtip vortices are far more stable and drift slowly downward over a long period of time.

Wingtip vortices occur when lift is being generated. Air from the higher pressure region below the wing is drawn up around the tip of the wing, spiraling off like a small, horizontal tornado.

In the airport environment, wake turbulence is common because aircraft that are taking off or landing operate at high angles of attack. The danger is compounded by the fact that aircraft are at low altitudes; if an aircraft is upset, there is little time to recover.

This modern, color-enhanced image from NASA shows that colored smoke rising from the ground is disturbed by the wake.

In 1948, Eisenhower becomes the first president ever to fly in a helicopter aboard a Bell H-13J. Two were purchased and modified to serve as evacuation vehicles for the president in event of an attack from the USSR.

The Berlin Airlift defies the Soviet blockade.

Soviet troops blockade supply shipments by road, rail, and water to the West German city of Berlin, which is an enclave within the Soviet Union. The U.S. and UK seek to outmaneuver the Soviets without giving up the city or starting a new war. The solution is the **Berlin Airlift**. C-54 and C-47 cargo planes begin landing food, water, fuel, and medical supplies in closely-timed 'stacks,' with some planes landing just three minutes apart. The operation leads to the suspension of the blockade by the Soviets within a year.

1948

Orville Wright dies of a heart attack in 1948.

The theory that the Universe is expanding from a point of origin is nicknamed **The Big Bang Theory** in 1949 by its staunchest critic.

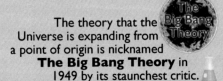

Bomb profiles take a lead from airship design.

The air-dropped Mark 3 nuclear bomb, better known as Fat Man (dropped on Nagasaki), is deemed to have performed terribly from a ballistics viewpoint. The next generation produced, the Mark 4, is redesigned for better targeted drops (relative aerodynamics), and better ballistics. The Mark 4 nuclear bombs' shape is based on the U.S. Navy's C-class blimps.

Commercial airliners get jet engines.

The prototype for the de Havilland DH 106 Comet commercial jetliner makes its first flight in 1949. It has a sleek aerodynamic design, pressurized cabin, and four turbo jet engines built into its wings but square cabin windows.

The Comet has square windows..

The Soviets introduce the Tupolev Tu-4 bomber, a unlicensed reverse engineered copy of the American B-29.

Donald Piccard founds the Ballooning Club of America in 1948. Son of Jean Felix and Jeannette Piccard, Don continues his explorer family's legacy of innovation while popularizing ballooning as a sport. He improves balloon materials and simplifies the techniques needed to operate a balloon safely.

The Soviets detonate an atomic bomb.

Nicknamed Joe-1 (for Joseph Stalin) by the Americans, the test in August 1949 proves the Soviet Union's has atomic weapons. The U.S. no longer has a monopoly on this technology.

Despite the officially-declared end of segregation within the U.S. military in 1948, the Tuskegee Airman still face racist harassment within the Air Force. At the 1949 U.S. Continental Gunnery Meet, four pilots from the 332nd Fighter Wing take first place in the conventional fighter class. Their perfect scores and previous admirable service records change the opinions of many white servicemen, including commanders and top brass.

American Overseas Airways (owned by American Airlines) is sold to Pan Am in 1950.

Cruise control is invented by engineer Ralph Teeter.

Bill Lear develops a more compact, precise autopilot device for use in fighter jets. The F-5 autopilot then earns the 1949 Collier aeronautics trophy.

Propeller driven airliners continue to improve.

The E77 Balloon Bomb is a biological weapon.

It is designed for the U.S. Army in 1950 as a vehicle for biological warfare targeting crops. Large amounts of feathers infected by cultures of anti-crop agents such as wheat stem rust would be released at high altitudes, disseminting the agents across a wide range. Despite being designated as deployment-ready, the E77 is never used.

Bombers and freighters are converted to passenger airliners.

The Korean War, 1950-1953, see extensive use of helicopters and jet aircraft.

Perhaps the first practical helicopter with only a single rotor, the Sikorsky H-19 Chickasaw is the first in the S-55 series. By moving the engine into the nose of the ship and the passenger cabin to just below the rotors, previous center-of-gravity issues are resolved. Originally designed for arctic rescue missions, choppers from the S-55 series will serve in all major U.S. military missions of the 1950's and 60's. Modified civilian versions are used in the helicopter airline services.

Sikorsky helicopters like the S-52 (left) and the Sikorsky H-5 serve as the primary medical evacuation vehicles during the Korean War. Wounded are carried inside, unlike on other models, which place the wounded in pods arranged alongside the fuselage. Notably, the layout of the S-52 solves many of the center-of-gravity issues that plague small utility helicopters, simply by putting the engine directly below the rotors.

Having worked for Sikorsky Aircarft Corp. after college, Charles Kaman forms **Kaman Aircraft,** in 1951. Kaman's first helicopter flies in 1947. The K-125 is first produced as a crop duster, with a pair of intermeshing rotors and servos incorporated into the rotor flaps. Modifications lead to the Kaman K-225, the first helicopter powered by a gas turbine. The K-225 proves the viability of gas turbines in helicopters and both the Navy and Coast Guard order models.

Britain becomes a nuclear power.

Operation Hurricane, developed in response to U.S. isolationism after the war, is the first test of an atomic weapon by the U.K. The weapon, a plutonium implosion device, is assembled at the Atomic Weapons Research Establishment on Foulness Island off the coast of Essex and transported via frigate to Australia's Montebello Islands. The bomb is detonated inside the hull of the HMS Plym to mimic the effects of a smuggled weapon. It explodes nearly 9 ft below the water line and leaves a 20 ft by 980 ft crater on the seabed. Britain is now officially the third nuclear superpower, after the Soviet Union and the U.S.

Jet aircraft dogfight.

In the early days of the war, Americans have undisputed air supremacy but Russian made MiG-15s soon enter the fray.

The first jet to jet skirmish soon follows when four MiGs fly across the Yalu River into South Korean airspace and USAF F-80C fighters engage them. Lt. Russel Brown gets the historic first kill.

The MiGs are agile and powerful and prevent the Americans from using their bombers, propeller driven B-29 Superfortresses, with impunity. The Americans soon add F86 Sabres to their fleets.

Thousands of planes will be flown on both sides and hundreds will be shot down. Americans refer to the area where most of the encounters occur as MiG Alley.

The Rogallo wing is patented.

In 1951, Dr. Francis Rogallo and his wife, Gertrude, are granted a patent for the "Flexi-Kite, the first flexible-wing kite to fly with the stability and shape of a parachute and the lift of an airplane wing. The patent is issued in Gertrude's name, to honor the significance of her role in the research and development of the project. The Flexi-kite is marketed as a toy, the proceeds from which finance the Rogallo's research.

A Cold War grips the planet in the west and in the east.

Radioactive elements fallout.

Testing is required to develop new nuclear weapons and their delivery systems. Radioactive fallout from Soviet and U.S. tests causes health concerns. The radioactive fallout from this period settles in sedimentary layers worldwide, providing an easily identified time horizon in the geologic record.

The Experimental Aircraft Association forms.

Airfields and airports for general aviation are plentiful and popular in America.

Many trained pilots are among the veterans returning from the war. Government surplus aircraft can be bought by enthusiasts of modest means.

In Milwaukee, Wisconsin, a group of pilots and engineers led by Paul Poberezny form the Experimental Aircraft Association (EAA) in 1953. The use of the term 'Experimental' comes from being required to display the word prominently on the door of home-built airplanes. The term is applied to 'Experimental Aircraft', which refers to airplanes used for educational or recreational purposes only. The EAA's first Annual Convention and Fly-In is held at Timmerman Field in Milwaukee, Wisconsin, with 150 people in attendance.

Jet engines propel by throwing air backwards at high speeds.

Jet engines, also called gas turbines, use rotary blades spinning at high speeds. Fresh air entering in the front is compressed by a series of fans and then sprayed with fuel in the combustion chamber and ignited with a spark. The burning gas/fuel mixture expands dramatically in volume and the pressure inside rises. As the gasses are released, blasting out through the nozzle at the back of the engine, the aircraft is propelled forward because, as Newton's third law states, every action has an equal and opposite reaction.

'Duck and Cover' is recommended.

American citizens, aware of the destruction caused by atomic bombs dropped by the U.S. on Hiroshima and Nagasaki, become terrified when the Soviets explode their first atomic bomb in 1949. In an attempt to achieve "emotion management," the newly formed Federal Civil Defense Administration (FCDA) comes up with the "Duck and Cover" campaign, which consists of public service announcements, classroom films, and army manuals. Though Duck and Cover provides no protection from radiation, it is considered effective in reassuring some of the public that it is possible to survive the tremendous heat and blast damage produced by an atomic bomb.

The "Cold War" between the democracies of the West (led by the U.S.) and the communist countries of eastern Europe (led by the Soviet Union) begins shortly after WWII ends. Although war is never officially declared, the two superpowers fight through proxy wars like the Korean War, the Vietnam War, the Yom Kippur War, and the Soviet Afghanistan War. The arms race ramps up, as does the space race.

The first jetliner crash is minor.

After flying over 30,000 passengers in its first year, a Comet 1 jetliner endures its first, but minor, crash in 1952. The Comet carries distinguished passengers such as the Queen of England.

The Electric Boat Company, becoming more involved in aerospace technology and development, changes its name to General Dynamics in 1952.

1953

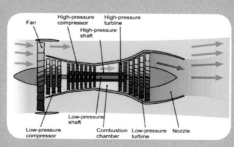

Not all of the power of expanding gas is used for thrust; some of the exhaust is used to turn a turbine that is connected to the intake compressor, enabling the process to continue.

French Colonial power in Vietnam is resoundingly defeated.

Ho Chi Mihn had argued for Vietnam's independence at Versailles but had been excluded from the official treaty negotiations and the Allies allowed the French to keep their Southeast Asian colonial possessions. Finding it increasingly difficult to manage this colony, the French adopt a new strategy of creating large military bases in remote locations. They hope that, by locating the bases far from population centers, they will not be subject to guerrilla warfare, and they assume they can keep the bases supplied by air.

At the battle of Dien Bien Phu, the French realize that they have underestimated the will of the Vietnamese people. The Vietnamese had dismantled their artillery into pieces which they transported by foot through hundreds of miles of roadless jungle to challenge the French base of Dien Bien Phu. After they install their artillery around the base and set up anti-aircraft guns to keep the French from resupplying, the French surrender and end their colonial aspirations for IndoChina.

The Comet is grounded.

20 minutes after taking off from Rome, the first Comet that had come off the production line, Comet G-ALYP, breaks up in midair. All 35 on board are killed. The cause of the disaster is a mystery because of a lack of witnesses and incomplete radio transmissions.

Later in the year, another Comet, G-ALYY (*Yoke Yoke*), crashes into the Mediterranean, killing all 21 on board. The fleet of Comets is grounded and production is halted. Investigation and testing reveal high stress concentrations on the air frame near the corners of the square windows.

Crimea is transferred from Russia to Ukraine.

Crimea had the designation of 'autonomous republic' within the Soviet Union until 1944 when its status was changed to 'province.' In 1954, Khrushchev transfers it to Ukraine as a friendly gesture to old supporters. This transfer seems of little consequence because all provinces are ultimately controlled by centralized Soviet authority. The port of Sevastopol, on the Crimean Peninsula, is the Soviet Union's only warm water port and a key base for Soviet Nuclear Submarines.

The U.S. Navy builds 4 super-carriers.

Four ships in the *Forrestal*-class of aircraft carriers are built between 1952 and 1955, the first true supercarriers.

Carrying up to 100 fighter jets and displacing up to 75,000 tons of water, these behemoths integrate bomb-proof armor plating into their flight and hangar decks. The original supercarriers have several design flaws that will be addressed in future modifications, most notably the placement of aircraft elevators (one of which was directly in the flight-path of the angled launch/recovery deck).

The Convair F-102 Delta Dagger features rocket-propelled ejection seats.

Aircraft speeds have been steadily climbing, generating a need for safer and faster emergency measures. At high speeds, manual bail-out from an aircraft is impossible, and the solid propellants used to eject in previous systems are not adequate to allow the pilot clear of the airframe in time.

Air Force One makes its first official flight.

The Air Force One designation is established after a civilian commercial flight with a call sign that is very similar to the previous presidential designation flies into the same airspace as the plane carrying Eisenhower.

Eisenhower orders 4 prop planes for presidential use, 2 Lockheed C-1212's and 2 Aero Commander Constellations.

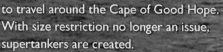
A Bell Model 47 helicopter flies the first television news flight for KTLA in Los Angeles, California.

General Dynamics creates a defense contractor division within the company to research and develop atomic-based technologies in July of 1955, named General Atomics. General Atomics will go on to create the TRIGA (Training, Research, Isotopes, General Atomics) class of small nuclear reactors. They are designed to be as safe as possible and to be used in scientific institutions, private and university research, and isotope production.

Hot air ballooning soars into a new renaissance.

This is made possible by the concentrated fuels kerosene and, later, propane, burned in portable 'can'-burners by innovators such as Ed Yost. The hot air balloon features prominently in the re-release of the movie The Wizard of Oz, in which the Wizard flees Oz in a hot air balloon.

Until 1956, all oil tankers were built to fit through the Suez Canal. The Suez Crisis forces oil tankers to travel around the Cape of Good Hope. With size restriction no longer an issue, supertankers are created.

1956

Meigs Field, Chicago is the busiest single-strip airport in the US.

The Boeing 707 jet airliner becomes a commercial success.

Pan American World Airlines becomes the first customer of the 707, ordering 20 jets to increase their passenger capacities from the prop airliners they already have.

The 707's biggest competitor, the Douglas DC-8, was rolling off the production line at the end of 1959, putting Boeing and its customers leagues ahead of other airliner operators.

Stellar nuclear fusion is described.

While searching for evidence of his Steady-State Universe Theory, Fred Hoyle figures out the mechanics of how stars work. In the cores of stars, many small atoms are fused into a lesser number of medium-sized ones, liberating energy and causing stars to shine. This information propels the sciences of astronomy, astrophysics, and nuclear physics forward and seems, at first, to help the Steady State Model by showing that new matter can be created. But the new matter created by stars uses hydrogen for the starting fuel and it is only the Big Bang Model that has an explanation for the origin of the hydrogen atoms.

1957

The Soviets launch Sputnik and win the first round of the Space Race.

Sputnik I is launched into space atop an R-7 Semyorka, the world's first intercontinental ballistic missile (ICBM). Controlled by radio and powered by two-stage rocket engines (one liquid oxygen, the other kerosene), this missile can carry its thermonuclear warhead up to 8,800 km.

The Soviets beat the Americans into space with the launch of the Sputnik I satellite in 1957. Its beeping radio signal can be detected by HAM radio operators in the US. It orbits Earth every hour and a half, and the 90 minute repetition of its incessant beep builds a frenzied tempo and is a psychological spark in the fire of the Cold War and the space race.

The Soviet R-7 is the world's first ICBM.

In August of 1957, the Soviet R-7 missile flies over 3700 miles, becoming the world's first ICBM capable of delivering a hydrogen bomb. The same R-7 launch vehicle is used later that year to send Sputnik, the first artificial satellite, into space. Vostok, a derivative of the R-7, will be used in 1961 for the first human spaceflight in history. 60 years after its first launch, a modernized version of the R-7 design will still be in use as a launch vehicle for the Soviet/Russian spacecraft Soyuz.

Attendance at the EAA's Annual Convention becomes too great for Timmerman Field in Milwaukee and it moves to Rockford, Illinois.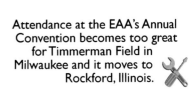

The Air Dock makes passenger access luxurious.

In 1954, United Airlines tests out their prototype of the "Air Dock," an enclosed metal walkway that attaches passenger planes to the airport terminal. Before this invention, passengers had to cross the tarmac and climb sets of removable "airstairs." While this was a fine way to board the plane in clear weather situations and provided an up-close experience with the plane itself, inclement weather often made the boarding process laborious. Although there is debate about which airport first debuted the modern "jetway," these pivoting hallways begin to be installed across the U.S. starting in 1959. Not only do they provide an all-weather entrance to the plane, but they also make the boarding process more efficient.

The National Aeronautics and Space Act of 1958 decommissions the NACA, and gives birth to the National Aeronautics and Space Administration, NASA.

The Federal Aviation Act of 1958 creates the Federal Aviation Agency (FAA), which takes over the responsibilities of the CAA and CAB.

The Soviet Union lands an unpiloted capsule on the moon.

Luna 2 becomes the first spacecraft to land on the surface of the Moon.

Eisenhower conducts a diplomatic tour of Asia by jet.

Early in 1959, Eisenhower decides that propeller-driven planes are not fit for presidential transport and permanently switches Air Force One to jet engine driven planes. In December of the same year, aboard a Boeing 707 carrying the title Special Air Mission 970 (SAM 970), Eisenhower makes a 22,000 mile goodwill tour, visiting 11 Asian countries in the "Flight to Peace."
The trip is made in roughly half the time it would have taken in a prop plane. Two more Boeing 707s are ordered for presidential use shortly thereafter, carrying the designations SAM 971 and SAM 972.

A voice message is relayed via satellite.

Project SCORE (Signal Communications by Orbiting Relay Equipment) is launched into low Earth orbit aboard a U.S. Atlas rocket in 1958. The Atlas program is the American response to the USSR's ICBM capabilities. Along with its Soviet counterpart, the Atlas rocket program sets the precedent of synergistic development between armament buildup and space-based scientific endeavors.

For years to come, most space missions –both piloted and unpiloted– will be launched aboard recommissioned ICBMs.

SCORE is the first U.S. test of a relay communications network by the US. SCORE can capture and forward voice messages from one location to another, making it the first 'store and forward' satellite launched by that government. SCORE captures the world's attention on Christmas Eve, 1958, when President Dwight D. Eisenhower sends out a Christmas message through the on-board voice recorder.

International communications are codified.

The Administrative Radio Conference of 1959 convenes in Geneva, Switzerland to codify international communications signals. Radio communications and alphabets, semaphore, and other flag-based communications are ratified. The conventions for phonetic alphabets set forth during this conference are used as the basis for all international radio communiques through the present.

The Atlas is the first American ICBM.

Many of the early tests in 1957-1958 are failures but data is gathered and modifications are made. The Atlas A (shown) is a test model which lacks a sustainer engine and separable stages. The Atlas B launches the SCORE satellite in December of 1958. The Atlas D is fully functional and capable of delivering a nuclear warhead in 1959.

Project Echo, a passive satellite communications system, reflects microwaves off huge metallic balloons deployed at high altitudes.

In 1960, NASA launches *Echo-1* into orbit but it fails to be deployed. Later that year *Echo-1A* is successfully launched. The balloon is inflated at altitude and acts as a reflector for a microwave signal emitted from the Jet Propulsion Laboratory in California and Bell Labs receives the signal at its 20-foot horn-shaped antenna in New Jersey.

World population reaches 3 billion.

Although demand for oil keeps rising, prices remain flat.

Oil-producing countries are not realizing a fair share of the profit for this resource that has become so important in the world economy. Oil prices have always been low; originally set by the oil companies and treaties imposed upon oil-producing countries decades ago. Oil-producing countries have been trying to get a larger share and to raise prices for a long time, and the formation of the Organization of Petroleum Exporting Countries (OPEC) in 1960 is the latest attempt to gain sovereign control over the resources within their borders. After the United States abandoned the Gold Standard (the Nixon Shock), the real value of the dollar declined, causing the real price of oil, which was already low, to decline as well, as it was paid for in U.S. dollars.

An active repeater satellite is launched.

Western Development Labs launches *Courier 1B*, the world's first active repeater satellite, in 1960. Preceded by a *Courier 1A*, which was lost in a launch failure only two and half minutes after liftoff, *1B* is contracted by the U.S. Air Force to expand Project SCORE's mission of improving real time communications over long distances. *Courier 1B* makes one orbit of the Earth before repeating a transmission from New Jersey to a station in Puerto Rico. Ground control will lose command of *Courier 1B* after 17 days, but the project's successes will inform the next generation of communications satellites. There are two major categories of communications satellites, passive and active. Previous to the *Courier 1B*, all satellites were **passive** and only able to bounce messages from Earth to another location, like a mirror. Due to the distances and the effect of Earth's atmosphere on the radio waves, these transmissions arrive at their destination as very weak signals. **Active satellites** instead receive transmissions and amplify them before sending them on to their destination.

Parachutes can be steered.

In 1961, French engineer Pierre Lemoigne produces the Para-Commander, a parachute with cutouts at the rear and on the sides, which allow it to be towed into the air and steered, leading to the practices of parasailing and parascending.

The Soviet satellite *Korabl-Sputnik 2* carries two dogs, 40 mice, 2 rats, and some plants into orbit and safely back to Earth in August 1960, paving the way for human space travel.

Piccard's bathyscape dives deep.

Record-setting balloonist Auguste Piccard designs deep sea bathyscapes, culminating in the *Trieste*, which is purchased by the U.S. Navy and modified for manned diving. Piccard's previous bathyscapes were lowered by cable, but the *Trieste* is self-powered. Auguste's son, Jacques Piccard, and U.S. Navy Lieutenant Don Walsh reach the deepest point on earth in the Marianas Trench, near Guam, in January of 1960. They achieve a depth of 10,911 meters, surviving water pressure equivalent to 1083 atmospheres.

Eisenhower warns of the Military-Industrial Complex.

In his farewell address, President Dwight Eisenhower warns the citizenry of the United States of the dangers of the Military-Industrial Complex.

The Military-Industrial Complex is a system of several components that interact and reinforce each other to become a politically powerful lobbying force. Industries that secure military contracts employ an army of engineers and other individuals and contractors. Research on and orders for raw materials as well as manufactured subassemblies are farmed out to corporations and institutions. Demand, or perceived need, is lobbied for as this existing system of organization naturally seeks to perpetuate itself. A vigilant and knowledgeable citizenry must monitor the military-industrial complex to keep it from defining our society and our economic system.

The Bay of Pigs invasion in Cuba is a fiasco.

In April, 1961, the U.S. attempts to overthrow Fidel Castro. Cuban nationalism has been steadily growing but many Americans and especially American business interests fail to distinguish a desire for sovereignty by third world nations from communism. Ironically, Castro's grasp on power is anything but secure until the foiled semi-covert invasion by the U.S.

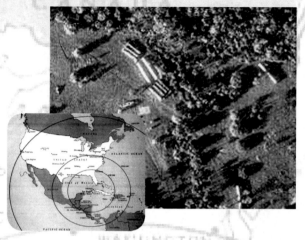

The Cuban Missile Crisis follows.

High quality photographs from high flying aircraft allow landscapes to be analyzed. One image, taken on October 14, 1962 by a U2 spy plane, shows missile transporters on the ground in Cuba. It sets off the 13 day crisis.

Another U2 spy plane, flown by Gary Powers, was shot down over the Soviet Union in 1960. The capture of Gary Powers motivates American Military and Intelligence agencies to develop better spy satellites as well as remotely piloted vehicles.

Kennedy promises to send an American to the Moon.

Satellites are put into geosynchronous and geostationary orbits.

The Hughes' family company of Syncom satellites are the first to achieve geosynchrony and geostationary orbits. *Syncom* 2 achieves geosynchronous orbit in 1963 and *Syncom* 3 achieves geostationary orbit a year later. With its position near the International Date Line, *Syncom 3* is used to broadcast a live feed of the 1964 Summer Olympics from their location in Tokyo, Japan, to the US.

OSCAR 1, the world's first amateur satellite, is launched into Low Earth Orbit as a ballast for another satellite, and transmits the message "HI" for the length of its three-week life.

The Soviet Union puts the first human in space.

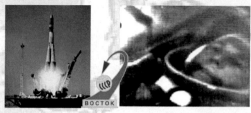

Russian Yuri Gagarin becomes the first human to enter space in April of 1961, in a Vostok spacecraft.

The Jetsons, a futuristic cartoon, premieres on ABC.

Airing at primetime, *The Jetsons* is the first show created for ABC TV to be produced entirely in color. Following the lives of the Jetson family, their dog, and their robot maid, the show displays whimsical space age dream machines.

The Soviet Union develops ABMs

The USSR conducts the the first successful Anti Ballistic Missile (ABM) tests in 1961. By 1970, they will deploy a fully operational system to defend Moscow.

Bell Labs develops the Nike-Zeus family of rockets for the U.S. military. These rockets are anti-ballistic missiles (ABM) capable of intercepting ICBMs in the upper atmosphere before they can reach their target. Initial models carry a 25 kiloton nuclear warhead, while later iterations carry 400 kiloton payloads and are able to intercept even low-orbit satellites.

An American reaches space.

Launched aboard a Mercury-Redstone rocket, Alan Shepard becomes the first American in space.

In the wake of WW II, the U.S. embarked on *Project Paperclip* and recruited more than 1,600 scientists and engineers, many of whom were involved in the Nazi regime. Among them are Wernher von Braun and Hermann Oberth, who develop the V2 rocket into the Mercury-Redstone.

A public- and privately-sponsored satellite is launched.

Developed by Bell Labs of New Jersey, operated by NASA, and partly funded by AT&T and the national post services of both Britain and France, *Telstar 1* is launched in 1962. In just a few months, it relays the first television broadcast, telephone calls, and faxes from space. Along with its sibling project, *Telstar 2*, this satellite is still in Earth's orbit, though out of commission.

The Limited Nuclear Test Ban Treaty is ratified.

The treaty prohibits nuclear explosion in the atmosphere, water, or space. Underground tests will still be allowed. Earlier versions of a test ban treaty sought to further slow the development of new weapons with a comprehensive test ban. The treaty is ratified by the Soviet Union, the US, and Britain in the fall of 1963.

Sport ballooning becomes more accessible

The earliest companies to manufacture affordable, innovative balloons are Ed Yost's *Raven Industries* and *Piccard Balloons*. The latter uses a new method for holding the weight of the basket and keeping the balloon together, using load-bearing tape along the envelope's seams. Together, Piccard and Yost become the first to cross the English Channel in a hot air balloon.

A paraglider flies.

David Barish, who was working to develop the "Sail Wing," a space capsule recovery device for NASA, tests his invention on Hunter Mountain NY. The device is a single surface airfoil, 90 ft long and 27 ft wide, made from one sheet of a boat's sail. Although Barish calls the activity "slope soaring," some say this is the first instance of paragliding. Barish later designed a smaller model - 27 ft long and 9 ft wide, that made it possible for people around the world to become paraglider.

America goes to war in Vietnam.

Commonly referred to as the *Huey*, *Bell Iroquois* helicopters fly medical evacuation missions in Vietnam and transport troops behind enemy lines.

Aluminum cans are recycled.

Although the aluminum atom is common in the Earth's crust, it takes a lot of energy to refine aluminum ore. In the 1960s, aluminum cans become not only prevalent but a waste disposal issue. Recycling of aluminum proves cost effective as it requires only 5% of the energy required to recycle ore.

Jean Felix Piccard dies in 1963 and will be commemorated on television's *Star Trek: The Next Generation* through character Captain Jean-Luc Picard.

Air Force One is a Boeing C-137 Stratoliner.

It arrives painted in gold and maroon, which JFK deems too regal and ornate for the leader of a democracy. With famous industrial designer Raymond Loewy, First Lady Jackie Kennedy redesigns the livery to be the more modest blue, white, and chrome that Air Force One will sport from now on. This plane carries the designation SAM 26000 when not transporting the president.

Shortly after Kennedy's assassination, Lyndon B Johnson is sworn into office aboard Air Force One as it carries JFK's body to the capital.

Americans are influenced by advertising.

Advertising products in order to stimulate demand is part of the American industrial economic system. Consumerism provides instant gratification as complex goods are purchased and put into use, all in the same day. Advertisements for these goods promise that the products will bring respect and happiness. Advertising also cultivates fear, implying that failure to consume certain products will lead to failure overall. The combination creates the expectation that it should be possible to accomplish great things easily without patience or perseverance, while at the same time cultivating a nagging fear of inadequacy.

1963

The first Learjet flies. Inventor Bill Lear is quoted, saying "They said I'd never build it; that if I built it, it wouldn't fly; that if it flew, I couldn't sell it. Well I did and it did and I could."

US Navy satellite *1963-38C* finally proves Kristian Birkeland's theory of the magnetosphere and the behavior of the aurora.

Spy planes fly at high altitudes.

The Strategic Reconnaissance airplane, the SR-71 Blackbird is developed in the late 1960s by Lockheed Martin's famous R&D department, commonly referred to as the Skunkworks.

The Gaia hypothesis is proposed.

J.E. Lovelock theorizes that living organisms interact with the inorganic environment to actively influence the conditions and composition of the biosphere. The hypothesis is further co-developed with micro-biologist Lynn Margulis.

Life seems to make its environment conducive to more life. For example, photosynthesizing bacteria produced free oxygen which enabled multi-cellular life to evolve. If the biosphere is disturbed, biologic responses tend to restore the environment to a nurturing state. For example, if global temperatures fall, more land is exposed (as sea level drops) giving termites more habitat and termites excrete methane which is a powerful green house gas.

The Cosmic Background Radiation is detected.

The horn-shaped antenna becomes obsolete after a new system replaces *Echo* and scientists are allowed to use it for research in astronomy in 1964. They seek to identify the different radio signals emitted by galaxies. In attempting to reduce the background static in the device, they realize that there is a low

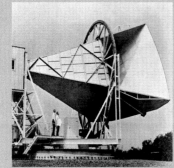

level of background radiation emanating from all directions of space.

They contact some astrophysicists for an explanation. They happen to contact the very scientists who are looking for the relic radiation signal of the Big Bang. The astrophysicists ask them the frequency of the ubiquitous static and immediately realize that the CBR has been found; the afterglow of the Big Bang has been detected!

Scientific balloons improve.

Echo 2 is launched in 1964. It is larger and more rigid than its predecessor. When fully inflated, it is 41 m in diameter but fits into a small, suitcase-sized packet for transport to orbit.

Dr. Strangelove debuts in 1964.

Dr. Strangelove or: How I Learned to Stop Worrying and Love the Bomb is a movie that satirizes the Cold War strategy of mutually assured destruction (MAD).

Cosmonaut Alexei Leonov becomes the first human to perform a space walk.

In early 1960, a new space program is envisioned as a follow up to *Project Mercury*. Only one astronaut was able to fit in the Mercury capsule, and this new project – *The Apollo Program* – will carry three.

A commercial satellite reaches geosynchronous orbit.

Built by the Hughes Aircraft Company, the *Intelsat 1* is the first commercial communications satellite in geosynchronous orbit.

Carrying the codename "Early Bird" (referring to the 'early bird gets the worm' proverb), *Intelsat 1* is launched in 1965 for NASA under the supervision of the Communications Satellite Corporation. With the Syncom family of satellites, the Hughes Corporation proves the feasibility of geosynchronous communications satellites. In operation for four years, this satellite will provide the first live television coverage of a spacecraft splashdown, for the *Gemini 6* craft.

A drone hunts submarines.

The Gyrodyne drone anti-sub helicopter (DASH) hunts Russian submarines. It carries two torpedoes, and was originally intended to be able to carry a nuclear depth charge. Mostly deployed from old destroyers that are too small to service full-sized helicopters, this drone is also used in Vietnam for spotting gunfire off ships.

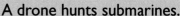

Helicopters become iconic in the skies of Vietnam.

The U.S. Marines' first turbine-powered assault helicopter, the Boeing-Vertol Sea Knight (left) is used extensively in Vietnam. The Sea Knight will see service in almost every major military action to come, including disaster and humanitarian relief.

The Bell Cobra (below) is expressly built as a gunship for U.S. military. Debuting in South Vietnam in 1967, it will remain a vital component of U.S. air strength until being replaced by the Apache in the 80's and 90's. Versions are still used by the U.S. Marines and other nations.

The Apollo 1 astronauts die.

During a pre launch test, *The Apollo 1* mission suffers a launchpad fire that kills the 3 astronauts aboard.

Surveyor 1, an unpiloted probe, performs the first U.S. soft-landing on the Moon.

Luna 9, an unpiloted USSR spacecraft, achieves the first ever soft-landing on the Moon in 1966, making it also the first spacecraft to send back data from the surface of a planetary body other than Earth.

The USSR's *Orbita* satellite family provides the satellite coverage for the world's first satellite-driven national television network, in 1967.

Hang-gliding becomes popular.

In the mid 1960's, plans begin to circulate for hang gliders that incorporate the Rogallo wing, which bends and flexes in the wind.

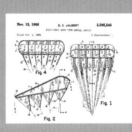

The parafoil is the precursor to the paraglider.

In 1966, Jalbert files a patent for the ram-air double-surfaced fully flexible airfoil that becomes the basis for all parafoils in use today and serves as the precursor to the paraglider.

The Saturn V makes its first unmanned flight

The Saturn V is a three-stage, liquid-fueled, super heavy-lift, expendable rocket developed to support the Apollo program. It is the tallest, heaviest, and most powerful rocket ever launched, and will become the only launch vehicle to carry humans beyond low earth orbit.

1967

In 1967, the U.S. Department of Transportation is expanded and reorganized as an umbrella organization for all "air and surface transportation" responsibilities, and the FAA is renamed the Federal Aviation Administration.

The Defense Department is the aerospace industry's biggest customer.

The Defense Department influences what the aerospace industry produces and who produces it. The large budgets produce jobs while jobs produce votes and politicians approve contracts for businesses that fund their campaigns. This web of relationships and flow of resources in the economy is known as the military industrial complex.

Israel destroys the Egyptian airforce.

Egyptian military forces are mobilized along the border of the Sinai Peninsula. In June, Israel launches a string of preemptive airstrikes against Egyptian airfields. Nearly the

entire Egyptian air force is destroyed on the ground, giving Israel air superiority in the subsequent Six-Day War (also known as the Third Arab-Israeli War). In tandem with these airstrikes, Israel attacks and takes the Gaza Strip. Syria and Jordan join the conflict. Israel is victorious and takes the West Bank and the Golan Heights, expanding its borders.

The Outer Space Treaty is signed.

This document, signed by 105 countries, outlines a moral and legal framework for international law in space. It bans the placement, testing, or storage of weapons of mass destruction in outer space or on a celestial body, such as the Moon. It does not, however, ban the use or placement of conventional weapons in outer space.

Fighter planes carry deployable ordinance.

Fighter planes are no longer limited to single-purpose use but now carry ordinance for limited bombing runs.

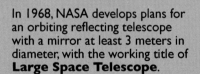

In 1968, NASA develops plans for an orbiting reflecting telescope with a mirror at least 3 meters in diameter, with the working title of **Large Space Telescope**.

Fossil fuels continue to burn.

World oil consumption keeps increasing at a fast pace, with the United States as the largest consumer. Oil companies eclipse medium sized countries in wealth and power. The temperature continues to rise, as it has since the 1850's.

Aircraft carrier systems.

Seeking to be create a defense industry independent of the British or Americans, the French design and build the *Clemenceau* aircraft carrier which is commissioned in 1961. Designed from scratch, it is state of the art and relatively smaller than its counterparts.

It incorporates features from existing carriers, like Catapult Assisted Take-Off Barrier Arrested Recovery. This system, known as CATOBAR, uses steam powered catapults to launch aircraft and another system to arrest landing aircraft.

Aircraft catchment or arresting gear consists of a series of braided steel cables or pendants that are laid across the deck of the carrier and attached to hydraulic damping systems. When an aircraft comes in for a landing, it deploys a tailhook along with its landing gear. The tailhook catches the pendants and transfers the kinetic energy of the incoming aircraft to the damping systems.

Throughout the decades, a variety of methods have been used to launch aircraft by catapult. Steam power is still the most common today but the newest generation of *Ford*-class supercarriers employ electromagnetic systems. Gunpowder, pressurized air cannons, hydraulics, and various weighted systems have all been used to assist in takeoff where long runways are not practical.

Capitalism and Communism are the only socioeconomic paradigms considered.

Humans often seem to think in just two categories; black and white, good and evil. During the cold war, the dichotomy of capitalism vs. communism will so dominate human thinking that other alternatives will rarely be considered.

Apollo 11, the first manned mission to the moon, lands in 1969.

Despite ringing computer and navigational alarms, Buzz Aldrin and Neil Armstrong land the *Eagle Lunar Lander* in the Sea of Tranquility on the moon.

We see our pale blue planet rising above the desolate lunar horizon.

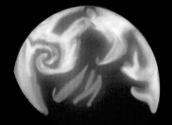

The Nimbus 3, a U.S. satellite for use in search and rescue, floats in its geosynchronous orbit after its launch in 1969.

M*A*S*H, the movie, debuts in 1970.

One of the most popular films of the early 1970s, the satirical black comedy M*A*S*H is set at a Mobile Army Surgical Hospital during the Korean War. Helicopters feature prominently in the film, their arrival signaling the start of the narrative as the characters, most of whom are doctors or nurses, spring into action to save the wounded passengers. A TV series emerges, discussing the politics of war.

1969

Groundwork for the internet is laid.

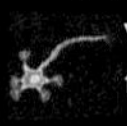

Research about "packet switching" begins: one packet switched network, ARPANET, would lead to what we now know as the internet.

With around 600 planes, attendance at EAA's Annual Convention and Fly-In again outgrows its location and moves to its permanent home in Oshkosh, Wisconsin.

The Boeing 747 debuts.

The 747's distinctive hump, wide body, and two passenger aisles gain it the nickname "Jumbo Jet." With two and a half times more capacity than the Boeing 707, the "Jumbo Jet" makes jet travel affordable to the middle class. Shown here in 1969, it makes its first commercial flights in 1970 for Pan Am.

The Soviets establish a space station.

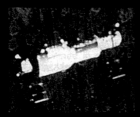

The Salyut is the first space station to enter low earth orbit. It is launched unmanned, with plans for the crew to come aboard later. The Soyuz 10 rocket carries the crew of three cosmonauts and manages to dock with the Salyut 1 but the crew is not able to transfer successfully to the station and simply returns to Earth.

The Soyuz 11 is then launched and successfully delivers a crew that stays aboard for 23 days, conducting research and experiments for both scientific and military purposes while orbiting the Earth 362 times and setting a record for time spent in space. The mission is cut short by malfunctions and the crew returns to Earth, dying upon reentry when a ventilation valve opens prematurely and depressurizes the interior of the ship. The mission is considered a success anyway.

Apollo 13 avoids disaster.

The Apollo 13 mission is launched in April of 1970, with the intention of exploring the Fra Mauro Highlands of the Moon. From the outset, the mission is plagued with hardships. When one of the second-stage engines cuts out two minutes early, the crew must compensate in order to return to the plotted course and successfully launch a third stage rocket toward a seismometer on the Moon (placed by Apollo 12) to measure seismic activity.

Just over two days into the mission, after a live television broadcast with Mission Control in Houston, an explosion occurs aboard the craft. Communications, electrical supply, and oxygen supplies within the command module are compromised, rendering the lunar landing infeasible as the Lunar Module must now act as the crew's primary source of oxygen and power. NASA's contingency plans call for trajectories that are no longer possible, most of which require ejecting the Lunar Module.

The crew and mission control devise a plan to take the Apollo 13 around the moon and use its gravity to slingshot them back toward Earth. With limited communication abilities and nothing but the supplies aboard the damaged command and lunar modules, it takes extreme cunning and ingenuity to bring the crew safely back to Earth.

Ad-hoc modifications to the CO_2 scrubbers are made to compensate for rising carbon dioxide levels. A jump starter for the powered-down command module is created, and a method of pressurizing the tunnel between modules to force the two to separate just before re-entry is devised.

The Apollo 13 splashes down in the South Pacific Ocean and the crew are aboard the recovery ship, USS Iwo Jima, in short order.

D.B. Cooper becomes the legendary hijacker.

Using the alias of Dan Cooper, a passenger boards a Northwest Orient Airlines flight from Portland, Oregon and hijacks the flight. Claiming to be in possession of a suitcase bomb, Cooper demands $200,000 in U.S. currency, four parachutes, and the means to refuel the flight on the tarmac in Seattle. The pilot tells the passengers that the flight is experiencing mechanical issues and circles the Seattle-Tacoma airport for two hours while authorities gather the demanded ransom. The flight lands on a remote area of tarmac and Cooper is given the ransom. He then releases all passengers and most flight attendants before ordering the remaining crew to head to Mexico City. With everyone but Cooper in the cockpit, the plane is depressurized and the aft airstair is lowered. When the plane lands at the Reno Airport several hours later, Cooper is nowhere to be found. Despite extensive investigations (including a blow-by-blow mid-air recreation of the events), Cooper was never found. This remains the only unresolved case of air hijacking or piracy in U.S. history.

The parafoil parachute debuts.

Theodore Hulsizer, a civilian prototype manufacturer for the US Air Force and NASA, works with Jalbert to create the first functional parafoil parachute. Previous attempts had produced such drag that the parachute was ripped to shreds. Hulsizer solved this by running the cords through rings that slid down as the parachute opened, slowing the opening.

The Vietnam war continues.

1972

Around the clock bombing missions devastate North Vietnam.

Operation Linebacker 1, conducted between May 9 and October 23, 1972, sees thousands of tons of bombs dropped on North Vietnam by B52s. Bridges and oil depots are taken out by F-4 Phantoms.

Henry Kissinger declares that 'Peace is at hand.'

Nixon's secretary of state, Henry Kissinger, makes his declaration on October 26th. Although North Vietnam has been forced to the negotiating table, talks break down without resolution.

Bombing is resumed with *Operation Linebacker 2*.

The campaign takes place between 18 and 29 December, 1972 and is nick-named *The Christmas Bombings*. In the city of Hanoi, thousands of civilians are killed. During the nights, B52s drop bombs from high altitudes and smaller bombers make the daytime raids.

In 1972, The Canadian *Anik 1* satellite is the world's first satellite-based domestic communications system to use geosynchronous orbit.

In March of 1973, American Airlines hires pilot Bonnie Tiburzi, making it the first major airline to employ a female pilot.

The first fly-by-wire flight is made.

NASA test pilot Gary Krier completes the world's first computerized fly-by-wire flight in an F-8 Crusader. The onboard computer controlling flight surfaces runs on only 38Kb of memory and is the same one used in the *Apollo 15* mission.

Hijackers threaten to use a passenger jet as a weapon.

Facing unrelated criminal charges, 3 men hijack a plane flying from Alabama to Florida. Armed with handguns and grenades, the three try to leverage their 34 hostages and a threat to fly the plane into a nuclear reactor for a $10 million U.S. ransom. This marks the first instance that hijackers threaten to use the plane itself as a weapon. The entire event will take over 30 hours and cover more than 4,000 miles, and provides the precedent required for physical screening of all U.S. airline passengers.

ABM and SALT Treaties are signed

In 1972, the US and USSR sign the Anti Ballistic Missile (ABM) treaty, limiting their strategic defense systems. Each country is allowed two defensive system sites; one for ICBM silos, and one for the capital. The treaty doesn't specifically define the word "strategic," which will later lead to misunderstandings between the two countries. They also sign the SALT treaty that freezes the number of ICBM launchers of both the countries at existing levels, and allows new submarine-based SLBM launchers only if an equal number of land-based ICBM launchers are dismantled.

Israel is invaded and oil is embargoed.

Seeking to reclaim territories lost in the Six-Day War, Egypt and Syria launch a surprise assault during the holiest day in Judaism and the Yom Kipper War begins. Egypt has acquired anti-aircraft missile defenses from the Soviet Union. American military support of Israel during this war triggers the OPEC states not only to increase oil prices but also to decrease oil production.

Airbus introduces its wide-body jet.

Beginning service in 1974, the wide-body Airbus jet becomes ubiquitous in short and medium distance flights and gains particular popularity with passenger air service in Europe. The A300 is the first twin-engine wide-body airliner and the first model produced by a consortium of aeronautical companies from Britain, France, and West Germany, **Airbus Industrie**.

The first cellular phone call is made.

In 1973, Martin Cooper of Motorola places the first cellular call to Joel S. Engel of Bell Labs. Cooper called Engel, who was also trying to build a mobile phone, to tell him that he had done it first.

Air Force One carries Nixon to the People's Republic of China in the first U.S. presidential visit to the Republic.

Executive One is a designation used only when the president travels aboard a plane that is primarily used for civilian transport. Nixon and family fly from Dulles Airport in DC to Los Angeles International Airport aboard a United Airlines DC-10 in order to "Set an example during the Energy Crisis."

Immediately after resigning, President Nixon boards *Air Force One* and flies home to California. Gerald Ford is sworn into office. While midair over Missouri, the pilot radios in to Kansas City airport to change their call sign from Air Force One to SAM 27000.

Civilian Super Sonic Transport is launched.

The Concorde flies at over twice the speed of sound. A Delta Wing helps to achieve aerodynamic efficiency in supersonic design.

Another flying car is attempted

Henry Smolinski and Hal Blake found Advanced Vehicle Engineers. The AVE Mizar combines a Ford Pinto and a Cessna Skymaster to create a car with detachable wings. It uses the engines of both the aircraft and the vehicle during takeoff, reducing the length of runway needed. Unfortunately, a wing support crumples during a test flight and both inventors are killed.

Skylab is launched.

Using a modified Saturn V rocket, the U.S. launches Skylab, an orbiting space station designed to explore how space flight may expand and enhance human well-being on Earth. Skylab is launched unmanned, equipped with the Apollo Telescope Mount and the Orbital workshop, as well as a Multiple Docking Adapter with two docking ports and an Airlock Module with extravehicular activity (EVA) hatches through which its crew will enter.

While holding the position of Vice Commander of the Military Airlift Command, former Tuskegee Airman pilot instructor Daniel "Chappie" James, Jr. is promoted, becoming the Commander in Chief, North American Air Defense Command. Along with this promotion, James becomes the first African-American to hold the rank of Four-Star General.

The Vietnam War ends with 'The Fall of Saigon' in 1975.

In their hasty departure, Americans scuttle some equipment.

The South Vietnamese Regime left in place by the Americans lingers on, but financial support is reduced in the wake of the recession. Although the South Vietnamese have more tanks than the North Vietnamese and have over 1400 aircraft, their use of this equipment is hampered by rising oil prices.

The first relay of satellite-to-satellite communications reaches its destination.

AO-6 and AO-7, or AMSAT-Oscar 6 and 7, are a pair of Phase Two amateur radio satellites of the OSCAR family, launched piggy-backed on other missions. Besides a slew of other firsts, the pair complete the first satellite-to-satellite relay (ground-AO6-AO7-ground) in January of 1975 and prove the viability and low cost of using satellites to transmit medical data.

1975

A new generation of aircraft carriers is introduced.

Named after U.S. Pacific Fleet Commander Chester W. Nimitz, there will eventually be 10 *Nimitz*-class supercarriers built. Powered by two Westinghouse A4W nuclear reactors, all are still in active use. These carriers are deployed during the Gulf War; in Iran, Iraq, and Afghanistan. With a maximum speed of 30 knots and employing the CATOBAR, Catapult Assisted Take-Off Barrier Arrested Recovery, flight deck arrangement, they typically operate 45 fighter jets, a dozen helicopters, 4 airborne early warning (AEW) aircraft, and 2 supply and cargo transport craft.

The carrier's nuclear reactors produce heat by nuclear fission. That heat is used to vaporize water into steam. The resulting increase in pressure powers turbines which turn each ship's 4 propellers.

The term **supercarrier**, although first coined by the *New York Times* in 1938 to describe a much smaller carrier, is an informal term used to refer to the largest aircraft carriers (usually 70,000+ tons of water displaced). The largest of the supercarriers are of the Ford class, which have a 100,000+ ton displacement.

The WASPs finally receive veteran status.

The Woman Airforce Service Pilots went unrecognized for many years, their records sealed and classified, and almost forgotten. When an Air Force press release erroneously states that the Air Force is training the first women ever to fly U.S. military aircraft, protest ensues. The WASPs records are released, and they are finally granted veterans status when President Jimmy Carter signs the GI Bill Improvement Act of 1977.

Promising straight talk, hard work, fair play, and justice, Jimmy Carter is elected president of the U.S.

The first of his agricultural family to pursue a professional career, Carter became a navy nuclear submarine officer. After the partial meltdown of The Chalk River Labs' experimental nuclear reactor in 1952, he headed one of the maintenance teams tasked with its cleanup. The extreme remedial measures necessitated by the spill of the radioactive materials will later influence his decision to avoid developing the neutron bomb.

On the second day of his presidency, Carter pardons all draft dodgers of the Vietnam War. During his presidency, Carter will have to deal with an energy crisis and then the Iranian Hostage Crisis.

An Indian satellite tracks shipping lanes.

Aryabhata, the Indian Space Research Organization's first communications satellite, achieves orbit aboard a rocket launched by the Soviet Union in 1975 and is used to track shipping lanes.

Pedaling above the English Channel.

US-based engineer Paul MacCready wins the second Kremer challenge to fly the first human-powered crossing of the English Channel. He had already won other prizes for his contraptions, most notably the first Kremer prize in 1977.

MacCready and his company, AeroVironment, build a craft known as *The Gossamer Albatross*. The *Albatross* has a carbon fiber frame, polystyrene wing ribs, and is wrapped in clear plastic mylar. With a canard wing in front and only a rearward single pusher propeller, it is powered by the pilot (Bryan Allen), who sits on a fixed, modified bicycle. Despite harsh headwinds, instrument failures, and fatigue, MacCready crosses the Channel in just 2 hours and 49 minutes.

Skylab does its job.

Between May 1973 and February 1974, NASA sends three manned expeditions to and from Skylab, each with a crew of three astronauts, in the Apollo Command/Service Module (Apollo CSM) launched atop the Saturn IB rocket. The crew must maneuver the CSM to the Docking Adapter while both are in low earth orbit. A backup Apollo CSM/Saturn IB is assembled for the last two expeditions in case an in-orbit rescue mission is required, but this vehicle never flies.

Gravity is used as a tool.

The *Voyager* spacecraft missions are launched 16 days apart, in 1977. They will use a gravitational assist from Jupiter before heading on different trajectories.

Star Wars debuts.

George Lucas' 1977 "epic space opera" is met with enthusiastic acclaim as well as biting criticism. Critics rail the two hour film by calling the plot shallow and banal, unable to stand on its own without special effects. The vast majority of feedback, however, is positive.

Its futuristic feel excites the audience and its storybook plot of good versus evil allows the audience to identify with the characters, who are compelled to find courage and to act decisively. But the plot is not so simple; the Galactic Empire seems as much like our own military industrial complex as it does the Soviet version. The film is a comic book come alive and sparks the imaginations of young and old alike.

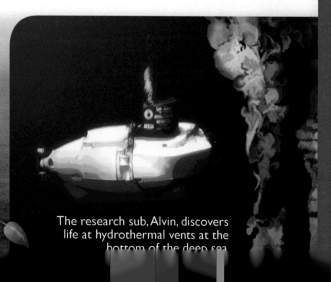

The research sub, Alvin, discovers life at hydrothermal vents at the bottom of the deep sea.

A Titan missile accidently launches.

A Titan II missile is accidentally launched in Arkanas
In September of 1980. Two members of a Propellant Transfer
System (PTS) team are checking the pressure on the oxidizer
tank of a Titan II missile at U.S. Air Force Launch complex 374-
7 in Arkansas when a socket falls off a ratchet and plummets
nearly 80 ft to the ground. The 8 lb socket bounces off a thrust
mount and pierces the exterior wall of the missile's first-stage
fuel tank, releasing a cloud of aerozine 50 fuel that, when
it comes into contact with the missile's nitrogen tetroxide
oxidizer, leads to an explosion in the silo. The explosion blows
the 740 ton door off the silo, ejecting the missile's second stage
and 9 megaton thermonuclear warhead, the most powerful
weapon in the US nuclear arsenal; more powerful than all the
bombs used in WWII combined and 600 times more powerful
than the bomb used in Hiroshima. The silo and surrounding
buildings are destroyed. The warhead cannot be found among
the wreckage until the next morning but luckily it did not
detonate, which would have destroyed the state of Arkansas
and released nuclear fallout across the entire East Coast. The
accident highlights issues with the chain of command and lack
of contingency planning. One crewman dies. 21 are injured.

Militaries continue to invest in multi-role fighter planes, like the F-16 Fighting Falcon.

Protests against Nuclear power plants occur in America.

In the 1980s, President Ronald Reagan launches the Strategic Defense Initiative (SDI) as well as the MX and Midgetman ICBM programs.

Voyager 1 flies by Saturn in November of 1980, passing within 125,000 km of its cloud tops.

Voyager 1 then flies by Jupiter. Five of its moons are studied and Io is found to be actively volcanic.

Pioneer 11 passes Saturn 21,000 km above its surface, the first spacecraft to visit the planet.

The Nimbus-7 measures the Ozone layer

Although the Nimbus satellite program had been measuring Ozone since the early 70's, the Nimbus-7, launched in 1978, is the first to provide comprehensive worldwide measurements.

Skylab falls.

Skylab is not equipped with control or navigation systems to bring it safely back to Earth, so NASA plans to use the Space Shuttle to boost it into a higher orbit where it can remain indefinitely. Facing delays in development, The Space Shuttle isn't launched in time and NASA scrambles to design a plan that, by strategically firing the station's booster rockets, will prevent Skylab from plunging uncontrolled to Earth and scattering debris across populated areas. On July 11, 1979, Skylab reenters Earth's atmosphere and burns up, somewhat more slowly than NASA expects, its debris landing east of Perth in Western Australia.

With new technologies, our understanding of Earth's atmosphere grows. Satellites, sounding rockets, weather balloons, and instruments on the ground help us to create a composite, more comprehensive picture of the Earth.

President Carter has solar panels installed on the White House roof in 1979.

A balloon crosses the Atlantic.

Double Eagle II successfully crosses the Atlantic, becoming the first balloon to do so.

BASE jumping is born.

In 1978, filmmaker Carl Boenish, along with his wife Jean Boenish, Phil Smith, and Phil Mayfield, filmed the first BASE jumps made from El Capitan in Yosemite National Park, with ram-air parachutes and a freefall tracking technique. BASE is an acronym for the act of parachuting or wing suit flying from Building, Antenna, Span (like a bridge), and Earth (like a cliff). Base jumping evolves into an extreme sport, and in the 1990s leads to the development of wing suits by Patrick de Gayardon, a French skydiver and BASE jumper.

Lithium-based batteries provide light weight power.

Physicists and engineers conduct research into new lithium-based battery systems, endeavoring to expand past the old lead-acid workhorse.

I want my MTV.

1981 sees the introduction of MTV, a 24-hour music video channel. The first images aired include a montage of the moon landing of the *Apollo 11* mission.

Lockheed Martin unveils the F-117 Nighthawk, a stealth attack aircraft.

The revolutionary technology of the internet debuts.

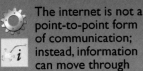

The internet is not a point-to-point form of communication; instead, information can move through a network of multiple relay stations. This network redundancy makes communication less vulnerable to single point failure. Much of the funding for its development came from the Department of Defense, which sought to insure military communications. The Internet Protocol Suite is standardized in 1982. Using TCP/IP protocol, networks anywhere in the world can transfer information.

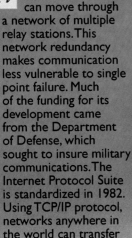

Salyut 7 orbits Earth for almost 9 years

The station is visited by 10 manned spacecraft carrying 6 long-term crews and 4 short-term crews. The station suffers electrical problems and a salvage mission, known as Soyuz T-13, is launched and successfully carries out repairs. The Soyuz T-15 is the last to visit Salyut and carries some of its equipment to the new Mir space station. It descends from orbit in 1991.

Climbers float down the French Alps.

Using small ram-air canopies as parachutes they "float" down the mountain, making the descent safer. These parachutes, weighing only 8 lbs, fly at about 20 mph, and drop the rider 3 feet for every foot traveled.

The era of the Space Shuttle begins.

Four orbital space flights take place in 1981. This class of spacecraft will buoy forward NASA's crewed missions from 1982 to 2011, with 133 successful launches and landings. Missions will cover everything from launching satellites and spacecraft to resupplying and exchanging space station crews.

NASA approves the COBE mission.

The COBE mission is designed to take precise measurements of the CBR. Measurements so far have identified the CBR, but have not been able to find the fluctuations that would have been produced in a quantum event such as the Big Bang. COBE is scheduled to launch with the space shuttle.

The Hubble telescope is under construction.

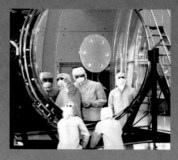

In 1978, Congress approves a budget to build a Large Space Telescope for the exploration of deep space. Construction of the telescope that will be placed in orbit, outside of Earth's atmosphere is exacting.

The **EAA AirVenture Museum** opens its doors in Oshkosh, Wisconsin.

Originally conceived by EAA founder Paul Poberezny in 1958 as a museum and education center, the fundraising and building campaign was taken up by his son, Tom Poberezny, in 1982. Wittman Regional Airport, adjacent to the museum and EAA's long-standing home airport, also houses EAA's national headquarters.

The quest for a unified theory of physics continues.

Scientists seek to find one force to encompass and replace the four currently recognized separate forces. Another breakthrough is made in 1983 as more evidence is found which shows the electromagnetic force to be related to the nuclear weak force, at least at high temperatures. Scientists working at the CERN particle collider verify the existence of the force carrying particles, called W and Z gauge bosons and predicted by earlier theory, during high energy collisions between protons and anti-protons.

RPGs prove effective against helicopters.

Muslims from all over the world journey to Afghanistan to repel the Soviet invasion. The U.S. supplies the 'freedom fighters' with arms and intelligence. The rebels learn to use Rocket Propelled Grenades with unexpected efficiency against the Soviet helicopter gunships.

Space Shuttle *Challenger* flies.

In April of 1983, the *Challenger* Space Shuttle is launched from Kennedy Space Center for its first flight. Carrying a payload satellite for 'tracking and data relay,' this flight was also the first instance of a spacewalk on a Space Shuttle mission.

In 1983, Sally Ride becomes the youngest astronaut to travel to space at the age of 32, and the first U.S. woman in space.

Reagan proposes a defense system to replace the paradigm of Mutually Assured Destruction.

The Strategic Defense Initiative, or SDI, is a proposed network of ground and space based sensors and missile launchers set to intercept nuclear ballistic missiles. Proponents of the plan are keen to create a defense network capable of removing the threat of a Soviet nuclear attack on American soil. The plan is nicknamed "Star Wars" due to the complicated technology required and the fictional-seeming nature of the proposal. Critics argue that the enemy will simply

send more missiles to overwhelm the system and if even a single missile gets through it could devastate an entire city or region. They warn that it will replace the deterrent effect of the Mutual Assured Destruction strategy while its capabilities are still a fantasy.

1983

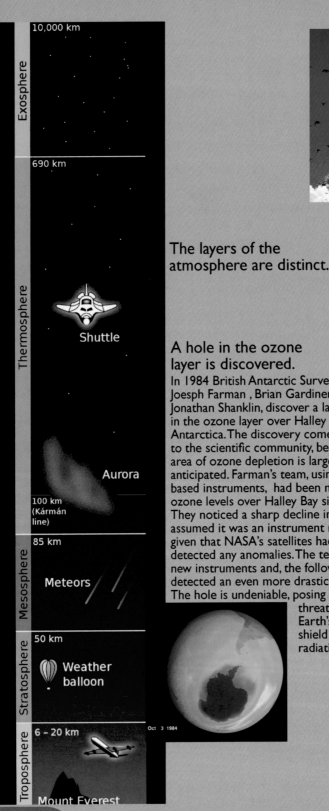

Exosphere

10,000 km

690 km

Thermosphere

Shuttle

Aurora

100 km
(Kármán
line)

85 km

Mesosphere

Meteors

50 km

Stratosphere

Weather
balloon

6 - 20 km

Troposphere

Oct 3 1984

Mount Everest

The space shuttle *Challenger* explodes.

In a disaster for the space program, a broken seal causes the right solid rocket booster to explode 73 seconds after launch. The crew of the shuttle includes a teacher, and millions of American school children watch as *Challenger* explodes, killing everyone aboard.

The layers of the atmosphere are distinct.

A hole in the ozone layer is discovered.

In 1984 British Antarctic Survey scientists, Joesph Farman , Brian Gardiner, and Jonathan Shanklin, discover a large "hole" in the ozone layer over Halley Bay, Antarctica. The discovery comes as a shock to the scientific community, because the area of ozone depletion is larger than anticipated. Farman's team, using ground-based instruments, had been measuring ozone levels over Halley Bay since 1957. They noticed a sharp decline in 1982 and assumed it was an instrument malfunction, given that NASA's satellites hadn't detected any anomalies. The team ordered new instruments and, the following year, detected an even more drastic decline. The hole is undeniable, posing a huge threat to the Earth's protective shield from solar radiation.

Paragliding takes off in Europe. By the mid-1980s, focus had shifts to the flight potential of rising air, which can used to increase flight duration and distance. Design improvements like increased wingspan, the use of nonporous fabric, and modifications in the shape and trim of the airfoil are made. By 1986, the sport is well established in Europe.

Hubble must wait.

After being approved in 1978 with the aim of a launch date in 1983, the building of the Hubble Space Telescope was beset by obstacles. NASA encountered problems with engineering, construction, and budget; the launch is rescheduled for October 1986. Unfortunately, the *Challenger* explosion causes much of the American space program to be put on hold, including the Hubble launch. The cost of keeping the Hubble Telescope in working condition, without launch, is about $6 million per month.

World population reaches 5 billion.

Airbus incorporates fly-by-wire.

The Airbus A320 becomes the first airliner in the industry to implement digital fly-by-wire controls into its design. The A320 is Airbus' first major effort to compete with airliner giants Boeing and Douglas. After years of collaborative plans and studies with many European corporations involved, the A320's design implements long, thin wings at a much higher aspect ratio than the 737 or MD-80, its US-built competition. Additionally, these single-aisle airliners are wider than other airliners on the market, with main fuel tanks residing in the wings. The A320 uses the most composite materials of any narrow body airliner on the market.

Voyager 2 reaches Uranus.

After nine years of travel, *Voyager 2* flies by Uranus. This marks the first and only short-distance flyby of the ice giant, with the craft

passing within 100,000 km of the lower atmosphere. In addition to studying its nine known rings, atmospheric composition, and magnetic field, *Voyager 2* also found two more rings and ten new moons.

Chernobyl melts down.

A toxic wind drifts over Ukraine and parts of Europe.

Brothers Alan and Dale Klapmeier test the Cirrus VK-30.

The single-engine push-propeller VK-30 is a success and kit deliveries will soon be fulfilled. Perhaps its biggest successes were the lessons learned concerning how to design and build Cirrus aircraft in the future; the Klapmeiers realize the benefits of following more conventional designs and creating certified production craft.

An oblique wing airplane is built.

First proposed in the 1940's by Richard Vogt, plans for an oblique wing aircraft have surfaced many times over the years. Only one craft has been built and tested in real time, however. A unique take on swing-wing design, an oblique wing is one that sweeps one wing forward and one aft. By modifying the angle of the wing's sweep, the pilot can reduce drag at high speeds. The AD-1 is built in 1979 as a collaboration between Ames Industrial Company, Burt Rutan, and Boeing. The AD-1 is flown and tested by NASA until 1982.

The Salyut program paved the way for the International Space Station

From 1971 to 1986, the Russians launched nine space stations and successfully transferred crews to six of them, using expendable Soyuz carrier rockets. Four Salyut stations conducted scientific research while two performed military reconnaissance. All offered cover for the highly classified Russian military Almaz program. The Salyut program evolved space technology, providing a model for multimodular space stations such as Mir and the International Space Station (ISS), both of which contain a Salyut-derived core module. The final craft from the Salyut series, Mir-2, becomes one of the first modules of the ISS.

Access to the internet increases.

In 1986, the National Science Foundation increases access to the internet by establishing the CSNET, Computer Science Network, which use its supercomputers at research and educational institutions.

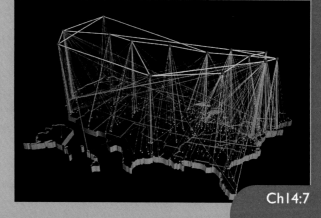

There is no central station for the internet.

On March 13, 1989 a large solar flare causes a coronal mass ejection.

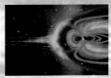

The Solar Burst travels away from the sun and toward Earth.

The entire province of Quebec, Canada, suffers an electrical power blackout. Hydro-Québec's power grid uses very long transmission lines to carry electrical power from distant dams. Its exposed continental rock shield seems to have been harder for the current to enter than its 735 kV power lines. Auroras are seen as far south as Florida.

NASA resumes the Space Shuttle program.

After much inquiry and public debate, NASA resumes the shuttle program, which had been grounded for two and a half years, since the tragedy of the *Challenger* explosion. The first new mission launches three commercial satellites and tests the OAST-1 solar array.

Unfolding from a package only 7 inches deep, this 102 ft long array of solar sheeting extends further into space from a spacecraft than any human-made structure has before. This demonstration helps prove the feasibility of large-scale solar arrays in space, paving the way for deploying such arrays on future endeavors, like the International Space Station.

Stephen Hawking publishes *A Brief History of Time: From the Big Bang to Black Holes.*

Voyager 2 flies by Neptune.

Seizing the opportunity to fly close to Neptune, NASA scientists route *Voyager* 2 between the ice giant and its largest (and only spheroid) moon, Triton. This not only marks the first and only mission to Neptune, but also permanently bends the trajectory of *Voyager* 2, sending it out into interstellar space below the plane of the solar ecliptic by about 30 degrees.

The *Exxon Valdez* runs aground in Prince William Sound, Alaska.

The oil tanker spills more than 10 million gallons of oil into the ocean.

The COBE satellite looks for the CBR.

After a series of setbacks and delays, The COBE mission launches in 1989, carrying instruments to search for, identify, and precisely measure the CBR and provide a better understanding of the birth of our Universe.

The first unofficial Paragliding World Championship is held in Verbier, Switzerland in 1987.

The first FAI World Paragliding Championship is held in Kössen, Australia.

The Berlin Wall falls in 1989.

ACHTUNG! SIE VERLASSEN wieder dann WEST BERLIN

380,000 Soviet troops remain in East Germany. The Soviet Union has the legal right to occupy East Germany, based on armistice treaties signed at the end of WWII.

1989

1990

The Hubble Telescope launches.

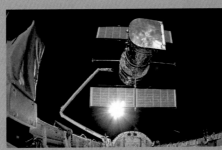

With the resumption of the Shuttle program, the Hubble telescope is launched from *Discovery*. Soon after launch, however, it becomes abundantly clear that something is wrong with the images it is producing. The blurry resolution of the images gives tham varying levels of usefulness, depending on the particular phenomenon being observed. Careful analysis finds that, although the mirror used was produced to perhaps the most exact specifications ever, its surface configuration was off by about 2.2 micrometers.

Sony debuts the first lithium-ion battery

The *Galileo* spacecraft performs the first flyby of an asteroid by a human satellite in October 1991.

Planets exist outside of our solar system.

Though detected in 1989, by indirect means, the existence of an Extrasolar planet (known as an exoplanet) orbiting the star Gamma Cephei is first confirmed in 1991.

In 1991, the USSR dissolves and the Cold War seems to come to an end.

Russia is promised that NATO will not expand eastward into formerly Soviet states.

Gorbachev proposes the creation of new institutions to replace NATO and the Warsaw Pact, but Washington does not want NATO replaced.

In February of 1990, U.S. Secretary of State James Baker and Chancellor Helmut Kohl of West Germany journey to Moscow to hash out an agreement.

To persuade the Soviets to withdraw their troops without the disbanding of NATO, Baker promises "that NATO's jurisdiction would not shift one inch eastward from its present position" Baker leaves a letter outlining the agreement, but it won't be made public until much later, when Kohl's official papers are released.

The COBE satellite detects slight nuances in the CBR, further supporting The Big Bang Theory.

The Cosmic Background Radiation would not be completely uniform if the Big Bang had really happened, because it would have been produced by a quantum event. Such small fluctuations are extremely difficult to discern, but COBE carries a detector that, in 1992, identifies tiny fluctuations, or ripples, in the CBR, further supporting the Big Bang Theory.

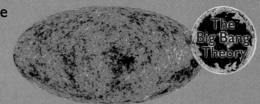

An actual map of CBR has an oval shape, due to the point of view of the detector.

Electronic Flight Bags are introduced.

In 1991, Shipping company FedEx first employs their "Airport Performance Laptop Computer" to aid aircraft inspectors in performance calculations. By the mid-1990's Fedex uses "Pilot Access Terminals" on their shipping airplanes. These devices are computers that mark a shift in air-travel's employment of an Electronic Flight Bag (EFB). An EFB is a computer/device that replaces the traditional pilot's flight bag, which is a heavy bag full of maps and documents. The implementation of electronic versions of this flight bag helps to reduce paper consumption, increase space in the cockpit, reduce pilot error, and increase the reliability of navigational charts by automatically updating them.

Paragliding and skydiving become popular sports.

By the 1990's, the sport of paragliding has evolved into two distinct practices - one is paragliding, in which the participant launches the craft by foot from the ground; and the other is skydiving, or parachuting, in which the participant jumps from an aircraft.

The *Pacific Flyer*, the largest hot air balloon ever built, crosses the Pacific.

With a volume of 74,000 cubic meters of hot air (2,600,000 ft³), the balloon flies in the jet stream from Japan to Canada in 1991. Flown by Per Lindstrand and Richard Branson, it attains the highest ever recorded speed for a piloted balloon, 394 km/hr, and sets a distance record.

Textron buys back Cessna in 1992 from General Dynamics. The same year, two of GD's major production facilities (both focused primarily on missile development and manufacture) are sold to General Motors-Hughes Aerospace.

Air Force One and Two receive an upgrade.

The aging 707's that had been operating as Air Force One through seven presidential administrations are replaced by a pair of Boeing 747s during the George H. W. Bush Administration. One is designed to be resistant to Electromagnetic Pulses (EMPs), and both have secure phone lines, computer communication systems, an office, conference room, private

staff quarters. The 707 carrying the designation SAM 27000 will be kept as a backup and will be in service until the G.W. Bush administration.

The USSR and U.S. sign the bilateral *START I* agreement.

The Strategic Arms Reduction Treaty limits both nations from stockpiling more than 6,000 nuclear warheads and 1,600 ICBMs. Additionally, the treaty prohibits each country from possessing more than 10,000 tanks, 20,000 pieces of heavy artillery, 2,000 attack helicopters, and 6,000 fighter aircraft.

Another roadable aircraft is attempted.

The Slovak aeronautics company, AeroMobil s.r.o., is founded and testing begins on the AeroMobil, a roadable aircraft. Designed by CEO Štefan Klein in 1990, the proof-of-concept prototype will take almost 20 years to develop.

The early version has a solid frame and accommodates only one person. Subsequent versions will include space for two, and wings that fold backward to run parallel with the road while in driving mode. All iterations include a rear-mounted pusher propeller.

Glasses for Hubble.

After much planning and designing, a solution to the Hubble dilemma is reached. Replacement of the mirror in space would be too complicated, and replacing it back on Earth would be too expensive and time consuming. Instead, the Corrective Optics Space Telescope Axial Replacement (COSTAR) is devised to correct the spherical aberration produced by the incorrect grind put on the primary mirror.

This instrument is connected to the back of the telescope and addresses the mis-grind like a pair of glasses. Instead of 'fixing' the issue, COSTAR is configured with the exact same issue, but in reverse, effectively correcting Hubble's vision. COSTAR is attached during the first scheduled service mission in 1993.

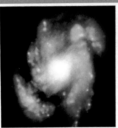 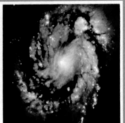

Before   After

Boeing and Airbus consider a joint project.

Airbus and Boeing begin a partnered feasibility study of a "Very Large Commercial Transport" (VLCT), an aircraft that would carry 500-1,000 passengers. It is predicted by Game Theory models that if both companies were to produce such a large airplane that neither would turn a profit. The two entities consider bridging their rivalry by forming partnership to build an aircraft for this niche market.

Apple introduces its first tablet, the Newton MessagePad, in 1993.

Caller ID devices are offered for sale on the general market in 1993.

General Dynamics sells its remaining two aerospace production facilities to Lockheed and Martin Marietta in 1993 and 1994, respectively. This closes the chapter on General Dynamics' contributions to aviation, and GD shifts its focus to land and sea production.

The 'Storm of the Century' in 1993 is the largest known to date.

At its maximum, the storm stretched from Canada to Central America. Cuba was badly damaged by winds in excess of 100 miles per hour, a foot of snow was dropped on the state of Georgia, and a mighty storm surge battered coastlines.

The Predator drone debuts.

GA-ASI develops unmanned aerial vehicles (UAVs) for aerial reconnaissance and later for tactical airstrikes. Perhaps best known for the MQ-1 Predator drone (1995-present), GA-ASI has been creating and testing UAVs since the late 1980's.

The Robinson is practical.

Even as gas-turbine engines are replacing the reciprocating piston engine models, Frank Robinson debuts the R44. The R44 is a high-performance, low-cost light utility copter employing a reciprocating engine and a simple teetering rotor system, making a perfect model for the commercial market.

Airbus continues alone.

Only two years into the VLCT feasibility study, Boeing drops out, maintaining that market trends in passenger travel wouldn't cover the projected $15 billion costs for developing such an aircraft. Airbus, however, takes this opportunity to begin to develop its own 'very large airliner,' code-named the A3XX.

This cell phone is smart.

In 1994, BellSouth places a mobile phone with PDA capabilities on the market. The Simon Personal Communicator is the first phone to be called a smartphone, with multiple applications. The Simon operates with a touch screen, an address book, calendar, and the ability to send and receive emails.

SOHO studies the sun.

In a joint venture between the European Space Agency and NASA, the Solar and Heliospheric Observatory is launched in 1995. Known simply as SOHO, the spacecraft primarily studies the outer layer of the Sun's atmosphere but has also provided solar data for space weather predictions concerning other spacecraft, and has discovered over 3000 comets.

 ## The internet takes off when it becomes fully commercialized.

Commercial internet providers emerged in the 1980's and early 1990's, and commercialized internet began to boom in Europe, Asia, and Australia.

In 1995, the internet in the United States is fully commercialized with the removal of the educational requirements that were on the National Science Foundation's Network.

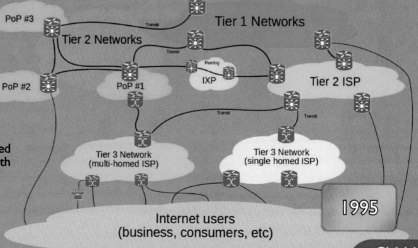

NASA's new UAV is solar-powered.

Low energy consumption and the ability to recharge using solar energy can enable drones to stay aloft for long periods of time. Created to act as a low-atmosphere, highly maneuverable satellite, Pathfinder is a solar-powered UAV capable of long-term, high-altitude flight. In 1997, Pathfinder sets altitude records for solar-powered aircraft, ascending to 21,800 meters. On this and other flights conducted in 1997, Pathfinder carries imaging systems to study terrestrial and coastline ecosystems of Kauai, Hawai'i.

Daily flights of airliners occur in patterns, international flights move with the sun.

Telescopes are time machines.

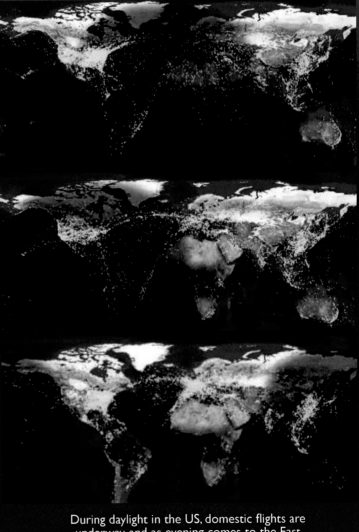

Telescopes allow us to see objects as they were in the past. The light from our sun takes 8 minutes to reach our eyes so we see the sun as it was 8 minutes ago. The next closest star, Alpha Centauri is 4.3 light-years away so we see it as it was 4.3 years ago. Andromeda is 2.5 million light years away. We can see galaxies that are more that 13 billion light-years away; when the light we see left those galaxies, the Universe was young. Our technological abilities and scientific understanding have evolved hand in hand.

During daylight in the US, domestic flights are underway, and as evening comes to the East Coast, planes bound for Europe head out

Tennekes publishes The Great Flight Diagram

Henk Tennekes first publishes an astonishing graph "The Great Flight Diagram" connecting all flying things in 1996 in his book The Simple Science of Flight. This graph shows that all birds and aircraft rely upon the same physics of flight to overcome gravity. Tennekes graphed weight, wing loading, and cruising speed to show that all flying beings and machines fall within one trend line across a range of 12 orders of magnitude of weight, 4 orders of wing loading and 2 orders of magnitude of airspeed. Wing loading is weight divided by the wing area and it increases the faster an aircraft travels. With greater speed, lift results more from airspeed than from the shape of the wing. Since lift always equals weight in equilibrium, faster aircraft are able to have smaller wings. This smaller wing area makes these faster aircraft have higher wing loading numbers. Birds that succeed evolutionarily and airplanes that fly all have wing loads, weight and airspeeds within the trendline (or there's a clear reason why they don't, such as eagles and vultures that have oversized wings to catch and soar on thermals).

Global energy use varies widely.

A picture of the Earth at night serves as a snapshot, showing where energy is used.

Assembly of the International Space Station begins.

Assembly of the ISS begins in November 1998, with the Russian module *Zarya*. About two weeks later, a NASA space shuttle delivers the module Unity. The two modules are permanently attached to one another using special pressurized adapters by astronauts during spacewalks, with another PMA (Pressurized Mating Adapter) left open to serve as a docking point for incoming shuttles. The ISS will remain unpopulated for two years, as the Russian space station Mir is taken out of operation.

Phones improve.

Nokia markets the first 'clamshell' style phone with PDA and mobile capabilities. *The Nokia 9000 Communicator* mobile phone can open on a hinge along its long side, revealing a screen and full QWERTY keyboard. This device can browse the internet (text-based), and send and receive both e-mail and faxes.

Global population is not evenly distributed, and some people use and have access to more kilowatts than others.

The Experimental Aircraft Association's yearly convention is renamed **AirVenture Oshkosh**.

The Unified Theory gets a boost.

A success in the quest for a Unified Theory is achieved. Although electromagnetism and the weak nuclear force seem very different in our typical everyday low energy environment, the theory of electroweak interaction proposes that, at higher energy levels, they merge into a single electroweak force. The existence of the electroweak force is established in stages. In 1973, the Gargamelle collaboration discovers neutral currents in neutrino scattering. In 1983, W and Z gauge bosons are discovered in proton–antiproton collisions at the converted Super Proton Synchrotron.

In 1999, Gerard 't Hooft and Martinus Veltman are awarded the Nobel prize for showing that the electroweak theory is renormalizable, thus bringing us one step closer to a Unified Theory by reducing the number of forces at work in the Universe from four to three.

Water is discovered on the moon.

After successfully detecting ice on the moon, the *Lunar Prospector* is intentionally crashed into a crater near its south pole, in hopes that the impact will release a plume of trapped water vapor detectable from Earth. Unfortunately, no such plume occurs.

NASA launches the *Stardust* spacecraft in 1999, with the mission of collecting dust samples from comet Wild 2 as well as cosmic dust.

The *Breitling Orbiter 3* carries Bertrand Piccard and Brian Jones and completes its transit in 1999.

Elon Musk is a successful entrepreneur

Long before he founded Space X, entrepreneur Elon Musk co-founded a company that made city guide software. He had taught himself computer programming as a child and moved to Canada to escape South Africa's compulsory military service. By 1998, the company, now called Zip2, provides software, directories, online calendars, and email to 160 newspapers. Zip2 is purchased by Compaq for more than 300 million dollars in 1999. Musk will go on to found X.com, which will later become Paypal and be sold to eBay for 1.5 billion dollars (U.S.) in 2002.

A hybrid-hot air balloon circumnavigates the globe.

The *Breitling Orbiter 3* uses both of the two usual balloon systems; contained lighter-than-air gas and heated air. Helium is contained in a sealed chamber and is never vented. To allow for additional buoyancy during the night when the helium has cooled and become more dense, a chamber containing atmospheric air is heated. Thus this balloon incorporates both a lighter-than-air gas and hot air.

A teenager hacks NASA.

After gaining access to computers at Bell South and the Miami-Dade School System, 15 year old Jonathan James hacks into the U.S. Department of Defense, the agency responsible for analyzing potential threats to the U.S. He intercepts usernames, passwords, and over 3000 messages between DTRA employees and ultimately obtains the source code that controls the life support systems of the International Space Station, causing NASA to shut down its computers for three weeks.

NATO expands into formerly Soviet Territory.

1949
1952
1955
1982
1990
1999
2004
2009

Poland, Hungary, and the Czech Republic join the North Atlantic Treaty Organization in 1999. Although NATO is supposed to be an alliance for mutual defense and none of its members are under immediate threat, and despite the concerns of some members and the virulent opposition of Russia, the new members are admitted.

Putin comes to power.

Vladimir Putin, a veteran KGB officer, becomes acting president of Russia in 1999, after the resignation of Boris Yeltsin. He then wins the subsequent election of 2000.

World Population hits 6 Billion.

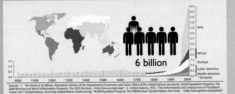

The Concorde crashes.

In July 2000, the Concorde exits the world stage with a crash. The on-takeoff crash of Air France flight #4590, which kills all 100 passengers and 4 people on the ground, is the only fatal accident in the 27 year history of the Concorde.

The **smartphone** is created.

Previously used only to run PDAs, the Symbian Operating System (OS) is applied to the Ericsson R380, the world's first GSM mobile phone specifically marketed as a 'smartphone.'

The R380 is as light and easy to use as any mobile phone currently on the market, but the conventional mobile phone touch pad flips open to reveal the rest of the phone's large touch-capable screen. Unfortunately, despite the extremely advanced User Interface (UI), the OS prevents users from installing their own software. The market price tag of $700 USD limits its popularity, but the R380 marks an innovation that will be built upon by all smartphones to come.

In order to get accurate enough figures to enable GPS location services on cell phones, Einstein's relativity equations must be used. Newton's cruder equations won't work well enough because the signals travel at almost the speed of light, up to the satellite and back.

The First resident crew to inhabit the **International Space Station** arrives on a Soyuz spacecraft.

In July of 2000, the Russian module *Zvezda* is launched and docks with the two existing modules of the International Space Station. As soon as the *Zvezda* module reaches "stationkeeping" orbit, the ISS become remotely activated as the primary vehicle, and the *Zarya-Unity* unit performs the maneuvering and docking. The *Zvezda* module is equipped with sleeping and mess quarters, CO_2 scrubbers, internal atmosphere controls, exercise equipment, and communications technologies (data, voice, and video). The attachment of this module provides the platform for permanent station habitation. November 2000 sees the first crew, consisting of U.S. and Russian astro(cosmo)nauts, take up residence in the station.

The AO-40 becomes the first satellite to employ GPS for altitude and navigation while in High Earth Orbit.

Pilot Jennifer Murray makes her second around-the-world flight. Her first was made in 1997 with her instructor, Quentin Smith. These two flights earn her the designations of first person to fly around the world in a piston-powered helicopter, first woman to fly a helicopter around the world, and first woman to fly around the world solo in a helicopter.

Businessman Dennis Tito spends an estimated $20 million as the world's first space tourist, onboard the International Space Station for a week in 2001.

On September 11, 2001, the United States is attacked.

Terrorists take advantage of the huge quantities of fuel in passenger jets embarked on transcontinental flights.

Four United Airlines flights are hijacked. One is aimed at the United States Capitol, but crashes into a field in Pennsylvania. Another crashes into the Pentagon, and the remaining two crash into the World Trade Center in New York City. Nearly 3,000 people are killed in this attack against American political, military, and financial targets.

America launches its War on Terror.

The United States launches the War on Terror, invading Afghanistan in October 2001 and Iraq in 2003, on the basis that both countries harbor terrorists. Laws protecting the rights and privacy of American citizens are suspended under emergency measures and the torture of prisoners will soon become official policy.

2001

Chapter 15: Space Probes, Drones, and Artificial Island Airstrips

SpaceX and Tesla are founded.

In 2002, Elon Musk founds Space Exploration Technologies Corp - SpaceX - a privately owned American aerospace manufacturer and space transport company, with the stated goal of reducing space transportation costs and, ultimately, allowing for colonization of Mars. Soon thereafter, he founds Tesla, Inc. to manufacture electric cars, residential solar panels, and lithium-battery energy storage systems, with the goal of making these technologies more affordable.

The Segway revolutionizes personal transport.

With two wheels and a vertical handlebar control system, the Segway uses a 'solid-state angular rate sensor' style gyroscope to keep the user and vehicle upright. Running on electric batteries, it has a maximum speed of 12.5 mph.

Within minutes most riders can learn to operate the Segway and find its direct translation of their simple body movements into motion to be almost effortless, bringing an unprecedented feeling of mobility and fluidity. These quiet, electric vehicles with zero tailpipe emissions will be appreciated by security personnel at conventions and in malls.

Another hack is revealed.

At the age of 19, Adrian Lamo, sometimes known as The Homeless Hacker, gains access to the internal computer network of the New York Times, infiltrating a database that contains social security numbers, home telephone numbers, and other personal information for over 3000 contributors to its Op-Ed page, and adding an entry that includes his own personal information, his cell-phone number, 415-505-HACK, and a description of his areas of expertise as: "computer hacking, national security, communications intelligence." He also adds five fictitious users to the database and uses them to conduct more than 3000 searches on LexisNexis.

Meigs Field is bulldozed.

Meigs Field is illegally destroyed in the middle of the night. Bulldozers are brought in to carve Xs into the runways. Organizations such as AOPA are prevented from having their day in court to keep this general aviation airport in Chicago open.

The proud granddaughter of a Women Airforce Service Pilot of WWII petitions for the burial of a WASP in Arlington National Cemetery.

The U.S. withdraws from the Anti-Ballistic Missile Treaty.

The U.S. withdraws from the Anti-Ballistic Missile Treaty that had been signed by the U.S. and the Soviet Union in 1972. Russia, China, and other nations protest, claiming that the treaty is a cornerstone to world security and that a new arms race will ensue, but U.S. President George W Bush asserts that America must have the flexibility and freedom to protect itself, especially against a limited number of missiles launched by rogue states or terrorists.

President George W. Bush becomes the first U.S. president to land on an aircraft carrier. When the Navy transports the President, the vehicle in use carries the designation Navy One. The Navy One that transported Bush was a Thirty-Five S-3B Viking that landed on the *USS Abe Lincoln*.

Wartime contract work can be lucrative.

Halliburton is awarded a contract for work in Iraq and Kuwait. Vice president Dick Cheney had been its CEO and is still a major stockholder. The company will make an estimated $39 billion from the war.

The BlackBerry smartphone debuts.

Although there are already BlackBerry built devices on the market, such as the BlackBerry 850 and BlackBerry 857; this new device, the BlackBerry 6210, released in 2003, usurps the name and becomes known simply as 'the BlackBerry.' Offering services such as a mobile phone, web browsing, fax, texting, and push e-mail notifications, the BlackBerry uses the point-to-point DataTAC wireless data network to connect. Although originally intended for business use, the BlackBerry is the first smartphone to see widespread consumer use.

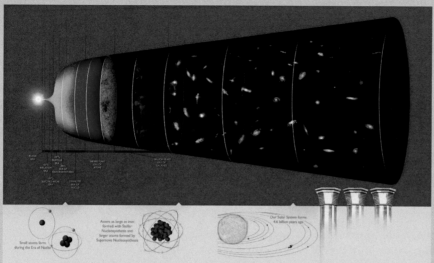

This model of the Universe, evolving through time from a singularity, has become the modern paradigm.

Three lines of evidence support the Big Bang model: the observed expansion of the universe, the abundances of the elements, and the CBR.

2004

Landing 21 days apart, Mars rovers *Spirit* and *Opportunity* explore the surface of Mars, sampling and testing its geology.

A new pylon air race is organized.

The producer of the beverage Red Bull organizes a modern pylon course air race. The Red Bull Air Race, established in 2003, has competitors flying an aerobatic obstacle course at high speeds. Pilots fly a slalom course between inflatable pylons. Failure to keep the plane far enough away from either pylon can rip the fabric of the pylon, disqualifying the pilot. Pilots are rated for speed and lose points if they fail to fly between the pylons in an exactly vertical or horizontal orientation.

Cassini, a NASA spacecraft launched back in 1997, enters Saturn's orbit in 2004.

A 121 million year old pterosaur egg is found in Argentina. The egg is part of a large cliffside colony of pterosaur remains, suggesting that some pterosaur species took care of their young in collective settings.

SpaceShipOne wins the X Prize.

White Knight carrying *SpaceShipOne*.

This non-government private project air-launches a manned spaceplane into orbit for approximately $25 million.

Cirrus Aircraft has a glass cockpit.

Cirrus Aircraft redesigns their popular SR22 with the industry's first standard glass cockpit. These primary flight displays are Avidyne's Entegra model instrument panels and include backup mechanical instruments. The term glass cockpit is used to differentiate modern digital multifunction flight control and management systems from traditional mechanical controls and gauges. The Cirrus SR22 is the first small aircraft to include an all-glass cockpit standard within a general aviation consumer's budget.

Additionally, the Cirrus SR22 models come standard with their Cirrus Airframe Parachute System (CAPS) installed. This ballistic recovery system is based on a solid fuel rocket housed in the fuselage behind the cockpit bubble, fired backwards to deploy a ballistic parachute large enough to slow the plane's descent.

Boeing CEO Stonecipher accuses Airbus of breaking a joint EU-US agreement limiting government support of large civil aircraft projects. The contract in question, between Airbus and various EU governments, allows for 33% of program costs to be subsidized with loans that must be paid back in under 2 years, with interest. Airbus argues that this loan system fully abides by the 1992 agreement, and counter-accuses Boeing of receiving pork barrel-style military contracts that act as a type of subsidy. Similar accusations will continue to fly.

Fighter jets incorporate stealth technology to maximize air superiority.

Isreal is an official member of the nuclear club.

Israel's Jericho III, a road mobile nuclear ICBM, enters service in 2008.

Spacecraft Cassini-Huygens lands its probe on the surface of Saturn's moon, Titan. Despite a software issue, pictures and atmosphere data are returned.

China's *Chang'e 1* lunar orbiter is launched. Using a microwave radiator, *Chang'e 1* will create the most comprehensive 3D map of the moon's surface to date.

Drones are deployed in growing numbers.

Drones are unmanned aerial vehicles - UAVs - and most are controlled from a remote location by pilots. As technology improves, more drones will be controlled autonomously by an onboard computer.

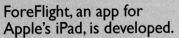

ForeFlight, an app for Apple's iPad, is developed.

Using cutting-edge mobile technologies, ForeFlight begins to develop applications for pilots for inplane navigation and planning.

In 2005, a planetary body, Eris, is discovered. Eris is 27% more massive than Pluto, making it the ninth-most-massive body to be orbiting the Sun.

The ozone hole is larger than ever before detected.

An explorer is missing.

Steve Fossett, known for breaking several aviation records, including flying around the world solo in a balloon in 2002 and gliding to more than 50,000 feet above the Andes in 2007, crashes in the Nevada desert.

The Airbus-Boeing rivalry continues.

Trade representatives from the EU and U.S. sit down to attempt to defuse the market tensions created by the Airbus - Boeing rivalry. Their efforts are unsuccessful and perhaps only create a more strained situation. Several months later, the U.S. files a suit against the EU for allegedly providing illegal subsidies to Airbus. Only 24 hours later, a counter-suit is filed by the EU against the U.S. for support given to Boeing.

European supplies of heating fuel dwindle.

The supply of natural gas flowing to consumers in Europe from Russia via pipelines in Ukraine is sharply reduced. The European Union purchases about a third of its gas from Gazprom, the Russian energy consortium.

Spacecraft *Stardust* returns its payload of cosmic dust. Samples collected from *Comet Wild-2* contain Glycine, an amino acid and fundamental building block of life. This find supports the *Panspermia Hypothesis*.

America's National security agency, the NSA, steps up its surveillance program.

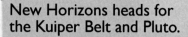

New Horizons heads for the Kuiper Belt and Pluto.

On January 19, 2006, New Horizons is launched. Carrying a payload of 7 different analysis instruments, the spacecraft is heading to the Kuiper Belt with a scheduled flyby of the Pluto system.

In February, 2006, a retired Russian Orlan spacesuit is deployed from the International Space Station with a radio transmitter attached to the helmet. As part of an experiment to repurpose decommissioned ISS gear as useful satellites, the empty suit drifts eerily before burning up on reentry.

Pluto is demoted to dwarf planet status.

The International Astronomical Union's 2006 decision to reclassify Pluto as a dwarf planet is met by unexpected outrage.

The IAU reclassifies its previous category of "minor planets" into "dwarf planets" and "small Solar System bodies" (SSSB). Hundreds of small bodies have been discovered in the solar system in recent decades but the discovery of Eris, a body that is larger than Pluto, precipitates the decision. Dwarf planets are objects that are in direct orbit around the Sun and posses enough mass to attain a spheroid shape, but not enough to clear their neighboring region of other material. Pluto is only marginally more massive than the other objects in its own orbit, disqualifying it from full "Planet" status.

China shoots down its own satellite.

China launches a ballistic missile in 2007, shooting down its own weather satellite. Modern military systems depend on satellites for communications, GPS, and high altitude reconnaissance. By destroying a satellite, China announces to the world that the weaponization of space is upon us. The weaponization of space is not about orbiting death rays or other weapons but rather about disrupting essential communications and GPS capabilities. The Chinese missile reaches an altitude of more than 500 miles in space, where the U.S. has been developing a missile defense network since withdrawing from the Anti-Ballistic Missile Treaty in 2002.

Apple debuts the iPhone in 2007.

Opting to use a finger-based touchscreen for use and navigation instead of a stylus or keyboard, the iPhone runs on the AT&T wireless network. Apple's CEO Steve Jobs announces the first generation iPhone at the Macworld Conference & Expo in San Francisco. Thousands of people camp out and form lines outside of retailers in anticipation days before the June 29th launch date. Running on the OS X, Apple's latest operating system that runs their laptop computers, Apple understands the need for brand-wide compatibility and will develop innovations across all of their devices as they go.

The iPhone comes locked into the AT&T wireless network. Soon a blackmarket industry will spring up to 'unlock' or 'crack' these phones for users to choose different network providers and plans.

At a cost of $473 million, the spacecraft *Dawn*, is launched in 2007. It will investigate the asteroids Ceres and Vesta.

Fierce competition between rivals continues to drive innovations in long-haul passenger service.

The Boeing 747 has been the largest airliner in the sky for almost 40 years, prompting Airbus to develop the A380 (code-named A3XX during development). While the 747 has a partial second passenger deck, the A380's design includes a second passenger deck that runs the full length of the plane. Able to serve the second longest nonstop scheduled flight and able to compete with the Boeing 747-8, the Airbus A380 is a double-decked widebody long-range airliner and the world's largest passenger airliner, with seating for up to 853 passengers. There are 200 A380 currently in service today.

Android, Inc. develops the Android OS for smartphones.

The first smartphone to hit the market running off of the open-source Android OS is the HTC Dream, as a competitor to Symbian, BlackBerry, and iOS (Apple's iPhone OS). The HTC Dream is a touchscreen mobile device with a screen that slides out to reveal a QWERTY type keyboard. One of the project's developers, Andy Rubin, comments that "smarter mobile devices [should be] more aware of its owner's location and preferences." The company will operate mostly in secret until being acquired by Google in 2005. Post-acquisition, the Android OS becomes the basis of many, W smartphones. Perhaps understanding that their major competitor is solely Apple, Android will strive to produce products that incorporate similar cross-platform applications and software, such as fully-integrated Google email and the Google Play Store.

The Solar Impulse takes flight.

Bertrand Piccard and André Borschberg began building the Solar Impulse in 2003 in a joint venture with a Swiss polytechnical university as a feasibility study for solar-powered long-range aircraft. By 2009, the two Swiss aeronauts have assembled a team of 50 engineers and specialists, and the photovoltaic monoplane completes its first flight in December of 2009.

The crash on the Hudson is not a disaster.

Shortly after takeoff from La Guardia on January 15, 2009, an Airbus A320 strikes a flock of geese. Rapidly losing power to both engines, U.S. Airways pilots Chesley Sullenberger and Jeffery Skiles are able to perform perhaps the most fortunate water landing in history. Landing in the Hudson River, just offshore of Lower Manhattan, all 150 passengers and five crew members are able to exit the aircraft safely to be saved by nearby ferries and sightseeing boats.

2009

Commercial airlines in the U.S. achieve an astonishingly good safety record.

In the years 2007 and 2008 not a single person in the United States dies on a commercial flight. This happens despite the fact that more people than ever are traveling by air.

The Falcon 1 reaches orbit.

SpaceX's privately funded liquid propellant rocket is the first of its kind to reach orbit. Later, the Falcon 9 will be the first orbital rocket to execute a propulsive landing , and the first to be re-used.

President Obama awards the WASPs the Congressional Gold Medal.

In 2009, President Barack Obama awards the WASPs the Congressional Gold Medal saying "The Women Airforce Service Pilots courageously answered their country's call in a time of need while blazing a trail for the brave women who have given and continue to give so much in service to this nation since. Every American should be grateful for their service, and I am honored to sign this bill to finally give them some of the hard-earned recognition they deserve."

A jet propelled human flies.

A Swiss ex-military and -commercial pilot makes his first public flight with a winged jetpack. Yves Rossy's six minute flight near Lake Geneva begins at an altitude of 7,500 ft from a single prop utility airplane, a Pilatus Porter. With the wings retracted, the four kerosene-fueled jet engines are ignited in the plane. While in freefall, the wings extend and horizontal flight can be maintained for an extended period of time. During this publicized flight, Rossy made several "effortless" loops, gaining more than 2,600 ft in altitude before landing with the aid of a parachute.

The U.S. and Russia sign the START II, prolonging the bilateral agreement to reign in both countries' nuclear weapons programs. This renewal limits the signers to only 1,550 nuclear warheads, 800 launchers, and 700 ICBMs and bombers.

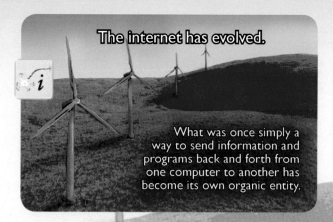

The internet has evolved.

What was once simply a way to send information and programs back and forth from one computer to another has become its own organic entity.

The Stuxnet computer worm destroys Iran's nuclear centrifuges.

In 2010, a computer worm is discovered deeply embedded in the computer systems of the Natanz nuclear facility in Iran. Nicknamed Stuxnet, the worm targets the centrifuges that are being used to enrich uranium, instructing them to spin faster, up to speeds that eventually destroy them. Over the course of a few years, about 20% of Iran's centrifuges are affected, leaving Iranian scientists wondering what went wrong until the worm is discovered. Attributed to Israel, the Stuxnet worm is likely the world's first digital weapon.

The largest commercial airliner built in the U.S. makes its first flight.

Taking off from Everett, Washington, the Boeing 747-8 features redesigned wings and new GE GenX jet engines. A full three ft longer than the longest airliner currently in the air, the first batch produced will be freighters. Subsequent passenger versions will be produced under the name 747-8 Intercontinental. Currently, Boeing has 108 orders for the 747-8, and Lufthansa will be the first to fly.

Apple releases the iPad.

With only four physical switches on them, two versions of the first generation of iPad are released in April of 2010: Wi-Fi only, and Wi-Fi plus 3G capabilities. On the first day of sales, Apple sells 300,000 iPads, and before the release of the iPad2, more than 15 million will be sold.

The *Gerald R Ford*-class of supercarriers (super aircraft carriers) have similar hulls to the previously prevailing *Nimitz*-class carriers, and build off of their technologies. Equipped with the EMALS (Electromagnetic Aircraft Launch System) the *Ford*-class carriers are more efficient, have smaller crew requirements, and more advanced missile and radar capabilities. With 25 decks and two A1B nuclear reactors, the *USS Gerald R. Ford* is the only existing example of this class of supercarrier, and is awaiting commission.

GE premieres their new GenX jet engine at the Paris Air Show.

The ice at the poles of the earth is melting at a highly accelerated rate; within the last twenty years, more ice has melted than in the last ten thousand years.

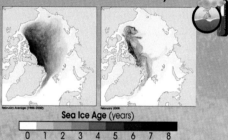

February Average (1995–2000)   February 2008

Sea Ice Age (years)

0 1 2 3 4 5 6 7 8

2010

Dragon Spacecraft is the first commercially operated and manufactured spacecraft to be recovered from orbit.

Dragon Spacecraft Program's maiden flight in December 2010 makes it the first commercially operated / manufactured spacecraft to be successfully recovered from orbit.

After the Space Shuttle program ends, Dragon (developed by SpaceX) will be the primary supplier of the ISS. SpaceX is now developing crewed versions of the Dragon, capable of transporting up to seven astronauts, or several crew members and cargo.

The Deepwater Horizon oil rig explodes in April 2010 in the Gulf of Mexico, creating an oil slick visible from space.

After almost 30 years of missions, the Space Shuttle program ceases operations.

 World Population grows by another billion.

7 billion

The spacecraft *Juno* is launched. With an expected lifespan of about 6 years, Juno is placed into orbit around the sun until 2013. The spacecraft is waiting for ideal conditions to head to Jupiter for study.

Cirrus Aircraft company is sold to the China Aviation Industry General Aircraft (CAIGA) for $210 million. CAIGA is a subsidiary of Aviation Industry Corporation of China, an aerospace and defense contracting company owned by the government of the People's Republic of China. $

The number of drones flying in the skies grows at a fast rate.

Drones become more efficient and are put to deadly use in Pakistan, Afghanistan, and Iraq. In the 21st century, drones are used for a number of civil applications, including police work, fire fighting, border patrol, and surveillance of pipeline inspections. Drones are expected to be approved for commercial use in the U.S. by 2015.

2012 - SpaceX sends the Dragon to the International Space Station

The U.S. Air Force announces that the Boeing 747-8 will serve as the next Air Force One. These jets will come equipped with better air-to-ground communications systems, will be hardened against Electromagnetic Pulses, and may very well carry an onboard missile defense system.

The much-improved iPad2 is released.

The new versions are lighter, thinner, and faster than their predecessors, and include two cameras (one forward-facing, and one user-facing), as well as a gyroscope.

NASA's *Curiosity* rover lands on Mars.

This is the first time that a video camera has ever landed on another planet. The rover's goals include determining if the planet could ever have supported life, studying the climate and geology of Mars, and preparing the way for future human exploration of the planet.

Mars possesses an atmosphere about 100 times thinner than Earth's, rendering parachutes alone inadequate for landing equipment on the rocky planet's surface. Previous rovers were small and light enough that a combination of parachutes and pre-impact airbags were adequate, but *Curiosity* is the largest mobile science laboratory ever landed on another planet and is far too heavy for airbags.

A new device is created to solve this and other potential landing problems, and it requires a new method of operation. The device is the sky crane, a specially-built platform attached above the *Curiosity* rover. Its use requires The Sky Crane maneuver, in which a ballistic parachute deploys when the descent module decelerates through the atmosphere. When the parachute has done all that it can, the sky crane and rover are released from the heatshield, and the surface-facing engines on the sky crane fire up. When the pair reach 25 ft above the Martian surface, the rover is lowered via a tether from the crane. The rover's own suspension system help create a soft landing and the tethers are detached via small explosives. Finally, the crane platform flies away to crash at a safe distance.

The World Trade Organization conducts an investigation into claims on both sides of the U.S. / Boeing - EU / Airbus controversy. In early findings, the WTO concludes that both companies have been unfairly subsidized. Finalized reports in 2011 conclude that research grants awarded to NASA were funneled into Boeing to subsidize civilian aircraft projects and must be paid back. The WTO also rules that Airbus's contracts with European governments must be reworked to reflect higher interest rates and shorter repayment cycles. Both sides of this trade dispute claim victory.

 The existence of the Higgs particle is confirmed by data from the Large Hadron Collider.

A 737 is powered by biofuel.

The biotech company, Solazyme, fills a 737 flown by United Airlines with their Solajet biofuel and makes their first commercial flight, in 2011

Solazyme has been cultivating sugar-fed algae to create a fuel to be mixed with conventional jet fuel, in a 60/40 proportion. 154 passengers arrive at Chicago O'Hare airport without ever feeling any difference in flight quality. Soon, more companies are searching for fuel additives derived from plants, animals, and algae.

Juno receives a boost.

Spacecraft *Juno* has been in orbit for two years, waiting for the ideal alignment of the planets. Scientists maneuver the craft to fly by Earth. By carefully planning when the engines fire as it passes into Earth's gravity well, *Juno* receives a speed boost of almost 2.5 mps with this slingshot tactic, and now heads on an intercept course with Jupiter.

Lithium is produced in large quantities by supernovas.

Lithium is a strategic material used in batteries for cellphones and other electronics. It is also used as a mood stabilizer.

Some lithium was produced in the Big Bang, some in the cores of low mass stars, some in supernovas, and some, perhaps, by the alteration effects of the mutation of other elements by cosmic rays. Japan's National Astronomical Observatory observes the explosion of *Nova Delphini 2013* and its production of a large amount of lithium. These observations suggest that classical novae are the greatest source of the Universe's lithium. Classical nova explosions occur on the surface of white dwarfs that exist in such close proximity to a main stage star (a star much like our own) that gas exchange occurs.

More countries develop ICBMs.

In 2012, India test fires the Agni V, with a strike range of more than 3,100 miles. Using the Unha-3 rocket, North Korea launches a satellite into space. The US is quick to suggest that the launch is, in a fact, a way to test an ICBM. In July 2014, China announces the development of the Dongfeng-41 (DF-41), an ICBM with a range of 7,500 miles, capable of reaching the United States and, some experts believe, capable of carrying multiple warheads.

The Tannkosh aviation festival continues to grow.

Located at the Tannheim Flugplatz in Germany, Tannkosh continues to attract more participants, becoming Europe's largest fly-in.

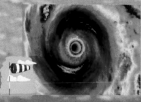

The strongest tropical cyclone ever known to make landfall, Super Typhoon Haiyan wreaks havoc on the Philippines in 2013.

Applications developers such as ForeFlight and Garmin make good use of tablet technology.

ForeFlight, and many of its competitors, uses the technology of tablets (primarily the iPad), to provide pilots with planning and navigations tools. The three-axis gyroscope and GPS capabilities of the iPad2 (and subsequent generations), allows these apps to provide synthetic vision, up-to-date weather and aviation charts, airport information, and attitude measurement. The tracking ability of these technologies will quickly catch on with professional and recreational pilots alike, replacing the traditional clipboard-style kneeboard with a responsive, touch-screen iPad version.

Yves Rossy, Jetman, flies over EAA's AirVenture.

2013

Just a few months after releasing the third-generation of iPads, Apple begins selling their 4th generation, along with the new iPad Mini.

The iPad Mini is just 7.9 inches across, comes with similar hardware as the iPad2, and quickly competes with other small-factor tablets.

Lufthansa enters the 747-8I into commercial service, and it is the first of its kind to carry passengers. On November 5, 2013, the ISRO, the Indian Space Research Organization, launches the *Mars Orbiter Mission*. Also known as 'Mangalyaan,' the project costs $74 million and carries five types of imaging instruments.

With more than 790 vendors, 10,000 aircraft, and 500,000 enthusiasts in attendance in 2014, EAA's AirVenture Oshkosh convention continues to set records.

The Solar Impulse 2 attempts to circumnavigate the globe on solar power.

Bertrand Piccard and André Borschberg have built a second solar-powered monoplane, the *Solar Impulse 2*, with vast improvements over its predecessor. After sunset, the plane relies on its batteries to fly through the night. During the day, it uses solar power to fly and to recharge the batteries. It gains altitude during the day and loses it at night.

In March, the plane takes off from Abu Dhabi, United Arab Emirates, heading east.

By May, the pair (trading off piloting) travel across Asia to Japan, reaching Hawai'i in early July. But the plane's batteries are damaged and some months elapse before the plane can fly the last legs to complete the journey.

Hacking is a political and military tool.

In November of 2014, a hacker group calling itself Guardians of Peace (GOP) demands that Sony pull *The Interview*, a comedy film about a plot to assassinate North Korean Leader Kim Jong-Un, threatening terrorist attacks on cinemas that screen the film. The hackers release confidential data hacked from Sony computers, including personal information about employees and their families, emails between employees, salary information, and copies of unreleased Sony films. Major U.S. theater chains cancel screenings of the film, and Sony decides to release it digitally, rather than in theaters nationwide. U.S. intelligence officials determine that North Korea is behind the GOP attack, but North Korea denies any involvement.

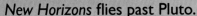

New Horizons flies past Pluto.

In July, 2015, *New Horizons* flies past the Pluto system, sending back the first clear images of these distant and mysterious rocks.

The Japanese Venusian orbiter reaches it target.

For five years, the craft has been orbiting the sun as JAXA scientists problem-solved an error that prevented insertion of the craft into orbit around Venus. In Late 2015, they make another attempt. After a short delay, as communications from the orbiter come in, JAXA confirms that Venusian orbit has been obtained. *Akatsuki*, which means *"Dawn"* in Japanese, will study weather patterns and electrical storms, and search for active volcanos on the surface of Venus.

Bob Hoover is honored.

Flying the Feathered Edge debuts. This film, by Kim Furst, explores the life of legendary pilot Bob Hoover. Perhaps the greatest pilot of all time, Hoover enjoyed pushing aircraft to the edge of their performance envelope as a WWII test pilot and on the air show circuit.

Power grids in Ukraine are hacked.

In December 2015, the Ukrainian power grid is the subject of an unprecedented cyber attack that causes a blackout for hundreds of thousands of people. The attack is sophisticated and coordinated, taking down six power providers at once, affecting computers, call centers, and internal systems designed to help restore power. The Ukrainian government blames Russia for the attack, claiming that the malware used was the BlackEnergy Trojan, which originates in Russia. U.S. investigators are unable to confirm the origin of the attack, but admit that it could have severe ramifications for power grids in the US, which are no more protected than those of Ukraine.

Boeing to build the next Air Force One.

The U.S. Air Force announces that the Boeing 747-8 will serve as the next presidential transport plane. This updated version in the 747 series has a longer fuselage and raked wing tips which decrease drag allowing it a larger payload and increase fuel efficiency.

Solar Impulse 2 resumes its epic journey.

Following the installation of new batteries and test flights, favorable flying conditions allow the solar-powered plane to take off from Hawai'i in April. Late in the evening of April 23, Impulse 2 lands near San Francisco, California. On May 2nd, the team again takes to the sky, heading across the continental U.S.

SpaceX carries out the first propulsive landing of an orbital rocket, the Falcon 9, in 2015.

SpaceX aims for Mars.

SpaceX announces plans to develop the Interplanetary Transport System program, with the goal of developing manned interplanetary spaceflight and eventually colonizing Mars.

Blue Origin CEO Jeff Bezos announces the company's plan for their first human space flights within a year.

Spacecraft Juno investigates Jupiter.

The Juno spacecraft achieves polar orbit of Jupiter on July 5, 2016 The spacecraft now begins its 20-month long mission to investigate Jupiter's atmospheric composition, gravitational field strength, and magnetosphere.

The *Cassini* spacecraft detects water on one of Saturn's moons.

Enceladus is a small icy moon in Saturn's orbit. Scientists propose that below its icy shell roils an ocean capable of supporting amino acids and other building blocks of life. As it flies through the water plumes, *Cassini* samples the effluent molecules for elements like hydrogen, which could indicate the existence of hydrothermal vents, the underwater incubators of life.

As of 2016, all five nations on the United Nations Security Council have operational long-range ballistic missile systems; Russia, the United States, and China also have land-based ICBMs (the US missiles are silo-based, while China and Russia have both silo and road-mobile (DF-31, RT-2PM2 Topol-M missiles).

Apps such as ForeFlight allow viewers to see traffic patterns in real time.

2016

Shinzo Abe visits Pearl Harbor.

75 years after the attack on Pearl Harbor, Prime Minister Shinzo Abe visits to commemorate the anniversary and to honor the peace that has been established between the two countries since the end of the war. Abe's visit comes on the heels of President Obama's visit to Hiroshima earlier in the year, and both visits mark a first for their respective countries. Abe does not apologize for the attack, but offers deep condolences and a renewed vow to keep Japan and the United States in this "Alliance of Hope."

A fifth Chinese island airstrip is built in the Spratly Islands.

In disputed ocean waters, claimed by The Philippines, Vietnam, and Taiwan, an artificial airstrip is built upon a reef. At 3,000 meters long, twice as long as the next largest artificial airstrip already built by China, it will be capable of accommodating the Chinese H-6G bomber, which could perform combat operations within a 3,500 mile radius of the island. Because of the island's location, 650 miles from China's current southern-most position at Hainan Island, China could potentially use the airbase for patrols or offensive operations, particularly against other South China Sea claimants.

An Indian satellite orbits Mars.

Eight months after its launch, Mangalyaan enters Mars orbit, making India the first country to successfully place an orbiter in Martian space on the first try.

An invasion of airliners brings a steady stream of tourists to Hawaii.

Was the U.S. election hacked?

U.S. intelligence agencies accuse Russia of hacking email and distributing online propaganda in order to influence the presidential election of 2016, by discrediting the Democratic presidential candidate, Hillary Clinton, in order to favor the election of Donald Trump. Questions arise about the possibility of collusion between the Trump campaign and the Russians, as well as the possibility of the Trump administration obstructing justice. Both Trump and Russia deny the allegations. A special investigator is appointed to get to the bottom of it.

Debate over crowd sizes is determined by satellite photography.

On Saturday, January 21, 2017 – one day after his inauguration – U.S. President Donald Trump accused the media of misrepresenting the size of the crowd at his inaugural proceedings. He insists that he saw a crowd that "looked like a million-and-a-half people" and "went all the way back to the Washington Monument." Satellite photos of the event, however, tell a different story, clearly depicting quite a bit of empty space in and around the inauguration.

Press Secretary Sean Spicer defends the President's assertion, coining the term "alternative facts" to account for the discrepancy. Controversy ensues, with the President insisting that his inauguration was attended by more people than any other in history. Side-by-side satellite photos of the crowd at his inauguration and the crowd at President Obama's are compared but the president refuses to amend his assertion.

2017   2009

North Korea claims to have an ICBM capable of carrying a large thermonuclear warhead

Regulations for drones are considered.

The FAA considers requiring every single drone, whether commercial or privately owned, to be registered and receive a serial number like a VIN. A pilots license might eventually be required to operate larger drones in sensitive areas.

Drones are already being used to assist humans in the dangerous jobs of inspecting smokestacks and high tension wires. They do a better job at a cheaper cost. More inspections lead to improved industrial efficiency as well as safety.

Concerns about drones are numerous. Many people are worried that camera-carrying drones will violate their personal privacy. While drones can, for instance, help deliver information to firefighters on the scene of a fire, drones launched by curious civilians can interfere with those efforts or jeopardize the ability of helicopters to deliver water. Careless pilots could injure bystanders and weapons could be mounted on drones operated by civilians.

Legislation is proposed to allow universities to pilot drones for research and education. Backed by two senators, the Higher Education UAS Modernization Act would negate effects of the current FAA regulations, which require colleges and universities to be treated as commercial operators, forcing faculty, staff, and students to be licensed pilots.

Cyberattacks can make you WannaCry.

In May, 2017 a ransomware cryptoworm, aptly called WannaCry, attacks. The worm is the result of malware called EternalBlue, which was developed by the United States National Security Agency and leaked by a group calling themselves the Shadow Brokers. It targets computers running the Microsoft Windows operating system and encrypts data so that users cannot see their own files. Ransom payments in the form of Bitcoin currency are demanded for an encryption key.

Within one day, more than 230,000 computers in 150 countries are infected. Hard hit is Britain's National Health Service, which is running an older, particularly vulnerable version of Windows OS. Almost immediately, Marcus Hutchins, a 22 year-old web security researcher from England, finds an effective "kill switch" in the code of the ransomware, allowing Microsoft to create and release a patch, greatly slowing the spread of the infection. Security experts also find ways to retrieve encrypted data without users having to pay the ransom.

The unprecedented attack serves to highlight the vulnerability of digital systems worldwide, especially since it is unusual that there happened to be a kill switch embedded in the worm and subsequent versions might not contain one. The NSA comes under fire for creating EternalBlue in the first place.

An electric plane sets a climb record.

In November 2017, over Dinslaken, Germany, the Extra 330LE climbs 3,000 meters in just 4 minutes and 22 seconds. Later that same day, the Extra 330LE sets another record, becoming the first electric plane to tow a glider.

Batteries are heavy, an obstacle that has been a challenge to electric flight. Engineers and mechanics swap out the heavy power plant of a high performance plane with a light Siemens electric motor and a collection of batteries. Weight and balance are important in airplanes, so the heavy batteries are put where the engine had been. On planes purpose-built for electric flight, the batteries are installed as close to the center of lift, which is in the wings, as possible.

The Extra 300 series planes are built for speed and aerobatic ability. Able to survive the stresses of up to 10 G, these light-weight planes are favorites for aerobatic competitions, like the Red Bull Air Races.

The Santa Monica Airport is threatened.

The city of Santa Monica has fought to close its airport, the oldest in operation in the country and long a favorite of celebrities and business interests alike, citing unsafe conditions, noise levels, and aircraft emissions. Since 1982, there have been at least 42 crashes within 5 miles of the airport, the most famous of which occurred in 2015, when actor Harrison Ford crashed a restored WWII-era trainer on a nearby golf course shortly after takeoff. Federal agreements from the end of WWII, when the airport was used by the military, require that it stay open at least until 2023, if not longer.

In 2017, the FAA announces a settlement to close the airport in 2028, returning the 227 acre parcel to the city of Santa Monica, which plans to turn it into a park. The agreement allows the city to immediately shorten the 4,973 ft runway to 3,500 ft, effectively reducing large jet traffic but allowing continued access for smaller aircraft. Both private and business aircraft interests vow to continue their efforts to keep the airport open.

NOAA's newest weather satellite, GOES-16, sends its first pictures back.

The ISS has been continuously occupied for more than 15 years.

The International Space Station has received many additions since the first resident crew took up habitation. Many Russian Soyuz capsules and three different Space Shuttles (*Atlantis*, *Discovery*, and *Endeavor*) have docked multiple times and facilitated crew rotation. More than a hundred uncrewed cargo-craft have delivered new supplies and additional components and modules. The ISS now totals 14 interlocked modules with numerous components, including cranes and solar panel arrays. Additional modules are in the planning, development, and research stages.

Instruments aboard satellites have been steadily advancing, allowing more and more detailed understandings of our planet and its atmospheric shell. At certain angles, the different layers of the atmosphere are visible to the naked eye.

This picture, taken from the International Space Station, shows the troposphere as red-orange, the stratosphere as dark blue, and the mesosphere lightening above.

Orbiting instruments tell us about ourselves.

Nasa's Orbiting Carbon Observatory-2, shown in this artist's depiction, is dedicated to measuring atmospheric carbon dioxide. Carbon dioxide emissions readily mix with other atmospheric gases as soon as they are released rendering them difficult to measure. But the detectors on board this satellite can measure the values within minutes allowing us to see our impact on the atmosphere as well as to measure the CO_2 emissions from natural sources such as volcanos.

The number of humans on Earth has been rising since the dawn of agriculture, when world population is estimated to have been about 5 million. It took all of human history until about 1800 for the population to reach a billion. The next billion came a little more than a century later, and the third followed in just a few decades. We reached 7 billion in 2011. Will we reach 8 by 2026, as most estimates predict?

Gravity kept us bound to the terrestrial realm throughout most of our evolution.

Flight has now become commonplace, and the allure of space beckons brightly. We have shown that we can land on the Moon, explore nearby planets, and, with our sophisticated telescopes and techniques, we can detect planets around other stars and observe thousands upon thousands of other galaxies.

Flight has allowed us to see our planet as a sphere in space and science has allowed us to discover much about ourselves and the Universe. Will this perspective bring us a new level of consciousness? Consciousness is when a being becomes aware of itself in its environment. Do we reach a new level of consciousness when we can see ourselves as a species on a planet in the Universe? Will this knowledge enable us to overcome our tendencies toward war and realize our dreams.

We have cultivated tools to help us explore new worlds and better understand the dynamics of our own, and, perhaps, to become a multi-planet species in the future.

Achieving our dreams of becoming an interplanetary species is probably only possible if we can apply these tools here on Earth. In order to make the next generation of space exploration technology, we will need to nurture the next generation of engineers and scientists, and to manage our resources thoughtfully.

Those of us who seek to venture farther into space must also devote ourselves to stewardship of our home planet.

Bibliography

Alexander, David E. *Nature's Flyers: Birds, Insects, and the Biomechanics of Flight.* Baltimore: Johns Hopkins University Press. 2002.

Alexander, David E. *On the Wing: Insects, Pterosaurs, Birds, Bats and the Evolution of Animal Flight.* New York: Oxford University Press. 2015.

Bennet, Donahue, Shneider, Voit. *The Cosmic Perspective* (6th ed.). San Francisco: Pearson Addison-Wesley. 2010.

Bowers, Peter M. and Ernest R. McDowell. *Triplanes: A Pictorial History of the World's Triplanes and Multiplanes.* Osceola, Wisconsin; Motorbooks International. 1993.

Brasier, Martin. *Darwin's Lost World: The Hidden History of Animal Life.* New York: Oxford University Press. 2009.

Brown, Cynthia S. *Big History: from the Big Bang to the Present.* New York; The New Press. 2007.

Bryson, Bill. *A Short History of Nearly Everything.* New York: Broadway Books. 2003.

Chaisson, Eric L. *Cosmic Evolution: The Rise of Complexity in Nature.* Boston: Harvard University Press. 2001.

Chaisson, Eric L. *Epic of Evolution: Seven Ages of the Cosmos.* New York: Columbia University Press. 2006.

Chatterjee, Sankar and R.J. Templin (ed). *Posture, Locomotion, and Paleobiology of Pterosaurs* (Special Paper 376). Boulder, Colorado; Geological Society of America. 2004.

Childers, Thomas (University of Pennsylvania). *A History of Hitler's Empire,* 2nd ed; The Great Courses. Chantilly, VA. The Teaching Company. 2001. Multimedia Learning Course.

Christian, David. *Maps of Time: an Introduction to Big History.* London: University of California Press. 2003.

Christian, David. (San Diego State University) *Big History: The Big Bang, Life on Earth, and the Rise of Humanity;* The Great Courses. Chantilly, VA: The Teaching Company. 2008. Multimedia Learning Course.

Cunningham, Jim. *John Monnett: From Sonerai to Sonex.* Stockton, CA: Wind Canyon Books. 2007.

Delsemme, Armand. *Our Cosmic Origins: From the Big Bang to the Emergence of Life and Intelligence.* New York: Cambridge University Press. 1998.

Eden, Paul E. *The World's Greatest Civil Aircraft.* New York: Metro Books. 2015.

FAA. *Airplane Flying Handbook.* (FAA-H-8083-3A) Jeppesen. 2004.

FAA. *Pilot's Handbook of Aeronautical Knowledge* (FAA-H-8083-25). Oklahoma City: FAA Publications. 2003.

FAA. *The Pilot's Handbook of Aeronautical Knowledge* (AC 61-23B). Aviation Supplies & Academics, Inc. 1980.

Filkin D. *Stephen Hawking's Universe: The Cosmos Explained;* 1st Ed. New York: Basic Books. 1997.

Fortey, Richard. *Life: A Natural History of the First Four Billion Years of Life on Earth.* New York: Vintage Books. 1997.

Gilbert, James. *The Great Planes.* New York: Ridge Press/Madison Square Press/Grosset & Dunlap Inc. 1970.

Goldstone, Lawrence. *Birdmen: The Wright Brothers, Glenn Curtiss, and the Battle to Control the Skies.* New York: Ballantine Books. 2014.

Goodnow, David. *How Birds Fly.* Columbia, Maryland: Periwinkle Books, Inc. 1992.

Goodsell, David. *The Machinery of Life* (2nd ed.). New York: Copernicus Books. 2009.

Gould, Stephen Jay. *The Book of Life.* New York: WW Norton & Co. LLC. 2001.

Hart, Roger. *Men in the Air.* New York: Praeger Publishers. 1973.

Hawks, John (University of Wisconsin – Madison). *The Rise of Humans: Great Scientific Debates;* The Great Courses. Chantilly, VA. The Teaching Company. 2011. Multimedia Learning Course.

Hazen, Robert M. *The Story of Earth: The First 4.5 Billion Years, From Stardust to Living Planet.* New York: Viking Books. 2012.

Hazen, M. (George Mason University and Carnegie Institution of Washington) *Origins of Life;* The Great Courses. Chantilly, VA: The Teaching Company. 2005. Multimedia Learning Course.

Jackson, Donald Dale. *The Epic of Flight: The Aeronauts.* Alexandria, Virginia: Time-Life Books. 1980.

Johnson, Norman A. *Darwinian Detectives: Revealing the Natural History of Genes and Genomes.* New York: Oxford University Press. 2007.

Holmes, Richard. *Falling Upwards: How We Took to the Air.* New York: Pantheon Books. 2013.

Jones B. *Discovering The Solar System;* 2nd Ed. Milton Keynes, UK: John Wiley & Sons Ltd. 2007.

Kemp T.S. *The Origin & Evolution of Mammals.* New York: Oxford University Press. 2005.

Kleppner, Daniel and Robert Kolenkow. *An Introduction to Mechanics.* New York: McGraw Hill. 1973.

Kleveman, Lutz. *The New Great Game: Blood and Oil in Central Asia.* New York: Grove Press. 2003.

Lane, Nick. *Oxygen: The Molecule that Made the World.* New York: Oxford University Press. 2002.

Lane, Nick. *Life Ascending: The Ten Great Inventions of Evolution.* New York & London: WW Norton & Co. LLC. 2009.

Long, John and Peter Schouten. *Feathered Dinosaurs: The Origin of Birds.* New York: Oxford University Press. 2008.

Lopez, Daniel S. *Aviation: A Smithsonian Guide.* New York: Macmillan. 1995.

Mackey, Sandra. *The Iranians: Persia, Islam, and the Soul of a Nation.* Plume Books. 1998.

Margulis, Lynn. *Symbiotic Planet: A New Look At Evolution.* New York: Basic Books. 1998.

Margulis, Lynn, Asikainen Celeste A., and Krumbein, Wolfgang E. (ed) *Chimeras and Consciousness: Evolution of the Sensory Self.* Cambridge, MA: MIT Press. 2011.

Marshak S. *Earth: Portrait of a Planet;* 3rd Ed. New York: WW Norton & Co. LLC. 2008

McMenamin M. *Science 101: Geology.* New York: Collins Press. 2007.

McNeill, William. *Plagues and Peoples.* New York: Anchor Press Books. 1976.

McNeil & McNeil. *The Human Web: A Bird's Eye View of World History*. New York: WW Norton & Co. LLC. 2003.

McWhorter, John (Professor Manhattan Institute) *The Story of Human Language*; The Great Courses. Chantilly, VA: The Teaching Company; 2004. Multimedia Learning Course

Mondey, David. *Aircraft: An All Color Story of Modern Flight*. New York: Octopus Books. 1973.

Mondey, David (editor). *The International Encyclopedia of Aviation*. New York: Crown Publishers Inc. 1977.

Muesse, Mark W. (Professor Rhodes College) *Religions of the Axial Age: An Approach to the World's Religions*; The Great Courses. Chantilly, VA: The Teaching Company. 2007. Multimedia Learning Course.

Munson, Kenneth. *The Pocket Encyclopedia of World Aircraft in Color: Airliners Since 1946*. New York: MacMillan Publishing Co, Inc. 1976.

Nørgaard, Eric. *The Book of Balloons*. New York: Crown Publishers Inc. 1970.

Owen, David. *Lighter than Air: An Illustrated History of the Development of Hot-Air Balloons and Airships*. Edison, New Jersey: Chartwell Books, Inc.1999.

Pacey, Arnold. *The Maze of Ingenuity: Ideas and Idealism in the Development of Technology*. London: Allen Lane Books. 1976.

Payne, Lee. *Lighter Than Air: An Illustrated History of the Airship*. New York: Orion Books. 1991.

Piccard, Auguste. *Between the Earth and Sky*. London: The Falcon Press. 1950

Rabinowitz, Harold. *Classic Airplanes: Pioneering Aircraft and the Visionaries Who Built Them*. New York: Metro Books. 1997.

Reilly, H.V. Pat. *From the Balloon to the Moon: New Jersey's Amazing Aviation History*. New Jersey: HV Publishers. 1992.

Rich, Patricia Vickers & David J. Bohaska. *The Ogygoptyngidae, a New Family of Owls from the Paleocene of North America*. Alcheringa 5: 95-102. 1981.

Rollinson, Hugh. *Early Earth Systems: A Geochemical Approach*. Malden, MA: Blackwell Publishing. 2007.

Roth, Jonathon P. (San José State University). *War and World History*; The Great Courses. Chantilly, VA. The Teaching Company. 2009. Multimedia Learning Course.

Scamehorn, Howard L. *Balloons to Jets: 1855-1955, A Century of Aeronautics in Illinois*. Chicago: Henry Regnery Co. 1957.

Southwood, R. *The Story of Life*. Oxford, England: Oxford University Press. 2003

Spier, Fred. *Big History and the Future of Humanity*. Boston: Wiley-Blackwell. 2011.

Steams, Peter N. (George Mason University) *A Brief History of the World*; The Great Courses. Chantilly, VA. The Teaching Company. 2007. Multimedia Learning Course.

Summers, Frank (Space Telescope Science Institute). *New Frontiers: Modern Perspectives on Our Solar System*; The Great Courses. Chantilly, VA. The Teaching Company. 2008. Multimedia Learning Course.

Taylor, John W.R. *A Picture History of Flight*. London: Edward Hulton. 1955.

Tennekes, Henk. *The Simple Science of Flight: From Insects to Jumbo Jets*. Revised and expanded edition. Cambridge, Massachusetts: MIT Press. 2009.

Tsiganis, K. et. al. *Origin of the Orbital Architecture of the Giant Planets of the Solar System*. Letters, Nature vol. 435, 26 May 2005 pp. 459-461.

Tyson, N. (Hayden Planetarium and Princeton University) *My Favorite Universe*; The Great Courses. Chantilly, VA: The Teaching Company. 2003. Multimedia Learning Course

Tyson, N. and Goldsmith D. *Origins: Fourteen Billion Years of Cosmic Evolution*. New York: WW Norton & Co. LLC. 2004.

Walker, Jearl, David Halliday and Robert Resnick. *Fundamentals of Physics*, 8th edition. New York: John Wiley & Sons. 2008.

Ward, Peter D. *Out of Thin Air*. Washington, DC: Joseph Henry Press. 2006.

Ward, Peter and Joe Kirschvink. *A New History of Life*. New York: Bloomsbury Books. 2015.

Watson, Alexander. *Ring of Steel: Germany and Austria-Hungary in World War I*. New York: Basic Books. 2014.

Whitehouse, Arch. *The Early Birds: The Wonders and Heroics of the First Decades of Flight*. New York: Curtis Books. 1965.

White Lynn Jr. *Medieval Technology and Social Change*. Oxford: Oxford University Press. 1966.

Wicander, Reed and James S. Monroe. *Historical Geology: Evolution of Earth and Life Through Time* (6th ed). New York: Brooks/Cole- Cengage Learning. 2010.

Wilson, Edward O. *The Social Conquest of Earth*. New York: WW Norton & Co. LLC. 2012.

Windsor, H. H. Jr. (editor). "Sky Hook Spirals from Plane." Popular Mechanics Magazine. Vol. 82, No. 6, December 1944, p.75.

Wirth, Dick and Jerry Young. *Ballooning: The Complete Guide to Riding the Winds*. New York: Random House. 1980.

Witton, Mark P. *Pterosaurs: Natural History, Anatomy and Evolution*. Princeton, NJ: Princeton University Press. 2013.

Wrangham, Richard. *Catching Fire: How Cooking Made Us Human*. New York: Basic Books. 2009.

Zimmer, Carl. *At The Water's Edge: Fish with Fingers, Whales with Legs, and How Life Came Ashore but Then Went Back to Sea*. New York: Touchstone. 1999.

Image Credits

5:1 – Curtis, John. "Xyela pusilla Symphyta." Illustration. Date unknown. [Public domain] Original Source: "British Entomology." Via Wikimedia Commons. Web.
5:3 – Martyniuk, Matt. "Life restoration (graphite) of Jinfengopteryx elegans." Illustration. 11 Dec 2006. [CC BY 2.5] Via WikiMedia Commons. Web.
5:3 – Martyniuk, Matt. "Life restoration of Tyrannosaurus rex based on specimen AMNH 5027." Illustration. 8 Aug 2013. [CC BY-SA 3.0] Via WikiMedia Commons. Web.
5:6 – ДиБгд. "Illustration of Rhamphorhynchus muensteri." Illustration. 2003. [Public Domain] Original held ДиБгд. Via WikiMedia Commons. Web.
5:7 – ДиБгд. "Isisaurus colberti in landscape." Illustration. 2007. [CC BY 2.5] Via Wikimedia Commons. Web.
7:4 – Hufstedler, Carla. "20,000 Year Old Cave Paintings, Hyena" Photograph. [Attribution-Share Alike 2.0] Original posted to Flickr. Via Wikimedia Commons.
7:5 – Saura, Pedro (Science/AAASD). "In El Castillo cave." Photograph. Via National Geographic News.
7:13 – Anon. "Ur Chariot." Image. [Public Domain] Via Wikimedia Commons. Web.
7:13 – WikiUser: "Rama." "Sphinx of Thutmose III." Photograph of goldened bronze statue. 2007. [CC BYS-SA 2.0] Original held by Louvre Museum. Via WikiMedia Commons. Web.
8:0 – Tissot, James Jacques Joseph. "Solomon Dedicates the Temple at Jerusalem." Painting. c. 1896-1902. [Public Domain] Original held by The Jewish Museum. Via WikiMedia Commons. Web.
8:0 – Gowy, Jacob Peter. "La caída de Ícaro." Painting. c. 1636. [Public Domain] Original held by Museo del Prado. Via WikiMedia Commons. Web.
8:1 – asurbanipal. "Portrait of Cyrus the Great." Image. Via kdix. ba. Web.
8:1 – Kāne, Herb Kawainui. "Ancient Polynesians in Outrigger Canoes Coming to Hawaii." Painting. Via bragg.com. Web.
8:1 – Nguyen, Marie-Lan. "Lamassu (Human-headed winged bull) heading left." Photograph of carving. 2005. [Public Domain] Via WikiMedia Commons.
8:1 – WikiUser: Trjames. "Right-facing Lammasu." Photograph of carving. 2007. [CC BY-SA 3.0] Via WikiMedia Commons. Web.
8:1 – Wright, John Henry. "Reconstructed Model of Palace of Sargon at Khorsabad." Etching. c. 1905. [Public Domain] Originally published in "A History of All Nations from the Earliest Times" (1905). Via WikiMedia Commons. Web.
8:1 – Horne, Charles F. (editor). "Portrait of Cyrus the Great." Image. 1917. [Public Domain] Original published in *The Sacred Books and Early Literature of the East*, (New York: Parke, Austin, & Lipscomb, 1917). Via WikiMedia Commons. Web.
8:2 – "Sunzi, author of the Art of War." Image. Via Suntzuart.com
8:3 – WikiUser: "Kaboldy." "The Persian horizontal windmill." Illustration. 2009. [CC BY-SA 3.0] Via WikiMedia Commons. Web.
8:3 – Woodcroft (editor). "Aeolipile Illustration." Illustration. c. 1876. [Public domain] Original Source: Knight's American Mechanical Dictionary, 1876, edited by Woodcroft, of London. Via WikiMedia Commons. Web.
8:3 – Schmidt, W. "Herons von Alexandria Druckwerke und Automatentheater." Illustration. 1899. [Public Domain] Originally printed: W. Schmidt: Herons von Alexandria Druckwerke und Automatentheater, Greek and German, 1899 (Heronis Alexandrini opera I, Reprint 1971), p. 205, fig. 44. Via WikiMedia Commons. Web.
8:3 – "Archimedes' screw." Illustration. 1875. [Public Domain] Original source: Chambers's Encyclopedia (Philadelphia: J. B. Lippincott Company, 1875). Via WikiMedia Commons. Web.
8:3 – Veronese, Paolo. "Jesus among the Doctors in the Temple". 1558. Painting. Via 1st Art Gallery. Web.
8:4 – "4th Century Christ." Image. Via AncientReign.com. Web.
8:4 – Apian, Peter. "16-Century representation of Ptolemy's Geocentric Model." Illustration. 1524. [Public Domain] Originally Edward Grant, "Celestial Orbs in the Latin Middle Ages", Isis, Vol. 78, No. 2. (Jun., 1987), pp. 152-173. Via WikiMedia.
8:4 – "Cameo of Sharpur I, humiliating Emperor Valerianus." Sardonyx carving. c. 260 CE. [CC BY-SA 2.5] Original held by Cabinet des Médailles. Via WikiMedia Commons. Web.
8:4 – Kāne, Herb Kawainui. "Ancient Polynesians in Outrigger Canoes Coming to Hawaii." Painting. Via bragg.com. Web.
8:4 – Sarkar, Arunava de. "Nalanda Univercity." Photograph. June 1, 2011. [CC SA 3.0] Original held by Arunava de Sarkar. Via Wikimedia Commons. Web.
8:5 – Lun, Cai. "An image of a Ming Dynasty woodcut describing major steps in ancient Chinese papermaking process." Woodcut. c. 105 CE. [Public Domain] Via WikiMedia Commons. Web.
8:5 – unknown. "Buraq on a reproduction of a 17th-century Indian Mughal miniature." Illustration. c. 17th-Century. [Public Domain] Via WikiMedia.
8:5 – Kāne, Herb Kawainui. "Ancient Polynesians in Outrigger Canoes Coming to Hawaii." Painting. Via bragg.com. Web.
8:6 – Sheng, Lanling Xiaoxiao. "An illustration of a fireworks display. . ." Illustration. c 1610. [Publi Domain] Originally published from 1628-1643 edition of the Ming Dynasty book Jin Ping Mei. Via WikiMedia Commons. Web.
8:8 – "Kneeling Knight, Westminster Psalter, London, c. 1250." Image. Original held by London, British Library ms. Royal 2A. XXII fol. 220. Via hubert-herald.
8:11 – Yoosai, Kikuchi. "MokoShurai." Image. [Public Domain] Original held by Tokyo National Museum - Dschingis Khan und seine Erben (exhibition catalogue), München 2005, p. 331. Via Wikimedia.
8:12 – Prout, Samuel. "A view of a windmill with a small ladder placed by the doorway." Engraving. 1815. [Public Domain] Original held by The National Library of Wales, call #1132339. Via WikiMedia Commons. Web.
8:13 – Kāne, Herb Kawainui. "Ancient Polynesians in Outrigger Canoes Coming to Hawaii." Painting. Via bragg.com. Web.
9:1 – Kee, Kang Byeong. "Shinkigeon-style Hwacha can fire 100 arrows at a time." Photograph. 14 Dec 2008. [CC BY 3.0] Via WikiMedia Commons. Web.
9:1 – Lodge, George Edward. "Lesser Megalapteryx." Illustration. 1907. [Public Domain] Originally published in "Extinct Birds" by Lionel Walter Rothschild. Via WikiMedia Commons. Web.
9:3 – unknown. "Fall of the City (Constantinople)." Painting. Via ballandalus.wordpress.com
9:3 – Da Vinci, Leonardo. "Helicopter (top) and experiment on lifting power of wing (bottom)." Illustration. c. 1440. [Public Domain] Original held by: British Museum, London. Via WikiMedia Commons.
9:4 – Da Vinci, Leonardo. "Study of horse." [Public Domain] Original held by Web Gallery of Art. Via Wikimedia Commons. Web.
9:4 – Da Vinci, Leonardo. "Paleodictyon." sketch. c. 1507. [Public Domain] Via fieldofscience.com. Web.
9:5 – Copernicus, Nicolas. "De revolutionibus." Illustration. c. 1520-1541. [Public Domain] Original held by Jagiellonian Library, Kraków (ID# 10,000). Via WikiMedia Commons. Web.
9:7 – de Loutherbourg, Phillipe-Jaques. "Defeat of the Spanish Armada. . ." Painting. c. 1589. [CC BY-SA 2.0] Via Maritime Museum, Greenwich, London. Web.
9:7 – Shaw, Byam. "The Adventures of Akbar Artillery." Illustration. 1913. [Public Domain] Original published in novel by the same name, authored by Flora Annie Steel. Via Wikimedia Commons. Web.
9:7 – Agricola, Georgius. "A water-powered mine hoist used for raising ore." Woodcut. 1555. [Public Domain] Via WikiMedia Commons. Web.
9:7 – Matham, Jacob. "A beached Sperm Whale on the Shore near Beverwijk." Engraving. 1601. [Public Domain] Original held by the Trustees of the British Museum (call #AN576810001). Via mercuriuspoliticus.wordpress.com. Web.
9:8 – Heydra. "Froskepollemolen." Photpgraph. 1969. [CC BY-SA 4.0] Original held by Rijksdienst voor het Cultureel Erfgoed (Call #24507). Via WikiMedia Commons. Web.
9:8 – "Peat Extraction ca. 1800." Image. c. 1800. [Public Domain] Via Encyclopedia Pictura. Web.
9:8 – "Whaling Fleet at Work." Painting. [Public Domain] Via Berkshire Fine Arts. Web.
9:8 – Galilei, Galileo. "Phases of the Moon." Image. [Public domain] Via Wikimedia Commons. Web.
9:9 - unknown. "William Gilbert's terrella." Illustration. c 1914. [Public Domain] Originally published in "Practical Physics," 1914, pub. by Macmillan and Company. Via WikiMedia Commons.
9:9 – "Chhen Li's diagram of Chinese windmills." Illustration. c. 1670. [Public Domain] Originially published in Joseph Needham's "Science and Civilization in China," Vol. 4 - 2, Physics and Physical Technology, Mechanical Engineering. 1971. Cambridge: Cambridge University Press. Web.
9:9 – Schott, Gaspar. "Engraving showing Otto von Guericke's 'Magdeburg hemispheres' experiment." Engraving. 1657. [Public Domain] Original published in "Experimenta nova (ut vocantur) magdeburgica de vacuo spatio" by Otto von Guericke, published 1672 by Amsterdam J. Jansson à Waesberge. Via WikiMedia.
9:10 – Thom, Robert. "Van Leeuwenheok at Work." Painting. Via ToLearn.com. Web.
9:10 – Borelli, Giovanni. "Borelli's Submarine." Illustration. 1680. [Public Domain] Originally published in "De Motu Animalism," 1680. Original held by Cite des Sciences de la Vilette, Paris. Via WikiMedia Commons. Web.
9:10 – Terzi, Francesco Lana de. "Vacuum Airship Sketch." Illustration. c. 1670. [Public Domain]. Via WikiMedia Commons. Web.
9:13 – WikiUser: Cnyborg. "Windmill in Sønderho, Fanø, Denmark. Dutch type, built in 1895 to replace an older mill destroyed by fire in 1894." Photograph. 2005. [CC BY-SA 3.0] Via WikiMedia Commons. Web.
10:0 - Desrais, Claude-Louis. "Montgolfier brothers flight. . ." Illustration. 1783. [Public Domain] Original held by Bildarchiv Preussischer Kulturbesitz, Berlin. Via WikiMedia Commons. Web.
10:0 – Zveg, V. (US Navy employee). "Battle Of Virginia Capes." Image. [Public Domain] Original held by US Navy Naval History and Heritage Command: Photo #: NH 73927-KN. Via Wikimedia Commons. Web.
10:1 – Raleigh, C.S. "The Whaling Schooner Amelia of New Bedford, Massachusetts." Drawing. Original held by NOAA. Via Cool Antarctica. Web.
10:1 – unknown. "The crossing of the Channel in balloon by Blanchard." Photograph of engraving. c. 18th century. [Public Domain] Via WikiMedia.
10:1 – de La Place, Jean-Baptiste Marie Meusnier. "Dirigere." Illustration. c. 1783. [Public domain] Via Wikimedia Commons. Web.
10:1 – David, Jacques-Louis. "Portrait of Monsieur Lavoisier and His Wife." Painting. [Public Domain] Original held by Metropolitan Museum of Art (call # 436106). Via Wikimedia Commons. Web.
10:2 – Smith, William. "Geological Map Britain." 1815. [Public Domain] Original held by LiveScience Image Gallery by the Library Foundation, Buffalo and Erie County Public Library. Via Wikimedia Commons. Web.
10:2 – Smith, William. "Fossils 2." Engraving. [Public Domain] Original William Smith's guide to classifying rock strata by characteristic fossils, 1815. Via Wikimedia Commons. Web.
10:3 – Bernard, Fred. "Dickens at the Blacking Warehouse." Image. [Public Domain] Original from "The Leisure Hour", 1904, London. Via Wikimedia.
10:3 – "McConnel & Company mills, about 1820." Watercolor image. [Public Domain] Original from A Century of fine Cotton Spinning, 1790-1913. McConnel & Co. Ltd. Frontispiece. Via Wikimedia.
10:3 – Heath, William. "Hobbies..." Hand-colored etching. 1819. Original held by the British Museum (ID# 1895,0408.23). Via Britishmuseum.org.
10:3 – Siegrist, Wilhelm. "Original draisine..." Image. 1817. [Public Domain] Via WikiMedia Commons. Web.
10:3 – Tuner, Joseph Mallord William. "The Battle of Trafalgar." Painting. 1806. [Public Domain] Original held by Tate Britain. Via WikiMedia Commons. Web.
10:4 – Huggins, William John. "The screw steamer SS Archimedes at sea." Painting. c. 1845. [Public Domain] Original source Intaglio Art Prints. Via WikiMedia.
10:4 – "Morse Telegraph Diagram." Image. [Public Domain] Via Wikimedia Commons. Web.
10:4 – "Ice Harvesting on Spy Pond." Print. 1854. [Public Domain] Via WikiMedia Commons. Web.
10:5 – Van Voorst, John. "A sketch of a South Sea Whaling Voyage, London." 1839. [Public Domain] Via Sothebys.com. Web.
10:5 – Porter, Rufus. "1849 ad for Rufus Porter's New-York-to-California transport." Illustration. 1849. [Public Domain] Via WikiMedia Commons. Web.
10:5 – WikiUser: WikiStefan. "Stellar Parallax." Illustration. 2004. [CC BY-SA 2.0] Via Wikimedia.
10:5 – unknown. "Chinese Ships in the Opium Wars." Via TimeToast. Web
10:6 – Parsons, William. "Drawing of the Whirlpool Galaxy." Sketch. 1845. [Public Domain] Via Wikimedia Commons. Web.
10:6 – Krassovsky, Nikolay. "Russian Black Sea Fleet after the battle of Synope, 1853." Painting. [Public Domain] Via Wikimedia Commons. Web.
10:6 – unknown. "Birr Castle 72 inch." Illustration. [Public Domain] Original Source: telescopes.stardate.org/ Via WikiMedia Commons. Web.
10:6 – Tallis. "The front entrance of the Crystal Palace, Hyde Park, London." Engraving. 1852. [Public Domain] Originally published in Tallis' "History and Criticism of the Crystal Palace." Via WikiMedia Commons. Web.
10:6 – Young, Mike. "Giffard Airship." Photograph. unknown. [Public

domain] Via Wikimedia Commons.
10:6 – Linehan, Sean. "A Hemispherical Cup Anemometer…" Photograph. 1899. [Public Domain] Original Source: "The Aims and Methods of Meteorological Work" by Cleveland Abbe, Johns Hopkins Press, Baltimore, 1899. Via WikiMedia.
10:6 – unknown. "Drake's Oil Well Pennsylvania, The Valley Where it All Began." Photograph. c 1904. [Fair Use] Via Titusville Shale Taskforce. Web.
10:7 – Heine, W. "Landing of Commodore Perry, Officers & Men of the Squadron…" Lithograph. 1853. [Public Domain] Original held by Library of Congress. Via Wikimedia Commons. Web.
10:7 – NASA. "Earth's Magneto Sphere and Solar Barrage." Image. [Pubic Domain] Via NASA Heliophysics Division. Web.
10:7 – WikiUser: Dhirad. "Taj Mahal, Agra, India." Photograph. 2004. [CC BY-SA 3.0] Via WikiMedia.
10:7 – Armistead, Wilson. "Husbands, wives, and families sold indiscriminately…" Illustration. c 1853. [Public Domain] Via WikiMedia Commons. Web.
10:7 – Alexander, W.A. "SS Hunley, Inboard profile and plan drawings." Illustration. 1863. [Public Domain] Via WikiMedia Commons. Web.
10:7 – "The balloon *Washington* aboard the *George Washington Parke Custis*." Image. c 1862. [Public Domain] Via WikiMedia Commons. Web.
10:7 – unknown. "The Union Army balloon Washington aboard…" Illustration. c. 1862. [Public Domain] Via WikiMedia Commons. Web.
10:7 – "From the Earth to the Moon." Scan. unknown. [Public domain] Original Soure: http://www.sil.si.edu/. Via WikiMedia Commons. Web.
10:8 – unknown. "Drake's Oil Well Pennsylvania, The Valley Where it All Began." Photograph. c 1904. [Fair Use] Via Titusville Shale Taskforce. Web.
10:8 - Cpt. Bullock. "Eclipse by Captain Bullock." Illustration. 1868. [Public Domain] Originally published in "Total Eclipses of the Sun" by Mabel Loomis Todd. Via WikiMedia Commons. Web.
10:9 – Unknown. "Front Cover of the 1871 pamphlet edition of Sir George Tomkyns Chesney's The Battle of Dorking." Photograph. 2011. [Public Domain] Original published by Edinburgh and London: William Blackwood and Sons, 1871. Via WikiMedia Commons.
10:10 – "Zoroaster." Photograph. 1878. [Public Domain] Original held by Swedish National Museum of Science and Technology. Via Wikimedia Commons.
10:10 – Reichard & Lindner. "Wilhelm II. on picture postcard." Photograph. 1905. [Public Domain] Original published by Gustav Liersch & Co. Via WikiMedia Commons. Web.
10:10 – Lueger, Otto. "Safety Bicycle and Penny-Farthing." Illustration. 1904. [Public Domain] Original Source: "Lexikon der gesamten Technik." Via WikiMedia Commons. Web.
10:10 – unknown. "Drake's Oil Well Pennsylvania, The Valley Where it All Began." Photograph. c 1904. [Fair Use] Via Titusville Shale Taskforce. Web.
10:11 – Chanute, Octave. "Biplane hang glider flown in the Chicago area." Photograph. 1896. [Public Domain] Via WikiMedia Commons. Web.
10:11 – Chanute, Octave. "A twelve-winged glider of Chanute's design…" Photograph. 1896. [Public Domain] Originally published in 1897 Aeronautical Annual. Via WikiMedia Commons. Web.
10:11 – Chanute, Octave. "William Avery at the St. Louis World's Fair in 1904…" Photograph. 1904. [Public Domain] Via WikiMedia Commons. Web.
10:11 – unknown. "Hannibal Bridge." Illustration. 1908. [Public Domain] Via WikiMedia Commons. Web.
10:11 – unknown. "Photograph of Albert Tissandier, left, Gaston Tissandier and…" Photograph. c. 1890. [Public domain] Via Wikimedia Commons. Web.
10:11 - "Lenkballon Albert Und Gaston Tissandier, Elektroluftschiff mit Elektromotor." Etching. c. 1883 [CC BY-SA 4.0] Via pictokon.net.
10:12 – Lueger, Otto. "Safety Bicycle and Penny-Farthing." Illustration. 1904. [Public Domain] Original Source: "Lexikon der gesamten Technik." Via WikiMedia Commons. Web.
10:12 – unknown. "Construction Tour Eiffel." Photograph. 1888. [Public Domain] Originally published in "Tour Eiffel: Montage de la deuxième plateforme." Via WikiMedia Commons. Web.
10:12 – "Octave A. Chanute." Photograph. c 1909. [Public Domain] Via WikiMedia Commons. Web.
10:13 – WikiUser: Nyttend. "The Wright Cycle Company offices." Photograph. 2010. [Public domain] Via Wikimedia Commons. Web.
10:13 – Grosvener, Gilbert H. "Alexander Graham Bell at the opening of the long-distance line from New York to Chicago." Photograph. 1892. [Public Domain] Original held by Library of Congress Archives, Prints & Photographs Division. Via WikiMedia Commons.
10:13 – Oomoto. "Japanese troops during the Sino-Japanese War." Photograph. [Public Domain] Originally published in "Bakumatsu Meiji no Shashin" by Ozawa Kenshin. Via WikiMedia Commons. Web.
10:13 – WikiUser: Pretzelpaws. "Clark Dome at Lowell Observatory." Photograph. 2005. [CC BY-SA 3.0] Via WikiMedia Commons. Web.
10:14 – Lilienthal, Otto. "Flügel eines Storches." Illustration. 1889. [Public Domain] Originally published in Der Vogelflug als Grundlage der Fliegekunst. Via WikiMedia Commons. Web.
10:14 – "Otto Lilienthal performing one of his gliding experiments." Photograph. c1895 [Public Domain] Original held by Library of Congress (Call # ppmsca.02546). Via WikiMedia Commons. Web.
10:14 – "Samuel Pierpont Langley - Potomac experiment." Photograph. 1903. [Public Domain] Original source: http://www.centennialofflight.gov/. Via WikiMedia Commons. Web.
10:15 – unknown. "Breaker Boys." Photograph. Via epubbud.com. Web.
10:15 – unknown. "David Schwarz' Airship." Photograph. c. 1897. [Public Domain] Via WikiMedia Commons. Web.
10:15 – Great Barrier Pigeongram Agency. "Pigeon-gam stamp from early pigeon-post service between Auckland and Great Barrier Island, New Zealand." Photograph. 1899. [Public Domain] Via WikiMedia.
11:0 – unknown. "Man-lifter War Kite" Photograph. c 1908. [Public Domain] Via WikiMedia Commons.
11:0 – l'Aerophile (staff). "Santos-Dumont no. 6, Rounding Tower." Photograph. 1901. [Public Domain] Original held by National Air and Space Museum (Neg.# 85-3941). Via WikiMedia Commons. Web.
11:1 – unknown. "Troops of the Eight nations alliance of 1900 in China." Photograph. 1900. [Public Domain] Via WikiMedia Commons. Web.
11:1 – Trost, John. "Lucas Gusher." Photograph. 1901. [Public Domain] Original held by The American Petroleum Institute. Via Wikimedia Commons. Web.
11:1 – Scherer, Peter. "First Zeppelin flight at Lake Constance." Photograph. c. 1900. [Public domain] Original Held by Print & Photographs (P&P) Online Catalog of the Library of Congress. Via WikiMedia.
11:1 – unknown. "Whitehead flying with power for a distance of 'one half mile'." Illustration. 1901. [Public Domain] Original published by The Bridgeport (CT) Sunday Herald. Via WikiMedia Commons. Web.
11:1 – Gribayedoff, Valerian. "Gustav Whitehead and his 1901 monoplane…" Photograph. 1901. [Public Domain] Via WikiMedia Commons. Web.
11:2 – Detroit Photographic Company. "Statue of Liberty c. 1900." Photochrom postcard. c. 1900. [Public Domain] Original held by Beinecke Rare Book & Manuscript Library, Yale University. Via WikiMedia Commons. Web.
11:3 – Daniels, John T. "First successful flight of the Wright Flyer, by the Wright brothers." Photograph. 1903. [Public domain] Original held by US Library of Congress's Prints and Photographs division, Call # IDppprs.00626. Via Wikimedia Commons. Web.
11:4 – unknown. "Steel Building and 60 inch reflector." Photograph. 1909. [Public Domain] Original held by Popular Science Monthly. Via WikiMedia Commons.
11:4 - unknown. "British Army Dirigible No 1…" Photograph. 1907. [Public Domain] Originally published in "Omhoog in het luchtruim! Praatje over het luchtvaartvraagstuk "De Aarde en haar volken." Via WikiMedia Commons.
11:4 – Beau, Jules. "*14-bis* de Alberto Santos-Dumont." Photograph. c1906. [Public Domain] Original held by Gallica Digital Library (Call #btv1b8433366m). Via WikiMedia Commons. Web.
11:4 – "Traian Vuia in his *Vuia I*." Photograph. 1906. [Public Domain] Via WikiMedia Commons. Web.
11:5 – "Sectional views of the Gnome Omega." Image. 1910. [CC BY-SA 4.0] Original held by FlightGlobal. Via WikiMedia Commons. Web.
11:5 – unknown. "Astronomer Edward Charles Pickering's Harvard computers." Photograph. c. 1890. [Public Domain] Original held by Harvard College Observatory. Via WikiMedia Commons. Web.
11:5 – Unknown. "Glenn Curtiss on his V-8 motorcycle, Ormond Beach, Florida." Photograph. 1907. [Public Domain] Originally published in the February 1907 issue of The Motorcycle Illustrated (magazine). Via Wikimedia Commons.
11:6 – unknown, "German Graf Zeppelin flies over St. Paul's Cathedral." Photograph. 1930. [Public Domain] Original held by The National Archives, UK. Via WikiMedia Commons. Web.
11:6 - Montauk, Ernest. "Advertising poster for the Grand Semaine d'Aviation." Graphical poster. 1909. [Public Domain] Via Wikimedia Commons. Web.
11:7 – French Navy. "Henri Fabre on Hydroplane." Photograph. 1910. [Public domain] Via Wikimedia.
11:7 – unknown. "General Map of Railways, India, 1909." Illustration. 1909. [Public Domain] Originally pub. in "The Imperial Gazetteer of India," vol. 25, Oxford University Press, 1909. Via WikiMedia.
11:7 – "Charles Weymann and his ..." Photograph. 1911. [Public Domain] Original held by FlightGlobal. Via Wikimedia Commons. Web.
11:8 – "A Caudron Type J 'Marine' seaplane being lifted on the Foudre." 1914. [Public Domain] Via WikiMedia Commons. Web.
11:8 – Ribeiro, Serra. "Hidroavião D.D.3, no rio Tejo, junto a Lisboa." Photograph. 1919. [Public Domain] Via WikiMedia Commons. Web.
11:8 – l'Aerophile (staff). "Santos-Dumont no. 6, Rounding Tower." Photograph. 1901. [Public Domain] Original held by Smithsonian Institution, National Air and Space Museum, SI Neg. No. 85-3941. Via WikiMedia Commons. Web.
11:9 - "An observer of the Royal Flying Corps…" Photograph. 1916. [Public Domain] Original held by Imperial War Museum (Call# Q 33850). WikiMedia.
11:9 – unknown. "Canadian soldiers fixing their bayonets to their rifles, Battle of Somme." Photograph. 1916. [Public Domain] Via http://elinorflorence.com. Web.
11:9 - RAF. "Aerial photograph, St Eloi, near Ypres, Belgium…" Photograph. 1916. [Public Domain] Original held by National Library of Scotland. Via WikiMedia Commons. Web.
11:9 – Brown, Charles E. "HMS Queen Elizabeth." Photograph. c1936. [Public Domain] Via Wikimedia Commons. Web.
11:9 – "German soldiers in a railway…" Photograph. 1914. [Public Domain] Via WikiMedia Commons. Web.
11:10 – "HMS Ark Royal after completion." Photograph. c. 1938. [Public Domain] Original held by Collections of the U.S. National Archives, Naval Historical Center. Catalog #: "19-SB-2J-1." Via WikiMedia Commons. Web.
11:11 – unknown. "Jasta 11 with Albatros D.III near Douai, France." Photograph. 1917. [Public Domain] Original held by the Imperial War Museum (ID# Q 50328). Via WikiMedia Commons.
11:11 – unknown. "Early attempt on a French Morane-Saulnier L to mount a forward-firing gun." Photograph. 1916. [Public Domain] Original held by Bibliothèque nationale de France (ID# EI-13-474). Via WikiMedia Commons. Web.
11:11 – "King George V and officials inspecting munitions factory." Photograph. 1917. [Public Domain] Via WikiMedia Commons. Web.
11:11 - unknown. "Curtiss Autoplane displayed at New York Aero Show." Photograph. 1917. [Public Domain] Originally published in Flight Magazine, 1917. Via WikiMedia Commons. Web.
11:12 – unknown. "The red Fokker Dr I of Manfred von Richthofen on the ground." Photograph. c. 1917. [Public Domain] Source: earlyaviator.com .
11:12 – unknown. "Aerial view of ruins of Vaux-devant-Damloup, France." Photograph. 1918. [Public Domain] Original held by National Archives and Records. Administration (ID# 512856). Via WikiMedia.
11:12 – Unknown. "Take-off of Alcock and Brown from St. John's..." Photograph. 1919. [Public Domain] Via WikiMedia Commons.
11:12 – US Army. "Men of U.S. 64th Regiment celebrate the news of the Armistice." Photograph. 1918. [Public Domain] Original held by US National Archive. Via Wikimedia Commons.
11:12 - unkown. "Junkers D.I German First World War all-metal fighter." Photograph. c. 1918. [Public Domain] Original held by San Diego Air and Space Museum Archives. Via WikiMedia Commons. Web.
11:13 – Orpen, William. "The Signing of Peace in the Hall of Mirrors, Versailles." Painting. 1919. [Public Domain] Original held by the Imperial War Museum (ID# IWM ART 2856). Via WikiMedia Commons. Web.
11:13 - unknown. "Neta Snook and Amelia Earhart..." Photograph. c. 1921. [Public Domain] Original held by Karsten Smedal. Via Wikimedia Commons. Web.
11:13 – Davidson, C., F.W. Dyson, and A.S. Eddington "1919 Eclipse Positive." Photograph. 1919. [Public Domain] Originally published in "A Determination of the Deflection of Light … Total Eclipse of May 29, 1919" Philosophical Transactions of the Royal Society of London. Via Wikimedia Commons. Web.
11:13 – Unknown. "Bessie Coleman." Photograph. 1921. [Public Domain] Original held by National Air and Space Museum. Via

Wikimedia Commons.Web.
11:14 – Unknown."G-AUED Airco DH 9c aeroplane." Photgraph. c1925. [Public Domain] Original held by John Oxley Library, State Library of Queensland.Via WikiMedia Commons. Web.
11:14 - unknown."C-Class Blimp, C-7." Photograph. c 1921. [Public Domain] Originally published in Grossnick, Roy A. (1986) "Kite Balloons to Airships... the Navy's Lighter-than-Air Experience." Via WikiMedia Commons.Web.
11:14 – Unknown. "Barnstormer/daredevil Carter Burton". Photograph. Unknown. [Public Domain] Original held by San Diego Air & Space Museum Archives / Carter Burton.Via Wikimedia.
11:14 – Unknown. "Daredevils Playing Tennis on a Biplane." 1925. Photograph. [Public Domain] Via Museum Syndicate.
11:15 – "San Rita Gusher." Photograph. c 1922. [Public Domain] Via WikiMedia Commons.Web.
11:15 – RAF (staff) "F2A in Dazzle Scheme." Photograph. c. 1917. [Public domain] Original held by Imperial War Museums, (ID# Q 27501.Via WikiMedia Commons.Web.
11:15 – WikiUser: Jaganath. "Flow separation." Image. 2006. [CC BY-SA 3.0] Via WikiMedia Commons.Web.
12:0 - WikiUser: Alexf. "EAA's Ford Trimotor landing at KTMB." Photograph. 2014. [CC BY-SA 3.0] Via WikiMedia Commons. Web.
12:0 - U.S. Navy. "A PAA S-42 taking offtaking off." Photograph. c. 1930. [Public Domain] Original held by U.S. Navy National Museum of Naval Aviation (ID# 2011.003.123.002).Via WikiMedia User.Web.
12:1 - unknown. "The maiden flight of the Pilgrim. . ." Photograph. 1925. [Public Domain] Original held by Goodyear Company (ID# H6051-63-25).Via airships.net .
12:1 – Royal Air Force (staff). "Supermarine Southampton, british seaplane." Photograph. 1933. [Public Domain] Original held by RAF.Via Wikimedia.
12:2 – Andromeda Galaxy (with h-alpha) by Adam Evans - M31, the Andromeda Galaxy (now with h-alpha) Uploaded by NotFromUtrecht. [CC BY2.0] via Wikimedia Commons.
12:2 – "1931 National Air Race poster." Image. 1931. [Public Domain] Via WikiMedia Commons.Web.
12:2 – "Hubble at Mt Wilson." Photograph. 1949.Via CalTech College of Astronomy
12:2 – Lemaitre. Licensed under Public domain via Wikimedia Commons.
12:2 – Long, Eric. "Sperry Artificial Horizon." Photograph. 2014. [Public Domain] Original held by Smithsonian National Air and Space Museum (ID# 2014-04796).Via NASM.
12:3 – unknown. "The Ford Flivver." Photograph. c 1927. [CC BY-SA 3.0] Original held by San Diego Air and Space Museum Archives.Via WikiMedia.
12:3 – unknown. "Empire State TV antenna..." Photograph. c 1931. [CC BY-SA 2.0] Originally published in Broadcast Engineering Magazine, August 1967, pg. 24-31.Via lnl.com/esbantennas.htm.
12:3 – Pan American Airways. "1936 Pan American Airways Route Map." Illustration. 1936. [Public Domain] Via WikiMedia Commons.Web.
12:4 – "Vorbereitung für Stratosphären-Flug." Photograph. 1930. [CC BY-SA 3.0] Original held by German Federal Archives (Call #102-11505).Via WikiMedia Commons.Web.
12:4 – Unknown. "HMS Ark Royal." Photograph. 1916. [Public Domain] Source: maritimequest.com
12:4 – Employee(s) of United Artists. "Poster for the American film Hell's Angels." Image. 1930. [Public Domain] Via WikiMedia Commons.Web.
12:4 – unknown. "Clarke and Roy Wilson flying airplanes in the movie Hell's Angels". Photograph. c 1930 [Public Domain] Original held by San Diego Air and Space Museum Archive.Via WikiMedia.
12:5 – Anton, Ottomar. "Hamburg-Amerika Linie Poster." Image. c1930. [Public Domain] Via WikiMedia Commons.Web.
12:5 – Pan American Airways. "1936 Pan American Airways Route Map." Illustration. 1936. [Public Domain] Via WikiMedia Commons.Web.
12:6 – "Goebbels speaks at a political rally." Photograph. 1932. [Public Domain] Original Held by German National Archives (Call #119-2406-01).Via WikiMedia Commons.Web.
12:6 – unknown. "Junkers Ju 49." Photograph. 1937. [Public Domain] Original Source: http://www.flug-revue.rotor.com/.Via WikiMedia Commons.Web.
12:6 – NACA/LaRC. "Stinson SR-8E Reliant." Photograph. 1936. [Public Domain] Original held by NASA/LaRC .Via WikiMedia Commons.Web.
12:6 – Unknown. "Century of Progress balloon, World's Fair, Chicago." Photograph. 1933. [Public Domain] Via WikiMedia Commons.Web.
12:6 – Siegel, Jerry and Joe Shuster. "The Reign of the Superman." Illustration. 1933. [Public Domain] Originally published in Siegel's 'Science Fiction #3.' Via WikiMedia Commons.Web.
12:7 - unknown. "The Hughes H-1 Racer." Photograph. 1945. [Public Domain] Original held by UNLV. Via Aero Telemetry.
12:7 – British Official Histories. "Chain Home Radar Coverage 1939–1940." Illustration. 1953. [Public Domain] Via WikiMedia Commons.Web.
12:8 – unknown. "URSS ANT-25 N025 in flight." Photograph. c. 1939. [Public Domain] Original held by: Tupolev Design Bureau. Via WikiMedia Commons.
12:8 – USAF employee. "Lockheed XC-35 USAF." Photograph. [Public Domain] Via WikiMedia Commons.Web.
12:8 – Unknown. "A Japanese Navy Mitsubishi A6M2 "Zero" fighter." 1941. Photograph. [Public Domain] Original held by Japanese Naval History and Heritage Command.Via Wikimedia Commons.
12:9 – Pasquerella, Gus. "The Zeppelin LZ 129 Hindenburg catching fire on May 6, 1937 at Lakehurst Naval Air Station in New Jersey." Photograph. 1937. [Public domain] Via Wikimedia Commons.Web.
12:9 – Ross, Alex. "Superman as depicted in 'The World's Greatest Super-Heroes'." 2005. [Fair Use] Original held by DC Comics. Via Wikimedia.
12:9 – "Deutsche Luftwaffe ist in fünf Jahren aufgebaut worden." Photograph. 1937. [CC-BY SA 3.0] Original held by German Federal Archives (ID # 146-1978-106-25).Via WikiMedia Commons.Web.
12:9 - HMSO. "Barrage balloons over London during World War II." Photograph. c 1942. [Public Domain] Originally published in "Air Publication 3003 - A Brief History of the Royal Air Force." Via WikiMedia.
12:10 - unknown. "Observer Corps aircraft spotter. . ." Photograph. 1940. [Public Domain] Original held by National Archives and Records Administration (ID# 541899). Via WikiMedia Commons.Web.
12:10 – "Friedrich Guggenberger." Photograph. 1941. [CC BY-SA 3.0] Original held by German Federal Archives (Call #183-B13197).Via WikiMedia Commons.Web.
12:10 – NACA/LaRC. "Stinson SR-8E Reliant." Photograph. 1936. [Public Domain] Original held by NASA/LaRC .Via WikiMedia Commons.Web.
12:10 – British Official Histories. "Chain Home Radar Coverage 1939–1940." Illustration. 1953. [Public Domain] Via WikiMedia Commons.Web.
12:10 - unknown. "Bombers over Britain." Photograph. 1940. [Public Domain] Original held by RAF Museum.Via WikiMedia Commons.Web.
12:11 - U.S. Navy. "General view of Pearl Harbor during the Japanese attack" Photograph. 1941. [Public Domain] Original held by National Museum of Naval Aviation (ID# 1996.488.029.034).Via WikiMedia.
12:11 - USAAF. "Pilots of the 332nd Fight Group. . ." Photograph. c. 1944. [Public Domain] Original held by National Archives and Records Administration (call # 535842).Via WikiMedia.
12:11 – WikiUser: Florida Memory. "Passengers aboard a Pan Am Boeing 307." Photograph. c. 1943. [Public Domain] Original held by State Library and Archives of Florida, Call # Rc15258.Via WikiMedia Commons.
12:11 – Windsor, H.H. Jr. (editor). "Sky Hook Spirals from Plane." Popular Mechanics Magazine.Vol. 82, No. 6, December 1944, p.75.Web.
12:11 – RAF. "WAAFs hauling in a kite balloon at a coastal site." Photograph. c. 1943. [Public Domain] Original held by Imperial War Museum, Air Ministry WWII Official Collection (ID# CH-21007).Via WikiMedia Commons.Web.
12:12 – "V-2 rocket on Meillerwagen at Operation Backfire near Cuxhaven. . ." Photograph. 1945. [Public Domain] Original held by Imperial War Museum ('S.I. Negative #76-2755).Via WikiMedia Commons.Web.
12:12 – "USS Lexington (CV-2) under air attack. . ." Photograph. 1942. [Public Domain] Original held by U.S. Naval Historical Center (ID# NH 95579).Via WikiMedia Commons.Web.
12:12 – Hollem, Howard R. "B-24s under construction at Willow Run." Photograph. c1942. [Public Domain] Original held by Library of Congress (Call # fsa.8b05939).Via WikiMedia Commons.Web.
12:13 – unknown. "Hill-copter." Photograph. c 1943. [Public Domain] via aerofiles.com.Web.
12:13 - unknown. "Stout SkyCar2." Photograph. 1941. [Public Domain] Via aerofiles.com
12:13 - unknown. "Please drive carefully, my bumpers are on the scrap..." Photograph. c. 1943. [Fair Use] Original held by U.S. Office of War.Via learnnc.org.
12:13 - unknown. "A Japanese Navy Mitsubishi A6M2 "Zero" fighter." 1941. Photograph. [Public Domain] Original held by Japanese Naval History and Heritage Command.Via Wikimedia Commons.
12:13 – Boeing Aircraft. "A Boeing 314 "Clipper" in flight." Photograph. c. 1941. [Public Domain] Via WikiMedia Commons. Web.
12:14 - SDASM Archives. "Heinkel, He 162, Spatz Volksjager." Photograph. c. 1946. [Public Domain] Original held by San Diego Air and Space Museum Archive.Via WikiMedia Commons.Web
12:14 – 11:20 - "Japanese fire balloon of mulberry paper. . ." Photograph. 1945. [Public Domain] Original source: http://web.umr.edu/.Via WikiMedia Commons.
12:14 – WikiUser: RuthAS. "Convair 440 D-ACAD of Lufthansa at Copenhagen (Kastrup) Airport." Photograph. 1968. [CC BY 3.0] Via WikiMedia.
12:15 – US Air Force (staff). "The Enola Gay." Photograph. c. 1945. [Public domain] Via Wikimedia.
12:15 - unknown. "H-4 Hercules 'Spruce Goose'." Photograph. 1947. [Public Domain] Original held by Alaskan FAA.Via WikiMedia Commons.Web.
12:15 - WikiUser: Meggar. "Bell 47G." Photograph. 2005. [CC-BY-SA 3.0] Via WikiMedia Commons.Web.
12:15 - Shaw, Wilbur and Devon Francis. "Airphibian Ad." Photograph. 1952. [Fair Use] Originally published in Popular Mechanics, July 1952, Vol. 161: No. 1.Via American-Automobiles.com
12:15 – "The first photos taken from space. . ." Photograph. 1946. [Public Domain] Original held by White Sands Missile Range/Applied Physics Laboratory, released by U.S. Army.Via WikiMedia.
12:15 – USAF. "Chuck Yeager next to experimental aircraft Bell X-1 #1 Glamorous Glennis." Photograph. c 1942. [Public Domain] Via WikiMedia Commons.
13:0 – USAF. "Berlin Civilians watching an airlift plane land at Templehof Airport." Photograph. 1948. [Public Domain] Original held by United States Air Force Historical Research Agency.Via Wikimedia Commons.
13:0 – USAF. "C-47 Skytrains unloading at Tempelhof Airport during the Berlin Airlift." Photograph. c 1948. [Public Domain] Original held by U.S. Museum of Naval Aviation (# 2000.043.012) Via Wikimedia.
13:0 – Beals, Cpl. Eugene, USMC. "A U.S. Marine Corps HO5S-1 evacuating wounded in Korea." Photograph. 1953. [Public Domain] Original held by U.S. Defense Imagery (ID#127-GK-13E-A173315.) Via Wikimedia.
13:1 – RAF. "Comet Prototype at Hatfield." Photograph. 1949. [Public Domain] Original held by the Imperial War Museum (Call #ATP 18376C).Via WikiMedia Commons.Web.
13:1 – unknown. "Boeing 377 Stratocruiser." Photograph. 2008. [Public Domain] Original held by San Diego Air and Space Museum Archive (ID# 00061828).Via WikiMedia Commons. Web.
13:1 - US Army. "A Mark IV 'Fat Man' bomb. . ." Photograph. c 1950. [Public Domain] Via WikiMedia.
13:2 - USMC. "A group of U.S. Marine Corp HO3S-1 helicopters." Photograph. 1951. [Public Domain] Via Wikimedia Commons.
13:2 - unknown. "World's FIRST Turbine-Powered Helicopter." Photograph. 1951. [CC-BY 2.0] Via WikiMedia Commons.Web.
13:2 - Beals, Cpl. Eugene, USMC. "A U.S. Marine Corps HO5S-1 evacuating wounded in Korea." Photograph. 1953. [Public Domain] U.S. DefenseImagery photo VIRIN: 127-GK-13E-A173315.Via Wikimedia.
13:2 - Kiser, Sgt. Robert E., Marine Corps. "A USMC HRS-2 of HMR-161 in Korea." Photograph. 1953. [Public Domain] Original held by US Marine Corps. (ID# HM-SN-98-06668). Via WikiMedia.
13:3 – Albertin, Walter. "P.S. 58 - Carroll & Smith Sts. Bklyn. hold a 'take cover' drill. . ." Photograph. 1962. [Public Domain] Original held by Library of Congress (ID # NYWTS - SUBJ/GEOG–U.S.–Civilian Defense–Tests—1962).Via WikiMedia Commons.Web.
13:4 – US Navy. "USS Forrestal." Photograph. 1957. [Public Domain] Original held by US Navy (Call #CVA-59-6321-L-7-57).Via WikiMedia Commons.Web.
13:5 – USAF. "Convair YF-102 on ramp E-1563." Photograph. c1955. [Public Domain] Via WikiMedia Commons.Web.
13:5 – USAF. "The VC-121 *Columbine III*." Photograph. 2007. [Public Domain] Original held by US Air Force (Call # 050322-F-1234P-024).Via WikiMedia Commons.Web.
13:5 – Freer, Mike. "A Boeing 707-320B of Pan American World Airways." Photograph. 1979. [GFDL 1.2] Via WikiMedia Commons.Web.
13:6 – Hoppers, Marcia. "Sputnik-1." Illustration. 2007. [CC BY-SA 2.0] Via futurism.com.Web.
13:7 – NASA/GSFC. "Luna 2 Soviet moon probe." Photograph. c. 1957. [Public Domain] Via WikiMedia.
13:7 – US Air Force. "An Atlas-B missile (s/n 10B) being prepared to launch the SCORE satellite from Cape Canaveral LC-11."

Photograph. 1958. [Public Domain] Via WikiMedia Commons. Web.
13:7 – USGS. "Meigs Field Airport, before demolition." Photograph. 2002. [Public Domain] Via WikiMedia Commons. Web.
13:8 – US Air Force. "Courier 1A communications satellite." Photograph. c. 1959. [Public Domain] Via WikiMedia Commons. Web.
13:8 – US Post Office. "US Postage stamp Echo 1." Hi-Res Scan of Stamp. 1960. [Public Domain] Via WikiMedia Commons. Web.
13:8 – NASA. "Echo-1 Balloon Satellite." Photograph. 1960. [Public Domain] Via WikiMedia Commons.
13:8 – NASA. "Horn Antenna." Photograph. 1962. [Public Domain] Via WikiMedia Commons. Web.
13:8 – US Navy. "The Bathyscaphe Trieste." Photograph. 1958. [Public Domain] Via WikiMedia Commons. Web.
13:9 – CIA. "Map of the . . . Cuban crisis." Image. 1962. [Public Domain] Via WikiMedia Commons. Web.
13:9 – CIA. "A U-2 reconnaissance photograph of Cuba." Photograph. 1962 [Public Domain] Via WikiMedia Commons. Web.
13:9 – NASA/GSFC. "Launch of Vostok 1, the first manned spaceflight." Photograph. 1961. [Public Domain] Via WikiMedia Commons. Web.
13:9 – unknown. "Mission insignia for Vostok 1, the first manned spaceflight in history." Illustration. c. 1961. [Public Domain] Via WikiMedia Commons. Web.
13:9 – Mission Photography. "Yuri Gagarin in Vostok 1." Photograph. 1961. [Public Domain] Via WikiMedia.
13:9 – "Project OSCAR Satellite." Photograph c. 1960. [Public Domain] Original held by the Smithsonian Institute, Air & Space Division. Via WikiMedia.
13:9 – NASA. "Syncom 2 - First Geosynchronous Satellite." Photograph. 1963. [Public Domain] Original published in NSSDC Master Catalog. Via WikiMedia.
13:9 – NASA. "Telstar, the first telecommunications satellite put into orbit." Photograph. 1962. [Public Domain] Via WikiMedia Commons. Web.
13:10 – Dung, James K.F. SFC Photographer. "UH-1Ds airlift members of the 2nd Battalion, 14th Infantry Regiment . . ." Photograph. 1966. [Public Domain] Original held by National Archives (ARC# 530610). Via Wikimedia Commons.
13:11 – NASA. "Horn Antenna." Photograph. 1962. [Public Domain] Via WikiMedia Commons. Web.
13:11 – NASA. "Echo-II." Photograph. 1961. [Public Domain] Via WikiMedia Commons. Web.
13:11 – Haggerty, Tech. Sgt. Michael (USAF). "An air-to-air overhead front view of an SR-71A . . ." Photograph. 1988. [Public Domain] Original released by USAF. Via WikiMedia Commons. Web.
13:12 – U.S. Army. "A U.S. Army Bell AH-1G HueyCobra in flight." Photograph. c1965. [Public Domain] Via Wikimedia Commons.
13:12 – D'Alessio, Sgt. Stephen (USMC). "CH-46 Helicopters & 3rd Battalion Marines." Photograph. 1973. [Public Domain] Via WikiMedia Commons. Web.
13:12 – Kellum, MSGT. Buster (USAF). "An air-to-air front overhead view of two FB-111 aircraft in formation." Photograph. 1983. [Public Domain] Original released by USAF. Via WikiMedia.
13:13 - WikiUser: "Ling.Nut." "Israel and the territories Israel occupied in the Six-Day War." Illustration. 2011. [CC BY-SA 3.0] Via WikiMedia Commons. Web.
13:14 – NASA. "Artist rendering of the general design of the Nimbus series of satellites." Illustration. 1978. [Public Domain] Via WikiMedia Commons.
13:14 – 20th Century Fox. "Poster of film MASH". 1970. [Fair Use] Via Wikimedia Commons.
13:14 – unknown. "ARPANET." Illustration. 1974. [Public Domain] via WikiMedia Commons.
13:14 – Scandinavian Airlines employee. "The prototype 747." Photograph. 1968. [Public Domain] Via WikiMedia Commons. Web.
13:15 – NASA. "Mission Control celebrates the successful splashdown of Apollo 13." Photograph. 1970. [Public Domain] Original held by NASA (ID# GPN-2000-001313). Via WikiMedia Commons.
13:15 – FBI. "One of several FBI composite sketches of D.B. Cooper." Illustration. c. 1971. [Public Domain] Via WikiMedia Commons. Web.
14:1 – Pingstone, Adrian. "Iran Air Airbus A300B4-605R (EP-IBA) arrives London Heathrow . . ." Photograph. 2014. [Public Domain] Via WikiMedia.
14:1 - US CIA. "Egyptian military trucks cross a bridge laid over the Suez Canal..." Photograph. 1973. [Public Domain] Via WikiMedia Commons. Web.
14:1 – Pingstone, Adrian. "Concorde's final flight." Photograph. 1979. [Public Domain] Via WikiMedia.
14:2 - unknown. "General Daniel 'Chappie' James, Jr." Photograph. c. 1975 [Public Domain] Original held by USAF. Via WikiMedia Commons. Web.
14:3 - 20th Century Fox. "Screenshot of the characters of the film Star Wars Episode IV: A New Hope . . ." Photograph. 1977. [Fair Use] Via Wikimedia.
14:3 – NASA. "The Gossamer Albatross II." 1980. Photograph. [Public Domain] Via Wikimedia.
14:4 - unknown. "Double Eagle II Flying the Atlantic." Photograph. 1978. [CC BY-SA 3.0] Original held by The Anderson-Abruzzo International Balloon Museum Foundation. Via adventureballoons.co.uk
14:4 – NASA. "Pioneer 11 image of Saturn (image F81), showing the satellite Rhea." 1979. Photograph. [Public Domain] Via Wikimedia Commons. Web.
14:4 – "Voyager 1 image of Saturn from 5.3 million km . . ." Photograph. 1980. [Public Domain] Original held by NASA. Via WikiMedia.
14:5 – NASA/Goddard. "Diagram of the layers within Earth's atmosphere." Illustration. 2013. [Public Domain] Via nasa.gov/ Web.
14:6 – "STS-1 Orbiter Columbia - arrival at Complex 39A." Photograph. 1980. [Public Domain] Original held by NASA (ID # KSC-80PC-0645). Via WikiMedia.
14:6 – MTV. "MTV's first promo featuring public domain images of the Apollo 11 moon landing." Photograph. 1981. [Fair Use] Via Wikimedia.
14:6 – Allmon II, Staff Sgt. Aaron (USAF). "A US Air Force (USAF) F-117A Nighthawk Stealth Fighter aircraft flies over Nellis Air Force Base . . ." Photograph. 2002. [Public Domain] Via WikiMedia.
14:7 – "Sally Ride America's first woman astronaut communicates . . ." Photograph. 1983. [Public Domain] Original held by National Archives and Records Administration (call # 541940). Via WikiMedia.
14:7 – U.S. federal government. "Strategic Defense Initiative logo." c 1983. Graphic. [Public Domain] Originally published in the biography of Lt. Gen James A. Abrahamson, USAF. Via Wikimedia Commons. Web.
14:8 – NASA. "Space Shuttle Challenger launches from launchpad 39B at the start of STS-51-L." 28 January 1986. Photograph. [Public Domain] Original held by Kennedy Space Center Photo Archive, Photo ID: KSC-86PC-0081. Via Wikimedia Commons.
14:9 - Pingstone, Adrian. "Iberia Airbus A320-200 . . ." Photograph. 2008. [Public Domain] Via WikiMedia.
14:9 - NASA/JPL. "A color photograph of Uranus, taken by Voyager II . . ." Photograph. 1986. [Public Domain] Via WikiMedia Commons. Web.
14:10 – NOAA. "Exxon Valdez, 1989" Photograph. 1989. [Public Domain] Original held by NOAA. Via Wikimedia Commons. Web.
14:12 - NASA. "Hubble is deployed from Discovery." Photograph. 1990. [Public Domain] Original held by NASA (ID# MSFC-9015550). Via WikiMedia.
14:13 – Aeromobil s.r.o. "The Aeromobil 1.0." Photograph. c. 2001. [Fair Use] Via aeromobil.com.
14:14 - WikiUser: Arpingstone. "R44 Raven at RIAT 2008." Photograph. 2008. [Public Domain] Via WikiMedia Commons. Web.
14:14 - NASA. "The core of spiral galaxy M100, imaged with Hubble before and after . . ." Photograph. 1993. [Public Domain] Original held by NASA (ID# GPN-2002-000064). Via WikiMedia Commons.
14:15 – Ferguson, Staff Sgt. Brian. "MQ-9 Reaper in flight." Photograph. 2007. [Public Domain] Original held by USAF Photographic Archives. Via WikiMedia.
14:15 – User: Ludovic.ferre. "Packet routing across the Internet." Illustration. 2010. [CC BY-SA 3.0] Via WikiMedia Commons. Web.
14:17 – NASA. "This is what the Earth looks like at night." Photograph. 2013. [Public Domain] Via WikiMedia Commons. Web.
15:0 – WikiUser: Patrickneil. "NATO has added 12 new members since . . ." Illustration. 2008. [CC BY-SA 3.0] Via WikiMedia Commons. Web.
15:0 – WikiUser: Kremlin.ru "Vladimir Putin." Photograph. unknown. [CC BY-SA] Original held by Russian Presidential Press and Information Office. Via WikiMedia Commons. Web.
15:1 – Sato, Toshihiko. "Concorde Air France Flight 4590 fire on runway." Photograph. 2000. [Fair Use] Via WikiMedia Commons. Web.
15:1 – Semendinger, Det. Greg. "NYC World Trade Center Attack from Air." Photograph. 2001. [Fair Use] NYC Police Aviation Unit. Via NYTimes. Web.
15:2 – WikiUser: Spinnick597. "Two tourists on a Segway tour in Florence, Italy." Photograph. 2007. [CC BY-SA 2.5] Via WikiMedia Commons. Web.
15:2 – WikiUser: ZargNut. "Meigs Field Runway a few days after destruction . . ." Photograph. 2003. [CC0 BY-SA 1.0] Via WikiMedia Commons. Web.
15:3 – WikiUser: Vectorstofinal. "Pre-2008 Cirrus instrument panel . . ." Photograph. 2006. [CC BY-SA 3.0] Via WikiMedia Commons. Web.
15:3 – NASA/JPL-Caltech. "Planet Saturn - Vortex and Rings." Photograph. 2014. [Public Domain] Original held by NASA/JPL (ID# PIA18274). Via WikiMedia.
15:3 – Logan, D Ramey. "SpaceShipOne Takes Off." Photograph. 2004. [CC BY-SA 3.0] Via WikiMedia.
15:4 – Ammons, Master Sgt. Michael (USAF). "This F-22A Raptor . . ." Photograph. 2006. [Public Domain] Original released on f-16.net. Via WikiMedia.
15:4 – "National Security Agency headquarters, Fort Meade, Maryland." Photograph. [Public Domain] Original held by the NSA. Via Wikimedia Commons.
15:4 - WikiUser: Timur Saban. "AirMule." Photograph. 2016. [CC BY-SA 4.0] Via WikiMedia Commons. Web.
15:4 - WikiUser: Capricorn4049. "DJI Phantom 2 Vision+ V3 . . ." Photograph. 2015. [CC BY-SA 4.0] Via WikiMedia Commons. Web.
15:4 – Bailus, Sam. "Major Russian gas pipelines to Europe." Image. [CC BY-SA 3.0] Via WikiMedia Commons. Web.
15:5 - FlickrUser: Axwel. "Airbus A380." Photograph. 2007. [CC BY-SA 2.0] Via WikiMedia.
15:5 – NASA. "Suitsat-1 in orbit ..." Photograph. 2006. [Public Domain] Via WikiMedia Commons. Web.
15:5 – WikiUser: John J Rice. "Lockheed Martin Atlas 5 launch vehicle (AV-010) . . ." Photograph. 2006. [CC BY-SA 3.0] Via WikiMedia Commons. Web.
15:6 – Brussels Airport. "Solar Impulse HB-SIA landing at Brussels Airport." Photograph. 2011. [CC BY-SA 2.0] Source: https://www.flickr.com/photos/brusselsairport/5726152313 . Via WikiMedia.
15:6 - Ng, Greg Lam Pak. "US Airways Flight 1549 in the Hudson River, New York, USA." Photograph. 2009. [CC BY-SA 2.0] Via WikiMedia Commons. Web.
15:6 - Jaguar MENA. "The Jetman Dubai pilot Yves Rossy . . ." Photograph. 2015. [CC BY-SA 2.0] Via WikiMedia Commons. Web.
15:7 – "Deepwater Horizon offshore drilling unit on fire." Photograph. 2010. [Public Domain] Original held by US Coast Guard (Call #100421-G-XXXXL). Via Wikimedia Commons. Web.
15:7 – "Age of Arctic Sea Ice in February 2008." Image. 2008. [Public domain] Original held by NASA. Via Wikimedia Commons. Web.
15:8 – NASA/JPL. "High-Resolution Self-Portrait by Curiosity Rover Arm Camera." Photograph. 2012. [Public Domain] Original held by NASA/JPL. Via WikiMedia Commons. Web.
15:8 – NASA/JPL-Caltech. "Artist's conception of Curiosity being lowered . . ." Illustration. 2011. [Public Domain] Via WikiMedia Commons. Web.
15:8 – Taylor, Lucas. "CMS Higgs-Event." Image. 2007. [CC BY-SA 4.0] Original held by CERN. Via Wikimedia Commons. Web.
15:9 - NASA. "Earth as seen by JunoCam . . ." Photograph. 2013. [Public Domain] Original held by NASA. Via WikiMedia Commons. Web.
15:9 - FlickrUser: Automobile Italia. "AeroMobil 3.0 ." Photograph. c 2010. [CC BY-SA 2.0] Via Flickr Commons. Web.
15:10 – NASA/JPL. "Pluto in True Color." Photograph. 2015. [Public Domain] Original held by NASA/JPL. Via WikiMedia Commons. Web.
15:11 - NASA/JPL-Caltech. "Jupiter's south pole." Photograph. 2016. [Public Domain] Original held by NASA (ID# PIA21032). Via WikiMedia Commons.
15:12 – US Navy. "Subi Reef being built up into an artificial island." Photograph. 2015. [Public Domain] Via WikiMedia Commons. Web.
15:12 – WikiUser: Dkroetsch. "Aeryon Scout UAV in flight." Photograph. [Public Domain] Via WikiMedia.
15:13 – NOAA/NASA. "GOES-16 captured this view . . ." Photograph. 2017. [Public Domain] Via NOAA.gov/. Web.
15:13 – NASA/JSC. "Earth's Atmospheric Layers." Photograph. 2011. [Public Domain] Via NASA/JSC Gateway to Astronaut Photography of Earth. Web.
15:13 – NASA. "Orbiting Carbon Observatory 2 (OCO-2)." Illustration. 2014. [Public Domain] Via NASA.gov/. Web.

Index

93795745R00128

Made in the USA
Lexington, KY
18 July 2018